CW00969913

Fairground Strollers and Showfolk

Also by Frances Brown:

FAIRFIELD FOLK – A HISTORY OF THE BRITISH FAIRGROUND AND ITS PEOPLE

Novels

THE HARESFOOT LEGACY

DANCING ON THE RAINBOW

THE OTHER SISTER

FAIRGROUND
STROLLERS and SHOWFOLK

FRANCES BROWN

RONDA
BOOKS

Copyright © Frances Brown, 2001

All rights reserved. No part of this publication may be reproduced, stored in a retrieval system, or transmitted in any form or by any means, electronic, mechanical, photocopying, recording or otherwise, without the prior written permission of the publisher and copyright holder.

The right of Frances Brown to be identified as the author of this work has been asserted by her in accordance with the Copyright, Designs and Patents Act 1988.

ISBN 0-9521282-1-7

First published in 2001 by:
Ronda Books
Sandings Farm
Lydeard St Lawrence
Taunton TA4 3RD
Tel/Fax: 01984 667276

Jacket design by:
P.Harris & T.A.Smith

Typesetting by:
Oakley Publishing
2 The High Street
Wiveliscombe TA4 2JX
Tel/Fax: 01984 624181
Oakleypub@virgin.net

Printed in Great Britain by:
Butler & Tanner, Frome, Somerset

Contents

Acknowledgements

My grateful thanks to all those travelling showfolk who have been so generous with their time, hospitality and information about the Freeman-Biddalls. My research has taken me over twenty years during which time the trail has often run cold, only to be revived by meeting members of other branches of the family who stirred my enthusiasm afresh. The sadness of my quest has been that several people who were most helpful did not live to see the book in print. Among these I should like to record my gratitude to my late aunts, Lilian Beldam and May Webb, to Walter (Dick) Harris and Victoria Sanger Freeman. I should also like to thank the following:

Leslie Biddall, Victor Biddall, Cyril Bloor, Malcolm Clay, Mrs B.Coneley, Michelle Day-Leonard, Professor Edwin Dawes, David Fitzroy, Marie Graham, Marilyn Graham, Grace Harding, Helga Harman, June Huntingdon, Mervyn Jones, Mrs V.L.Lambert, Mitchell Miller, Roger Newbery, Paul Newman, Carolyn Prola, Ann Ramsbottom, John Reeves, Patricia Robinson, Meriel Stokoe, Barbara Stroud, Ernie Taylor, Dr Vanessa Toulmin, Dr John Turner, Peter Wells, and Alan Wilkins.

Libraries, Museums and Record Offices throughout the country have been invariably helpful, but I am particularly indebted to the staffs of Annan Historic Archives; The Beacon Museum, Whitehaven; Buckinghamshire and Gloucestershire Record Offices; Tower Hamlets Local History Library and Archives; the National Fairground Archive, Sheffield; the British Library and the Theatre Museum, Covent Garden. I should particularly like to thank Graham Downie, Chairman of the Fairground Association of Great Britain, for providing encouragement and advice, and Cyril Bloor for sending me much valuable material. Special thanks are due to Paul Harris for being so generous with his time and talents. And to my husband, Henry, who has supported me every step of the way in researching this history, my love and deepest gratitude.

Illustrations

I am grateful to Miss Barbara Stroud, Mrs Margaret Ramsey and Dr Henry Stroud for making available many of the family photographs in this book. Other illustrations have been taken from my own collection or are reproduced with the kind permission of the following:

Annan Historic Archives, Bank Street, Annan: *43,44,45,47,52,59,60,64,65,75,76,77,78,84,85;* The Beacon, Copeland Borough Council: *18,19,38,48,51,53,54,61,62,63,70,72,73,74,157;* London Borough of Lambeth Archives Department: *90;* The Collections of Merton Library Services: *133;* Oxfordshire County Council Photographic Archive: *3;* Vestry House Museum, London Borough of Waltham Forest: *4,87,88,91,93,94,95,96,103,115,116,119,120,121,127,128,131,132,134,139; World's Fair*, P O Box 57, Albert Mill, Albert St, Oldham OL8 3QL: *14,15,16,17,24,25,27,28,29,30,31,32,56, 67,68,71,79,83,107;* Cyril Bloor: *34,35,36;* Michelle Day-Leonard: *123;* Marilyn Graham: *37,39,40, 46,80,81,82,109,110;* Mrs V.L.Lambert: *11,12,13,42,66,69;* Mitch Miller: *41;* Carolyn Prola: *114,117*. For the back jacket Chris Wickenden has kindly allowed me to reproduce his evocative painting of St Giles Fair, Oxford.

For Violet Lorraine and Andrew

Honour and fame from no condition rise,
Act well your part, there all the honour lies

Alexander Pope quoted by P.T. Barnum at Stockport, 1877

Biddall family at the Royal Agricultural Hall, Islington, c1888
Rebecca and her mother Rosie Biddall in foreground.

Preface

Oh, no! Not again. Not the same old trick we had last year! As a little girl I felt embarrassed when Dad started begging for the use of someone's hat at Christmas, and aunts, uncles, cousins and friends grouped themselves around a table to watch. And to listen. Because Dad never performed straightforward magic. There were always jokes and a tale to be told. I don't remember any words, only the sight of his hands moving around the table shuffling four trilby hats and carefully placing corks, covering first one, then another, until every cork had its own hat. One under each. With hands shuffling all the time as he talked, corks started mysteriously to disappear and reappear until there were three empty hats and one hat with four corks underneath it – without anyone apparently putting them there! How? They had passed through the solid table-top, would you believe? And of course I didn't. But how else to explain the fact that Dad would take up a cork and ostentatiously pass it under the table, knock it against the wood until he declared it 'through', and then lift a hat to reveal the cork's presence? A trick, of course. And I would certainly see how it was done next time if I watched every move he made and never once took my eyes off his hands. So, next time, I did watch every move he made – saw him lift a hat, extract a cork, pass it under the table, rap the wood (some corks proved more difficult than others to push through, Dad said). Then I would see his hand raise the hat on the table to show all four corks sitting neatly underneath it – and still I wouldn't know how on earth they had got there!

My father was Harry Stroud who, although descended from generations of fairground folk and married to a travelling showman's daughter, had chosen to settle down after 1945 and raise his family as house-dwellers. He thus enabled me to attend school (all the year round!) and eventually pursue my love of history by securing a place at Queen Mary College, part of the University of London based in the Mile End Road. In the course of my first week as a student there I set out on foot to explore the East End, for me exciting virgin territory. Unwittingly my steps led me to St Dunstan's Church, Stepney, where – had I but known it – my paternal grandmother, Rebecca Biddall, had been christened in 1869 when her family was overwintering in nearby World's End Yard. At eighteen I scarcely remembered this grandmother who died when I was a toddler. All I knew was that Rebecca had travelled the fairs, owner of a splendid set of chairoplanes, and that earlier in her life she had performed in a circus.

Two decades later I set out to discover more about her family and was surprised to find that, although always referred to as the 'Biddalls' their real name was Freeman. How, I wondered, had the name Biddall come into the family and how long had they been involved with travelling shows?

Attempts to find answers brought me into contact with the age-old and world-wide traditions of strollers and showfolk whose range of talents was astounding. The quest has led me to explore many unusual byways of popular entertainment and in the course of my research I have been amazed by Wizards in their Temples of Magic, suffered with Pantomime Babes, trembled at exploits of Female Blondins, puzzled over Professor Pepper's Ghost Illusion, and agonised at disasters in travelling menageries. Nowadays I feel a thrill of pride to be even remotely connected with people like the clown who, having mastered every act in circus, still hauled on ropes, sewed up storm-ripped canvas and shoed horses – all to keep the show on the road. I only hope that I can do justice to the memory of such a performer and to all those who, at the drop of a hat and whatever the weather, would leap onto a platform and entice audience after audience into the show.

Rebecca Biddall with her granddaughter

1

The Wizard That Was

> The effect of this terrible shock was to turn the survivor's hair white and when he afterwards started in show business and impersonated a wizard, his appearance as such was much enhanced by his snowy locks.
>
> *World's Fair*, 19th May 1934

The appearance of the great Signor Bosco having been advertised all week, the Wentworth Assembly Rooms in Peterborough were packed one Monday evening in November, 1864. Citizens had paid well to see the famous magician perform. Imagine, then, their chagrin when regaled with the kind of tricks commonly seen outside a penny show at fairs.[1]

Was the great Bosco having an off day? Or had they been duped by some charlatan? It was probably the latter. And the perpetrator of the hoax might well have been Henry Freeman, also known as Biddall. By all accounts a wild-looking man, much of Henry Freeman's life is shrouded in mystery, but what is known is that early in life he turned his prematurely white hair to good account by impersonating a wizard.

Born at Iver, Buckinghamshire, on 20th December 1800, Henry was the son of Moses and Mary Freeman, labourers who had fallen on hard times. In recent years Mary had borne and buried three infant daughters, the family being described as 'poor' by the sexton when he came to calculate his fees.[2] Living in such reduced circumstances must have hit the parents hard because, before moving to Iver from their native Gloucestershire in the 1790s, both Moses and Mary had known better times.

Moses Freeman had been born in 1753 in the village of Bisley where his forebears had lived for generations and his grandfather, John Freeman, a prosperous clothier, had bequeathed him a cottage in his will dated 1763.[3] Moses was still living in Bisley in July 1775 when, at the age of twenty-one, he contracted to marry a local girl, Martha Butt. Their banns were called on three occasions. The wedding, however, never took place and so Moses was free to go through the ceremony at Stonehouse parish church on 9th November 1779 when he married Mary Bedel (also spelt Biddle).

Mary had been born at Stonehouse in 1758, daughter of William and Mary, and hers was not the first marriage to link Freemans and Bedels, for her father's cousin, Rebekah Bedel, had married William Freeman at Stonehouse in 1760. A year after their marriage Moses and Mary were blessed with a son and named him Samuel after Mary's brother. Five years later, a second son, William, was christened at Bisley, but the parents' joy must have been cut short by the death of their firstborn. When Samuel was buried at Bisley in November 1786, the parish register marked the decline in Moses Freeman's fortunes by classifying his family as poor. Possibly victims of those recent changes in the cloth industry which were causing workers to leave the Cotswold valleys in droves to seek employment elsewhere, Moses, Mary, and little William left the area and by 1792 had arrived in Iver.

Henry, born nearly a decade later, was only eight years old when his father died in 1809. His mother died two years later. Both were laid to rest in the churchyard at Iver. What happened to Henry next is not clear until he strolls onto the stage of a company of travelling showfolk.

According to Henry, the showman, what had happened was this:

As a young man he had been seized by a naval press-gang and forced to sail the high seas. It was a hard life made dramatically more so when, whilst sailing the Pacific, his ship ran short of drinking water and he was sent ashore in a company to find fresh supplies. A storm blew up and the ship had to put to sea, leaving the shore party stranded. In the ship's absence, that little group was attacked by cannibals and – yes – eaten! All but one, and he, poor soul, was found by the ship's crew on their return, standing on the beach haggard, prematurely aged and with hair turned snowy white. Henry Freeman, of course. Back in England Henry made a living by training birds to perform in a sideshow until he stumbled on a way to profit from his startling white beard and hair. He turned to 'wizardry'.[4]

This is how Henry told the tale on the tober. But another version of the story was handed down in his family. This tells how young Henry Freeman whilst serving in the navy was shipwrecked on a foreign shore where natives slashed his face with ritual cuts that left him scarred for life. So horrific was his visage that on his return he was reduced to exhibiting himself in a freak show.

A grimmer story this, but one that finished with a happy ending when the owner of the freak show, Hannah Baker, grew fond of her exhibit and entered on a courtship that resulted in marriage.

What, if any, truth there is in either story is questionable. Suffice to say, Henry Freeman married Hannah Baker (from an old-established family of travelling showfolk[5]) and both made their presence felt in Biddall's hanky-panky show – a 'walk-up wagon' that they took into towns, driving up to the end of a road or factory gate to give a show. Once customers were satisfied, they would drive off to find another audience in another street. Among the entertainments on offer were juggling, tumbling and conjuring, all performed by the Freeman children, for over the years Henry and Hannah developed their show to employ the whole family. Charles, born 1828, proved a natural gymnast. Benjamin, their second son, had a talent for clowning. William could hold any audience with his patter. Sam became a musician and tumbler. Mary Ann (Polly), born in 1846, was the mind-reader in what became known as their Grand Temple of Magic. George, their youngest son, was set to emulate his siblings as soon as he could walk.

But children grow up and, no matter how loyal, will meet and mate and go their own ways. If for a time some marriage alliance brought in fresh blood and new talent, that was welcome. But any travelling company had its optimum size – there was only so much accommodation, so many mouths who could be fed from one week's takings. Expanding young families had eventually to hive off from parents to form themselves anew.

So it was with the Biddalls. At Sudbury in July 1848 Charles married Charlotte, daughter of John Lincon, fairkeeper. In the next ten years Ben married Mary, daughter of James Scott, musician; William married Mary Ann, daughter of John Fairweather, actor; Samuel married Augusta, daughter of Joseph Smith, circus proprietor.

Christmas 1860 found several members of the Freeman family in their usual winter-quarters in London's Mile End Road. That it was a very different Mile End from the stark grey street of today is evidenced by an old Eastender's memories reprinted in *World's Fair,* 26th June 1909.

> In those times, Mile End and Stepney were really good residential neighbourhoods, where well-to-do City men lived. Arbour Square was the haunt of lawyers, ship's brokers, bankers and other professional men. Not far away stood the Green Dragon, famous for its pleasure and tea gardens and country lanes. They extended up to

> Stepney Green, where at election times the hustings were erected for voting. The last hustings was on a cold November day in 1868 ...
>
> The great event of those days was STEPNEY FAIR, which was not restricted only to the Fairfield, but stretched from Mile End Road to Commercial Road, and from Stepney Church to the London Hospital, with stalls, booths and tents pitched on every available inch of ground ...
>
> THE STROLLERS
>
> Menageries, waxworks, Richardson's Show, boxing booths, jugglers, acrobats, singers, and dancers who today would have made a fortune on the music-hall stage – all were there. Those were the days when the strolling players, almost extinct now, flourished with their brethren, the strolling minstrels.

Not renowned for sophistication, in the early 1860s Stepney Fair usually boasted a number of acting booths featuring *The Red Barn, or Murder of Maria Marten* as their stock piece, a waxwork exhibition, conjuring booth, and a roundabout worked by boys eager to offer their services in return for free rides. There were also simple cockshies – three sticks stuck in bags of sand with a twopenny piece balanced on one stick, a tobacco-box on another, a knife on the third. You had three sticks for a penny to throw at them and, if the object fell *in* the sandbag, you *lost*!

But it was not just Old Stepney fair which brought Henry and Hannah, their children and grandchildren to winter here year after year. It was that something like a continuous fair took place in this part of London during winter months. As Whimsical Walker, famous Drury Lane clown, later recalled in his autobiography, *From Sawdust to Windsor Castle*:[6]

> To my boyish fancy a perpetual fair went on in the great stretch of no man's land – afterwards I believe called Mile End 'Waste' – extending nearly a mile along the side of the Mile End Road. Penny shows, stalls where everything which no one could possibly want was sold, hosts of penny merchants living on their wits – and most ingenious they were in tickling the fancy of the public – excited groups hotly discussing any topic which might be in the air at the time – it did not seem to matter much what – and above all, the Cheap Jack and his Dutch auction! The Cheap Jack with his glib tongue, ready wit, and unlimited stock of impudence, was a joy, and one could stand for an hour enjoying the fun and not spend a penny.

1. Whimsical Walker as Pantomime clown at Theatre Royal, Drury Lane

Travelling showmen also valued Mile End Road for the ease with which they could park up on this busy highway. On Census night in April 1861 there were seven vans recorded in King Harry Yard, Mile End, in one of which slept Henry and Hannah Biddle [sic] and their youngest son. Henry gave his age as 61 and his birthplace Buckinghamshire; Hannah, 56, her birthplace Oxfordshire, and George, 13, his birthplace Swavesea in Cambridgeshire. The menfolk were described as 'musicians', a generic term covering the profession of strolling player. Among those living nearby in caravans were Charles Miller, aged 55, and Charles H. White, 26, also described as 'musicians', the Blanchflowers with their niece, Elizabeth Jenkins, and nephew, Joseph Nichols, and William and Hariet Barker described as 'general dealers' from Norfolk.

Calling ten years earlier, a census enumerator had found the families of George and John Sanger, circus proprietors, in this same congenial stopping place.

'We wintered at this time in a big yard attached to the King Harry public house in the Mile End Road, where cattle were brought weekly from all parts of the country for Friday's market at Old Smithfield,' wrote George Sanger in *Seventy Years A Showman,*[7] going on to describe its landlord, old Packwood, as 'a stout man with a jolly, round red face, always in his shirt-sleeves and always wearing a short white apron.'

The Sangers, Bakers and Biddalls were of similar stock. Performers *par excellence*, trained from the cradle, they formed a coterie of strollers and showfolk who for generations would make their living from a talent to amuse. Cleaving to their own, these families would intermarry until their blood had mingled in the veins of enough entertainers to put a smile on the face of the world. Innovative and energetic, later generations would be quick to seize on the latest inventions and technological advances, but they owed their success in showbusiness to the talents inherited from their forebears, men who had set out as boys with a carpet-bag on their backs containing a scrap of matting – the only equipment needed to establish themselves as tumblers in a travelling show.

By 1861 Henry and Hannah were left with only their two youngest at home – fifteen year old Polly and thirteen year old George. Not that it mattered when they were on the road, for there were always one or two faithfuls who joined them every year and many young hopefuls keen to do the same. Luckily for us, one such left a vivid description of the Biddalls' show as he experienced it in 1861.

Born in 1851, son of the manager of Cooke's circus, young Thomas Dawson Walker ran away from his home in Stockport at the age of nine and joined a tumbling booth at Knott Mill Fair, Manchester. 'Put on some togs,' said the proprietor. 'Knock about on the front of the booth and let me see how you get on.'

The lad got on surprisingly well, with the help of a broomstick soon bending back until his head touched his heels in his effort to be an acrobat. With greater skill came ambition and dissatisfaction with the twopence a week he was being paid. He left and joined a travelling photographer. Then at Ashton Fair came his big break. Randall Williams wanted a boy to play 'A living head without a body' and Master Walker, with wig and false whiskers, agreed to creep under the stage and poke his head through a trap door.

'Open your eyes. Can you see?' demanded the exhibitor.

'Yes,' murmured the head.

'Turn your eyes to the right.'

The head obeyed.

'Then to the left.'

The head did as it was told.

'Smoke a cigarette.'

The head obliged.

And all went well until a mischievous little boy stuck a pin in the head's bottom. When its owner dived down to punch the offender, he was sacked on the spot.

Which is where the Biddalls came in. For resourceful young Walker now joined their hanky-panky show. With his face blackened, he was called Jumbo and encouraged to develop his talents as a clown, a role that fitted him like a glove.

'I imagine I then "found" myself. I certainly was a huge success and suddenly became the greatest boy on the parade,' wrote the future Whimsical Walker in his autobiography.

By the time they reached Whitby that winter the ten year old had also mastered the art of conjuring and must have felt on the road to glory when Hannah Biddall announced that she had rented the town's Theatre Royal for the season. They were to open three nights a week with the 'legitimate' – *Maria Marten – or Murder in the Red Barn*, *East Lynne*, all the usual favourites. For their pantomime Hannah chose *Babes in the Wood* starring her daughter Polly and little Whimsical Walker as the babes. The scene painter was Biddall's clown, Billy Baker, who also made the properties. It seemed a promising venture until they saw the venue.

The Theatre Royal, Whitby, was a ramshackle wooden building on West Cliff which let in so much rain that there could be up to three feet of water under the stage. So, picture the scene after several days of wet weather:

The company are playing out their drama and have reached the part where two little darlings are lying on the ground being covered with leaves by robins (one of which was a huge property bird that became a codfish in the harlequinade). The audience is hushed by the sight of these poor little children dying and being taken up to heaven. Except that on this particular night a rope breaks and the box containing the babes crashes through the stage and plunges them into a watery grave! End of panto. Pronto.

But heigh-ho, life on the road! What made it special was the people.

> The travelling from town to town, the buzz, the din, the excitement of fairs, the admiration and wonder of the gaping rustics, the jovial meeting of old chums ... Then there were the catastrophes which were bound to occur even in the best-regulated shows, and the expedients to be thought out at a moment's notice ... the chances whether expenses were going to be paid or not – the vagaries of the weather – the bad or good temper as the case might be of the proprietor! All was delightfully uncertain; sometimes disappointing, sometimes exhilarating, but one thing was never absent – the sense of freedom – and so long as we pleased our audiences our mission in life was fulfilled! (Whimsical Walker in *From Sawdust to Windsor Castle*)

Young as he was, Whimsical Walker had already noticed that every company of strolling players had its 'character'. Biddall's 'character' at this time (and for years to come) was their cornet player, Jim Stokes, who comprised the entire orchestra. He had a wooden tooth and could play only when this was in his mouth. Often mislaid, the tooth provided an element of uncertainty that gave his performance edge.

Not long after the *débâcle* at Whitby Whimsical Walker left the Biddalls and made his way to London where an emissary of his family caught up with him in the Mile End Road and took him back home. Not that he stayed long. How could he, once blooded by show business? His father, unable to ignore the signs, took him along to Stockport fair and apprenticed him to Pablo Fanque. By this

2. Whimsical Walker in his seventies

master showman young Whimsical was taught the skills of circus life – to ride, vault over horses, and perform on trapeze.

But sixty years later, when asked who first made him up as a clown, Whimsical Walker gave the credit to Billy Wallser, a fellow performer with Biddalls. Billy Wallser came from another family of travelling showfolk who wintered at Mile End. Unlike Whimsical, however, when Billy joined the Biddall show he linked his fortunes with the family for life. Hence he was still with them when they arrived in Oldham at Christmas 1865. Despite the festival the atmosphere in town seemed dismal, the *Oldham Chronicle*, 6th January 1866, reporting that 'The usual Christmas and New Year's tea-parties and entertainments have taken place. There were a few booths in Tommy Field but beyond this there was indeed very little display.'

Certainly the people running one of those booths were in no mood to celebrate. They were preparing for the funeral of its owner, Henry St Clair[8] Freeman, aged 64, who had just died of phthisis. His death, formally witnessed by William Wallser, was followed by interment in a public grave in Chadderton cemetery.

It was a sad end to a hard life and it can only be hoped that before he died Henry had drawn some satisfaction from knowing that his offspring were achieving the kind of success that would bring honour and fame to the name of Freeman-Biddall.

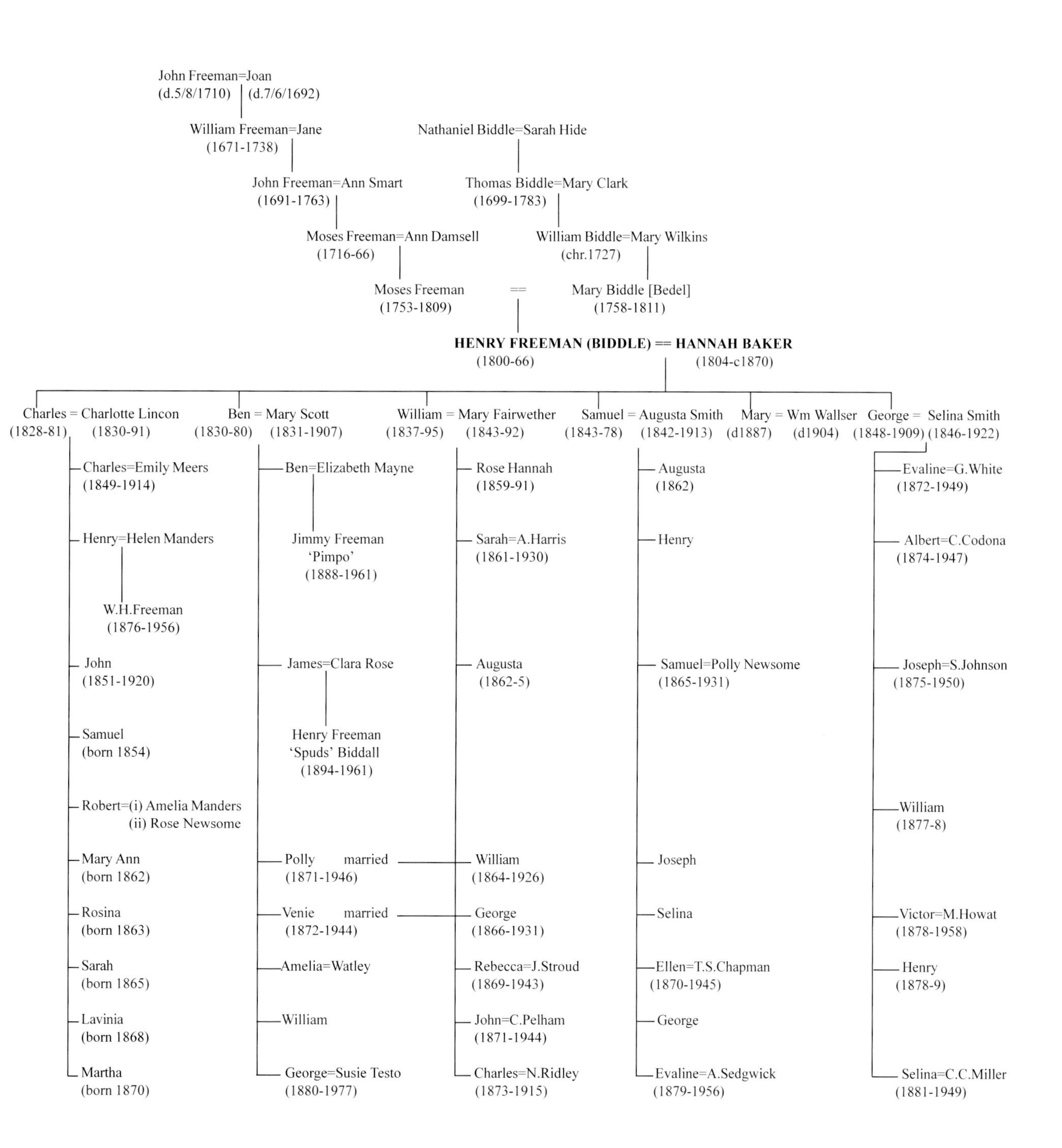

Freeman-Biddall Family Tree

2

Rise To Fame

MADAME BOUTELLE The most accomplished TIGHTROPE ARTISTE extant will produce her most daring exploits ... SIG. ANTONIO BOUTELLE the INIMITABLE CLOWN will perform New and Extraordinary Feats.

Worcester Arboretum Poster, 23rd July 1860

Benjamin Freeman, eldest son of Henry and Hannah, gave his age as twenty-two when he married Mary Scott at Cowley parish church, Oxford, on 6th September 1852. Time and place were significant. They marked the date of St Giles's Fair.

> This large annual pleasure fair, which was held in that part of our city from whence it takes its name, on Monday and Tuesday last, passed off with unusual *éclat,* amid sunshine and shower ... While in most places what may strictly be termed 'pleasure' fairs have been for some years rather on the decline, St Giles's forms a striking exception; indeed, its popularity is evidently on the increase, and this is doubtless to be ascribed in a great measure to the railways ... Many hundreds from the town of Banbury and intermediate places availed themselves of the liberality of the Great Western Company in running an excursion train for the occasion.
>
> Altogether several thousands paid a visit to this celebrated gathering, among whom were many a buxom farmer's wife and blooming daughters, dressed all in their best, some happy under the "protection" of their future lords; also a large number of clean and neatly-clad agricultural labourers, evidently bent on enjoying the fruits of their labour in the harvest field. Indeed the caterers for public amusement seemed to anticipate a successful fair, for there was a greater number of shows and stalls than on any previous occasion in the memory of the oldest inhabitant.
>
> (*Oxford Chronicle,* 11th September 1852)

Among the shows were Edmonds's (late Wombwell's) Menagerie – a treat selected by the Reverend Jacob Lee for local school children so that they might witness some of the wonderful works 'of Him whom they are taught to love, reverence, and obey.' There were portable theatres, in one of which Shakespeare's *Richard III*, together with a comic song, a couple of dances, a good dose of clowning business, and a tableau were 'done' in twenty minutes.

Peepshows provided authentic glimpses of the Kaffir war, Banbury murder and similar atrocities whilst in other booths clever birds, performing ponies, and giants amused and astonished. Photographic studios offered facsimiles of people's 'own dear selves'. In Ben Clarke's sparring academy from Norwich, the 'noble art' of self-defence was displayed and lads invited to put on the gloves. Elsewhere were bold displays of horsemanship, a dance pavilion, and long rows of stalls selling sweets and toys.

3. Shows lined up at St Giles Fair, Oxford, 1868

4. Children at a toy stall, late 19th century

People who took advantage of warm, sultry weather to visit the fair on Monday afternoon had to rush for cover when a thunderstorm struck soon after four o'clock. Strolling players too dived behind their scenes to leave St Giles's looking like a deserted village. But once the rain had passed, the fairground revived and filled with pleasure-seekers whose noses were assailed by the reek of fried sausages while their feet trampled through mud the consistency of a half-baked pudding.

The fact that among all this throng only one man was arrested for drunkenness and nobody for pickpocketing led the *Oxford Chronicle*'s reporter to applaud the event and suggest that, 'we should regret the day when country fairs, conducted as this has been, should cease to amuse for a while the working classes, and to rub off a little of the corroding rust of every-day life. We think all those who furnished entertainment in the fair and elsewhere have had no reason to complain of want of custom; undoubtedly a good deal of money was circulated – the natural effect of plenty of work, good wages, and cheap bread.'

From St Giles some showfolk went on to Wychwood Forest Fair founded about sixty years earlier by a group of friends trying to avoid the boisterous activities of the Wake. But others heard of their pleasant retreat and followed, swelling the gathering into an annual fair with all the pomp and din its originators had been hoping to escape. In 1853 the opening of the Oxford, Worcester and Wolverhampton line provided chance to visit the fair by train with return tickets being offered at single fares. Result?

> The Oxford station presented an animated scene of bustle on the occasion of the starting of the first train for Charlbury on Wednesday morning, the platform being densely crowded with young and old of both sexes in holiday attire and their countenances lit up with the smile of satisfaction anticipative of a pleasant holiday...
>
> At Charlbury the company found various vehicles waiting to convey them to the "Plain", as the scene of the fair is called ... On the Plain "streets" for the shows and stalls were formed as usual by means of ropes extended from tree to tree – one main line being conspicuous, with others diverging in various directions. The shows were numerous and gay to a degree defying verbal delineation. There was Wombwell's establishment with a powerful brass band in front, Bruton's extensive theatrical company, including a performer who, clinging to a rope stretching between two poles at a great elevation, performs feats of a seemingly perilous and most astonishing character ...
>
> The ringing sounds of laughter and buzz of conversation filled the air on all sides in cadences mingling with the boisterous din of the showfolks, the solicitations of the itinerant vendors of small wares, and the notes of strolling musicians and ballad-singers, the majority of whose ditties, whether joyous or lachrymose, formed a strange discord, above which the ear was assailed in never-ending iteration with the efforts used by a large proportion of the number for giving effect to the popular but somewhat unmeaning strain of *Pop goes the weasel.*
>
> And not less striking were the bye-scenes of the fair – the endless diversity of little domestic groups formed by the representatives of town and country, or of gipsy semi-civilisation, squatted on the green sward in quiet sheltered nooks of the forest scenery, enjoying themselves with refreshments and music after their own fashion, or strolling amid the dim *chiaroscuro* of deep vistas streaked with golden gleams of broken light as the rays of the sun casually penetrated such retreats.[1]

With this idyllic scene the journalist of the *Oxford Chronicle* painted a sunset picture of the world of strollers and showfolk as it was before the advent of steam and road locomotives made heavy, more sophisticated equipment the order of the day. But there were other reasons why fairs like Wychwood Forest were under threat. A Bill had already been passed for the area's disafforestation and enclosure for cultivation. The population was increasing and people had to eat.

In marrying Mary Scott, Benjamin Freeman was marrying into one of the oldest circus families in the land. Since childhood Mary had been performing in the little fairground tumbling booth owned by her father, James Scott. James was a pal of George Sanger who was then travelling with 'nut boards', a small stall with something like a spinning dart board at which customers fired guns and received a number of nuts or a cigar if they hit the bull's eye. When George acquired a hanky-panky booth he asked James Scott if he could have his slanging pony for fortune-telling.

'My old pony is about done,' said Scott. 'But as we're going to Barnet fair, what do you say if we buy two ponies and I'll break them in and you can have your pick?'

It was agreed. Sanger paid for the ponies. James Scott trained them and, besides keeping one for his trouble, was later able to boast that he had broken in the first performing pony for Sanger's.[2] Such intimacy and cooperation between the two families would echo down the generations.

A close connection also existed between Scotts and Hannefords. James claimed descent from a John Scott who supposedly competed with Ned Hanneford as a juggler before George III in 1777. Thus started a family rivalry which lasted over a hundred years, ceasing only when James's grand-daughter Elizabeth Scott married Ned Hanneford at Leeds in 1890, forming a union that would produce a famous bareback riding act and earn renown in America.

5. Elizabeth Hanneford, née Scott, aged 76, with son, Poodles, and granddaughter, Grace

But that was for the future. In 1852 it was James's daughter Mary who was about to make a name for herself – not by juggling, or horse-riding, but by walking the rope.

Rope-walking was known in ancient Greece under four different names: the *Neurobat* crossed at a great height, the *Oribat* danced on the rope, the *Schoenobat* slid down the rope, the *Acrobat* did acrobatics on the rope. Romans used the one word *Funambulus* (from *funis*, a rope and *ambulare,* to walk) to describe this activity which strollers and showfolk have included in their repertoire since medieval times. Rope-dancing had always been popular in small tenting shows with the artistes

In July 1860, however, there was still a mood of optimism and posters triumphantly proclaimed that Madame Boutelle 'the most accomplished tightrope artiste extant will produce her most daring exploits during the afternoon concluding in the evening with her Terrific Ascent on the Rope amidst a Display of Fireworks!' Signor Antonio Boutelle 'the inimitable clown will perform new and extraordinary feats.' There was also a Marionette Theatre, possibly the one being travelled by Ben's brother, William Biddall, whose wife was also expecting a child. Certainly the tightrope artistes and the marionettes were still together a month later at Dudley Castle Fêtes organised for the benefit of the Working Men's Institute.

No less than five bands had been engaged for this grand occasion. In the courtyard Signor Giuseppe Operti, pianist to King Emmanuel of Sardinia, conducted concerts by local artistes. Paths winding around caves and ruins in the castle grounds were illuminated with thousands of lamps. There were marionettes, balloon contests, dancing, fireworks, and way above their heads Signor Persiani's daring 'pyrobolic flight' and Madame Boutelle's acrobatics on the tightrope.[3]

Whether she went on to give more performances before returning to winter quarters is not known. What is recorded is that Mary Freeman gave birth to a son on 15th November 1860 at Globe Road, Mile End. Benjamin Henry's birth was registered on Christmas Eve. Up the road in King Harry's Yard, William Biddall's wife, Rosie, gave birth to a baby daughter six weeks later.

If 1859 had been *annus mirabilis* for rope-walkers, 1861 saw the phenomenon peak. And since time and the rope waited for no man, even a nursing mother had to be up there competing with the best if she was to stay at the top. Christmas 1861 saw Madame Boutelle appearing at the fine double-tiered building with its imposing tower that was Sheffield's Surrey Music Hall before it was destroyed by fire in 1865. Here she remained for a month before moving on to the Victoria Music Gallery, Manchester, and thence to Stockport Music Hall for twenty-four nights. It was a gruelling schedule, the pace being set by Blondin (Jean François Gravelet) always pressing the bounds of possibility. Many rivals were maimed or killed in their attempts to emulate his routines. Small wonder – if his performance at Malvern in 1862 was anything to go by.

The original idea for Blondin to walk from one hill to another having been ditched because of difficulties in exacting payment, organisers settled for a field screened by canvas – only to find that the rope could be seen from several vantage points by those wanting to avoid admission charges (1/- generally, 6d for labourers, half price for children). The coiled cable, 2¼ inches diameter, was delivered by rail well in advance and carried to the field where it was hoisted through holes made in two masts 130 yards apart and made fast to trees, the centre span being kept steady by sandbags and small guy-ropes.

At five o'clock on the big day Blondin arrived by carriage from the Foley Arms Hotel, saluted the crowds, and was winched up to a platform on top of one of the masts. He was dressed in tunic, silk tights and feathered cap. His pole, already at the platform, was made from lancewood weighted at both ends with iron. Carrying this before him, he began to walk at an elevation of seventy feet, his first movement being downhill.

As he went along he threw first one foot in the air and then the other, and seemed so much at ease, that the anxiety which was depicted on many faces at the outset soon disappeared. When he had walked over about one-third of the length of the rope, he stood for some time on one leg, then he sat down for a moment, and next lay down on his back, with the pole across his chest. Then he ran as far as the middle of the rope, sat down and untied and retied a cord which was lashed round the middle of his pole. Then he stood on his head and beat his feet together, and next lay down on his back to rest himself. Whilst he lay, he performed the extraordinary feat of placing the pole across the rope beyond his head so that it nearly balanced itself, and whenever it appeared inclined to tip over, he threw his hand behind his head to steady it. As he lay extended on the rope, he had nothing to rely on but his skill in balancing his body, and the least mistake might have turned him off the rope.

7. Blondin's 'various feats' on the rope

Suddenly he caught hold of the pole, flung himself from his back, heels over head, and alighted on his feet on the rope ... After a pause, he produced a white handkerchief, which he folded and placed over his eyes; then he took a bag, made of some striped material, put it over his head, and thrust his arms through holes in its sides. The bag reached to his knees and gave him a very grotesque appearance. Then taking his pole, he began to walk along the rope, descending the steeply inclined part apparently in great trepidation; trembling violently, and now and then pretending to slip, allowing one foot to descend considerably below the rope ... At length he fell down on the rope ... pretended again to have lost his balance, and struggled in a manner that must have rendered it difficult for him to stand on the rope. Next he lay down on the rope, and after various feats walked to the southern end of it and rested. Here he pulled off the sack and showed that he still had the handkerchief over his eyes.

(*Worcester Journal,* 13th July 1861)

A hard act to follow, but this is what Madame Boutelle did when she returned to Worcester in 1862. Blondin performed at the town's Pleasure Grounds on the last day of June; Madame Boutelle starred at the Odd Fellows' Fete in July. Four thousand turned out to watch Blondin in an exhibition which local newspapers described as 'productive of fright and terror from the danger always imminent to the performance of a man on a naked rope stretched at a great height.' (*Worcester Herald*, 5th July 1862)

So why would people return to see similar tricks? The answer was simple. These tricks would be attempted by one of the famous Female Blondins whose recent crossings of the Thames had attracted so much attention in the press.

GRAND MIDLAND FESTIVAL
Fête of the Wolverhampton Order of Oddfellows
on MONDAY, 28th July Instant
PROCESSION OF THE LODGES through the principal Streets
of Worcester to the Arboretum.
FOUR MILITARY BANDS.
The HEROINE OF THE THAMES, MADAME BOUTELL,
the Female Blondin, will perform on a Rope 600 feet long, purchased for the occasion.

8. The Female Blondin crossing the Thames, 1861

Advertisements such as this coupled with fine weather attracted nearly eight thousand people to the Arboretum where 'The Female Blondin MADAME BOUTELL performed on a rope raised to a considerable height, and in the evening walked amidst fireworks, an excellent pyrotechnic display terminating this, one of the most successful fetes ever held in these grounds.' (*Worcester Herald*, 2nd August 1862)

It was the kind of success that the hard-pressed Arboretum Company was anxious to repeat. On Monday, 18th August 1862, they advertised a Grand Firework Fête at the Worcester Pleasure Grounds with the gardens to be illuminated during the evening with Italian Lights and numerous fire balloons to lift off. At seven o'clock the Female Blondin would make her first ascent on a rope six hundred feet long at a height of a hundred feet and her second at half-past nine amidst fireworks accompanied by the band of the Worcestershire Yeomanry Cavalry. Again Madame Boutelle completed the act successfully, no doubt causing alarm and excitement as her routine included a simulated fall. It had really caught the crowd's imagination when Selina Young tried to make a rope crossing of the Thames from Battersea to Cremorne in August 1861 – a feat which ended in dramatic failure when the rope sagged and started to sway too violently for her to continue. After standing marooned in mid-air while attendants tried to tighten the remaining section, it was announced that some rogue had cut the guys to steal their lead weights and there was nothing Miss Young could do but jettison her pole and slide down one of the sway ropes into a boat.

Next day enormous crowds turned out to see her repeat the attempt. This time the crossing was successful. As the performer was greeted by strains of *See the Conquering Hero Comes,* cynics suggested that her previous failure had been a carefully staged publicity stunt. Be that as it may, there was nothing premeditated about her fall from a forty foot high rope rigged at the Highbury Barn Pleasure Gardens the following August. A fractured thigh left poor Miss Young with one leg three inches shorter than the other. Amidst mounting public disquiet about what the *Era* newspaper called 'the morbid and romantic desire of the present age for perilous adventures' a subscription was raised for the crippled performer, but her misfortune did nothing to deter fellow artistes.

In June 1863 Carlo Valerio fell to his death from a sixty-foot wire in Cremorne Gardens and Mr E.T. Smith vowed that no such exhibitions would take place there again while he was Proprietor.

A month later the *Era* announced: 'A fête in connection with the Ancient Order of Foresters will be held at Aston Park, Birmingham, on July 20th at which another Female Blondin will endanger her life on the high rope.'

The performer on this occasion was Madame Genevieve, alias Mrs Edward Powell, thirty-six year old mother of five. She had undertaken to appear twice – once in the afternoon and the other at night with fireworks – for the sum of £15. Concern was expressed about the safety of her rope after it snapped whilst being erected. Discarding the smaller piece, her husband had re-tied the main portion to the mast, while his wife was heard to murmur, 'If Mr Powell says it's all right, I am satisfied.' (*Era,* 26th July 1863)

There was immense cheering as Madame Genevieve mounted the platform and stepped boldly onto the rope. Cheers when she returned to the landing stage, loaded her ankles and wrists with chains, walked the length of the rope again. Then, divesting herself of the chains, she bound her eyes with a scarf, covered her head and set out again. Three or four steps later the rope broke and she plunged to her death. At the inquest it was suggested by a surgeon that 'she might have lived had she not been six months in pregnancy at the time of the accident.'

Society was outraged.

'Sir,' wrote Queen Victoria's private secretary to the Mayor of Birmingham, 'Her Majesty cannot refrain from making known through you her personal feelings of horror that one of her subjects – a female – should have been sacrificed to the gratification of the demoralising taste, unfortunately prevalent, for exhibitions attended with the greatest danger to the performers.' (*Era*, 2nd August 1863) The Mayor added his voice to the clamour against this 'barbarous species of amusement which unhappily has become popular, not only in the Metropolis, but in all parts of Her Majesty's home dominions.'

Although the inquest resulted in a verdict of accidental death, the jury expressed their opinion 'that parties are greatly to blame who engage people for performances which are dangerous to life for the amusement of the public. They think all dangerous and degrading performances by either sex should be discouraged.' (*Era,* 26th July 1863)

To avoid future opprobrium, managers of theatres and pleasure gardens hastily cancelled all planned exhibitions of high rope-walking. At Kidderminster, when a circus applied to visit the town on Friday, 25th July, the Mayor objected to a proposed performance in which two Female Blondins were to run along a rope fifty feet from the ground, starting from opposite ends, one to vault over the other when they met in the centre. The applicant explained that the rope would be stretched above a tent so that, in case of a slip, the performer would be caught on canvas. The Mayor still objected. Eventually this 'sensation feat' (as posters had it) was left out and amended bills proclaimed that a 'rational entertainment' would be provided, including pugilistic encounters.

Female Blondins had clearly fallen from favour. Whether for this reason, or the possibility that Polly was again pregnant, her name did not appear alongside her husband's in advertisements for Dudley Castle Fêtes in 1868.

1-3 June 1868 Dudley Castle Fetes
Caverns open and illuminated by gas,
with performances by a band of South Carolina minstrels;
SIGNOR ANTONIO on the elastic wire;
feats of swordsmanship by Sergeant W. Fawke;
balloon ascents.'

(*Blocksidge's Dudley Almanack,* 1st June1868)

By the time Polly was in her late forties she had given birth to at least six children. Benjamin Henry having been named after his father and Freeman grandfather, her second son was called James after his Scott grandfather. Next came William and Mary Ann. Lavinia was born on 13th April 1872 at St Helens fairground. Then, after the birth of another daughter, Amelia, Polly was expecting again when she realised that Ben was very ill. The family moved into rented accommodation in Prestwich near Manchester so that she could nurse him through the difficult last stages of phthisis, the disease that had killed his father and brother Samuel. When Ben died on 19th January 1880, his widow was left in desperate straits. Fortunately help was on hand. Her brother James Scott took the fatherless family under his wing and it was in the front wagon of his marionette show on Wanstead Flats that Polly's youngest son, George, was born on 20th May 1880. By a curious coincidence George's future wife would be born the following year also in the front wagon of a marionette show on Wanstead Flats.

George, born at a tragic time for his family, survived a challenging childhood. Three years old and he was on the payroll of a travelling theatre, earning a shilling a week as the Cat in *Dick Whittington*. After that he became part of his mother and brother's tumbling act and appeared at Balmoral Castle in John Scott's British Royal Circus owned by his uncles.

Life was often very hard for the lad and the woman who had once been fêted as Madame Boutelle. On one occasion in Wigan with no money to pay for transport to Wales, where they were to join Polly's brother, the pair had no option but to walk. They tramped for miles. With blistered feet and boots in a shocking state they reached a village where a reservoir was being built. Because it was pouring with rain a crowd of Irish navvies had congregated in the pub that George and his mother entered, cold and wet and with only a few coppers left. Seeing that George was carrying a violin case, the foreman said, 'Give us a tune then, lad.' George obliged. Suddenly the day turned brighter. The landlady brought them some dinner. The foreman went round with a hat demanding a silver collection for the pair and amassed thirty shillings. George announced that the first thing he would buy was new boots for his mother.

9. Madame Boutelle's youngest son, George Biddall, as tumbler

10. George Biddall aged eighteen

Adventures like this encouraged in George an unusual resourcefulness. His talents were all-round. When occasion demanded he could be clown, tumbler, trapeze artiste, musician, groom, expert decorator or sign writer. On his own admission, only two circus skills eluded him – he could neither juggle nor walk the tightrope. For a while he went into business on his own account and opened a cinematograph show.

'The first picture I showed was the longest film on earth,' he later recalled. 'There were about 100 feet of film and it lasted three minutes ... I had the show for about six months and it was a complete failure. I lost every penny I had.'

After a tour of the fairs with various shows and stalls, George went back to circus life. 'I joined Fossett's Circus and Madame Paulo's and made the circus a profession and a study.'

In July 1906 George was performing with his Uncle John Scott's Circus at Beith when Ellen Scott (John's wife) died suddenly and it fell to George to sign as witness present at her death. In January 1907 his own mother died and one month later George married Susannah Testo at Gosforth parish church. Susannah was daughter of the late William Testo, famous for his marionette show, and granddaughter of Felix Testot, who had reputedly come to England during the French Revolution. George and Susannah went on to have four sons and a daughter.

On his ninetieth birthday George was interviewed at Hetton in a caravan which he had built for himself over forty years before at the Lake Ground, Houghton-le-Spring. Asked to what he attributed his long life, he replied: 'Youthful outlook, good food, and keeping fit.'[4] After he died in 1977, his ashes together with those of his wife were scattered on Newcastle Town Moor, ancient site of one of Britain's greatest fairs.

3

Tumbling Into Life

> Wanted, Engagement for the Winter Season, Biddall's Famous Circus Family with Male and Female Equestrian Acts. The Finest in the Business. Performing horses. Trick Acts. Ground and Aerial Acts. Remember we ride every act in the profession ... Apply to James Biddall, the Circus, Dalmellington, Ayrshire.
>
> *World's Fair*, 10th October 1914

When Mary Freeman (Madame Boutelle) died at Tynemouth in January 1907 it was in the presence of her second son, James Freeman. Drawing on the talent of his family and assuming the name Biddall, James had already established a popular travelling circus in the north. For example, in 1902 his show was a star attraction at Longsight Wakes, a 'made-up do' to cater for the new urban population that had sprung up between Stockport and Manchester. Among the rides at this fair were Whiting's whirling gondolas, lit by hundreds of electric lights, and Thomas Hurst's two novelty roundabouts: his ride a cock-horse patent set (three saddled birds) and his flying ostriches from Cape Town. But it was the shows which attracted most attention, especially Biddall's circus with its attractive outside parade and programme, as described in the *Era*, 2nd August 1902:

> The Biddall Family are famous on the road as fearless riders, daring vaulters, and expert acrobats. Miss Rosina Biddall on the tight and the slack wire surprised and delighted us. Another Miss Biddall as the female jockey did some clever bareback horsemanship. The Brothers Biddall, clowns and acrobats, did a capital Risley turn. Master Benjamin Biddall, the boy bareback horse rider, created quite a sensation by daring exploits. Mr Biddall introduced his clever pony, Tommie Dodd, in menage and comic turns, the grand wind-up of a first-rate sawdust performance being episodes from the Boer War by the whole strength of the Biddall Family.

In August 1906 Biddall's circus was one of the attractions at Seaham Harbour's Flower Show and the following Easter it opened at Durham alongside the Freak Exhibition belonging to Sam Biddall, son of Samuel and Augusta. After that the cousins often travelled together, both shows appearing at Larkhall and Dunfermline in July. In late September 1907 they met up with their Uncle George Biddall when he brought his famous Ghost Show to Dumfries Rood Fair. James Biddall's Circus with their grand Continental Riders and Sam Biddall's Living Novelties then moved on to Stranraer Fair.

Scotland featured large in James Biddall's calendar again the following year. He was at Vinegar Hill in July, opening at Gallowgate next to George Green's Carnival Ground. In September Biddall's Circus gave performances in Balfron's Recreation Park for two days. In November James Biddall

11. Thomas Stephenson Chapman (1843-1913) on left. In 1894 his son married Ellen Freeman, daughter of Sam & Augusta, and the couple joined Biddall's Ghost Show.

12. Four generations:
Ellen Chapman with Selina (daughter),
Ellen Claudina (granddaughter),
and Elaine (great granddaughter)

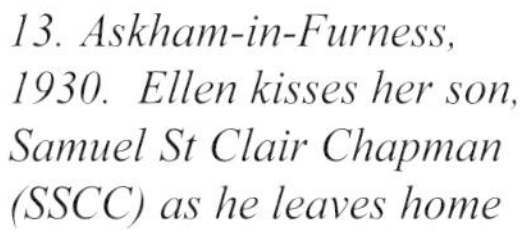

13. Askham-in-Furness, 1930. Ellen kisses her son, Samuel St Clair Chapman (SSCC) as he leaves home

14. Sam Biddall (1865-1931)

opened at Carlisle Fair with Sam Biddall and his mother, Augusta Palmer, also there with their shooting galleries.

So often did these different branches of Biddalls meet at fairs in the north that people tended to think they were the same concern. James Biddall's Circus, George Biddall's Ghost Show and No.2 Cinematograph, Sam Biddall's Novelty or Freak Show – all were referred to as Biddall's Shows. At Dunfermline Fair in July 1909 (after George Biddall's death) Biddall's Circus and Biddall's Cinematograph were present together with Mrs G. Biddall's cakewalk machine, Manders' Menagerie, Johnson's Varieties and Palmer's Novelty Booth, shooting gallery and variety frames. When Dumbarton held its historic fair in the last week of August, the *Era* (11th September 1909) reported that some of the best shows and machines on the Scottish round attended and 'The famous entertainers of the people included the Biddall family and company, with circus.'

In November, after a disappointing turn-out at Carlisle Fair, Biddall's Circus moved to the Cumbrian coast taking in Workington and Whitehaven Fair where Biddall's Ghost appeared, a shadow of its former self since George's death earlier that year. Biddall's Circus, Ghost Show and cake walk were still together at Cleator Moor the following week before the Circus finished its season well by attracting good audiences at Frizington where it opened in December.

James Freeman-Biddall had married Clara, daughter of George Rose, a circus proprietor who had been born at Banff. By 1910 the couple's large family had developed into a talented circus troupe known for its equestrian skills. After touring Aberdeenshire that summer James placed an advert in *World's Fair,* 24th September 1910: 'The Biddall Family of circus artistes are at liberty for the winter season with their well-known number of acts.' A month later he thanked all enquirers and announced that he had settled with Mr W. Codona.

This set the pattern for future years. After a winter engagement in music hall or Christmas carnival, in summer James toured with his circus. By 1912 he had moved his headquarters from Newcastle to Bridgend in Fife where his brother-in-law, William Rose, had a permanent address useful when advertising: 'Wanted, three Bandsmen, to join at once (two Ist Cornets and Trombone) for tenting. State lowest terms in first letter. No fancy salaries, but money sure. Biddall's Circus, Bridge End, Ceres, Fife.' (*World's Fair*, 15th June 1912) To this address came sad news that July of the death of James's eldest brother, Ben, in Belfast.

In August 1912 Biddall's Circus toured as far north as the Wick district in Scotland where it was remarked that Misses Clara and Florence Biddall were becoming great favourites. Returning south an urgent call went out: 'Wanted, Agent to join at once for a short season. Biddall's Circus, Stanley, Perthshire. Write or Wire.' (*World's Fair*, 7th September 1912) At the same time James started advertising for an engagement for the winter season, calling upon managers to come and see for themselves the Biddall Family's equestrian acts. Having repeated this advertisement twice, by October he was sounding desperate:

'The Biddall Family will shortly be at liberty for the Winter Season to accept engagements, with the number of first class acts: Jockey Act, Bar Act, Trick Act, Double Act, four in number. With own horses, and trick pony, good clowns, and entrees, if required. All letters addressed to: James Biddall, c/o Mr Rose, Bridgend, Fife.' (*World's Fair*, 5th October 1912)

Perhaps aware that he had left things rather late, he advertised as early as June the following year:

> Wanted Known to Managers and Agents, Music Hall or Circus, the Biddall Family are at liberty in November for the winter season, male and female equestrians, with own horses, trick and liberty horses, rocking ladders, vaulting over horses, aerial and ground acts. Come and see our numbers and pick out what you require. Can be seen any time. Now touring with Manders and Bailey's Circus. Those who are looking for workers and know their business, communicate at once to James Biddall, c/o W. Rose, Bridgend.
>
> (*World's Fair*, 7th June 1913)

Of course this address for correspondence gave no clue as to the Circus's whereabouts. In fact they had travelled south that summer ready to open at Skegness for August Bank Holiday.

It might have been only August but James was already thinking ahead and announcing to circus proprietors, music hall and carnival agents: 'I have at liberty for the winter season any of the following first class talent: Jockey with own horse; Trick Horse; Contortionist; Aerial Gymnasts; Lady Equestrienne with own horse; Double Act, two males, two females, and two horses, one of the latest acts in the business. All these acts are good, and bluff. Managers and agents especially invited to see these acts. A week's route sent to those who would like to see us.' (*World's Fair*, 16th August 1913)

By October James Biddall had travelled north again to tour Kirkudbright and Dumfries. Drawing heavy loads over such a distance was obviously proving too much for the traction engine which he decided to sell in favour of something more powerful. On 25th October 1913 he advertised in *World's Fair*:

> For Sale, a Steam Motor Tractor, made by Ruston & Proctor, two speeds, wire rope, spuds, water tank, dynamo on front of engine for electric light, to be sold with or without electric plant, now pulling load and driving light; also, for sale, a good Green Circus Tent, 70 ft, with a 21 ft centre, red and white wallings, all in good condition. Can be seen any time. Now on tour. All applications to James Biddall, The Circus, New Galloway, Saturday; Moniaive, Monday; Thornhill, Tuesday.

In the course of the next season he took possession of a Burrell road locomotive, engine number 2173. Known as the *Empress* when owned by Smith and Whittle, James Biddall renamed her *Flora*.

Cowboys being the current craze, throughout early months of that summer James was advertising for good lariat spinners, stock whip crackers or anything in the Wild West business that could be done in the ring. In May he travelled north from Coupar Angus via Stonehaven, Banchory and Aboyne, to reach Banff and Buckie by early June.

As the time for seeking a winter engagement approached, James must have been in expansive mood or simply determined not to be overlooked. Part of his advertisement in *World's Fair* (15th August 1914) appeared in triplicate:

Wanted Known
Wanted Known
Wanted Known
At Liberty for the Winter Season
At Liberty for the Winter Season
At Liberty for the Winter Season
Male & Female Equestrians
with own horses, also Trick Horse, Good Auguste and Clowns with good entries.
Show can be seen at any time on application to
James Biddall, Circus, Bridgend, Ceres, Fife.

Repeating the advert a fortnight later to no effect, in October he reverted to the usual format.

> Wanted, Engagement for the Winter Season, Biddall's Famous Circus Family with Male and Female Equestrian Acts. The Finest in the Business. Performing horses. Trick Acts. Ground and Aerial Acts. Remember we ride every act in the profession. If you are needing circus talent write to us. We can accommodate you with anything you require, as we have the People, and we have the Goods, and all are at liberty for the Winter Season. Apply to James Biddall, the Circus, Dalmellington, Ayrshire.
>
> (*World's Fair*, 10th October 1914)

But people had other things on their minds that autumn, and there were no takers. By the end of the month James was sounding desperate again.

> Wanted known At Liberty for the Winter Season Male and Female Equestrians. Jockey Act. Lady Banner Act. Ragtime Trio – three on one horse. We ride every act in the business. Also the Rocking Ladders. Trick horse. Funny Clowns. Joey Pony. Aerial and Ground acts. If you want good talent we are the people. We have the talent and the horses and everything we use in the ring. We don't ask for the earth. All we ask for is a fair wage.
>
> (*World's Fair*, 31st October 1914)

Perhaps this difficult situation exacerbated tensions and triggered the departure of James's son from the family enterprise. At the beginning of the next touring season he advertised: 'Wanted Engagement as Advance Agent. Enough said. Address: J.F.Biddall, c/o WF, Oldham.' In the same column his father was advertising: 'Wanted, Agent, Also Band of four. A good Gag for Tenting. A Couple of Grooms, start in March. State lowest terms in first letter. Apply: Biddall's Circus, Darnconner, Ayrshire.' (*World's Fair*, 20th February 1915)

A good agent, especially one who knew Scotland, was hard to find and Biddall's Circus continued to advertise at Newburgh in April, then Old Meldrum and New Deer (Aberdeenshire), and at Keith (Banff) in May. In July they were still in need of an 'Agent to join at once. One that knows Scotland preferred. State lowest terms in first letter. Also apply, 1st & 2nd Cornet Players. Biddall's Circus, Strathaven (for Monday only), nr. Glasgow, Scotland.' (*World's Fair*, 17th July 1915)

Biddall's Circus was at Lochmaben about to move on to Lockerbie for another one day stand when the usual advertisement was posted in August:

'The Biddall Family. Male and Female Equestrians. Three in number and with own horses. Double act, jockey act, bar act, trick act and trick horse act. The above can be seen now on tour.' (*World's Fair*, 7th August 1915)

They must have blessed the new Burrell when a week later they were climbing up to the market town of Alston at an altitude of 900 feet in the Pennines. Even more so the following day when they reached Nenthead at 1500 feet. Three weeks later they arrived at Boroughbridge and Knaresborough still advertising for a winter engagement. They spent Christmas in Gretna where a secret township was growing up to house the thirty thousand women and men who came from all over the world to work in the massive new cordite factory. Among the workers James might have spotted his cousin, Victor Biddall, driving a transport lorry.

By now the younger generation of James and Clara's family had made their mark. All were acclaimed for their circus skills; one daughter and son-in-law known as 'The Omars' were famous for their wire and acrobatic act. But war was about to take its toll. Benny joined the Lancashire Fusiliers, Henry the Army Ordnance Corps, their brother-in-law Tommy Hall the Royal Scots Fusiliers. All three were sent to France.

15. The Two Omars, 1915

In March 1916, James and Clara's fears for their lads overseas were suddenly eclipsed by the death of their daughter, Lizzie Hall, at Bonnybridge. She was only twenty-two. Seven months later her widowed husband was killed in action.

Reunited after the war, thankfully sound in wind and limb, the brothers took the family show back on the road. A pre-war tour had seen them as far north as John o' Groats. In the summer of 1920 they set out for Land's End. The programme, mostly provided by Biddalls, comprised over a dozen items:

1 Overture
2 Canadian rough rider
3 Lariat throwing and stock-whip manipulation
4 Lady wire walker
5 Master Biddall, jockey-act
6 Flying ring experts
7 Comical entree by clowns
8 Miss Biddall in trick act on horseback
9 High leaping and vaulting act over horses
10 Liberty and waltzing horse
11 'Grant', contortionist and hand balancer
12 Brothers Biddall in double riding act
13 Riding act, assisted by the clowns

16. *Four generations: James Biddall with his family, 1936*

17. *Lenoma Biddall*

18. *Bingo's Car, advertising his cinematograph*

Nightly I dream of the dear old show [Biddall's Ghost Illusion] and often see myself in clown attire or otherwise strutting across its stage. And what glorious days these were. I often sit and bring back dear recollections of the past when I had all the enjoyment of life ...
(Bingo's Book, *page 14*)

BINGO'S 1919 BOOK

Of Funny Stories, Poems, & Songs.

New Series] [Edition 1.

Little Stories.

Long Stories.

A Chat with Kingston.

Short Poems.

Long Poems.

A Chat with Bingo.

KEEP SMILING

Price 6d. Worth 6s. You're sure to smile!

19. *Bingo's Book, published 1919*

Reviewing it for *World's Fair* (28th August 1920), *Onlooker* wrote:

> One of the finest circuses that has been down in the west for several years is Biddall's Circus which has taken Devon and Cornwall by storm this season. The Biddalls' Quartette of ragtime dancers on bareback horses brings down the house; also does Master Henry who does a very tricky jockey act.
>
> John Lowden the heavy weight lifter also meets with hearty applause; also the Clowns ... The Arab troupe of high leapers over horses is another pleasing item on the programme.
>
> The show has a very good appearance and the three-pole tent looks well inside and out, and the way the show is handled is marvellous. There is one thing Mr Biddall can boast of, and that is that he has a family that is not afraid of work. Also the agent, Mr W. Fowler, is a man who seems to have his heart's interest in the show.

Mr Fowler may have had his heart in the show but tended to greet people always with the same doleful cry: "I had to miss such-and-such a place. They wanted too much money for the tober and I couldn't get another one."

The problem was, Biddalls were following behind Bostock's and grounds that used to be 30/- or £2 had risen to as much as £20. For this reason they had to find alternative tobers at Penzance, Helston and Budleigh Salterton.

In retrospect, their triumphal tour of the west in 1920 cast a sunset glow over Biddall's Circus. Neither James nor Clara was in good health and in 1922 both went into hospital for serious operations. James made a full recovery but Clara died. She was buried at Buckie. Among the chief mourners were her son Ben and his wife Lenoma.

Lenoma had been connected with the Biddalls all her life because her father, Bob Coady, had been attached to George Biddall's Ghost Show and her brother, Harry Coady, partnered her husband Ben in the clown duo known as the Freeman Brothers. Whilst on the road early in the morning of Wednesday, 6th June 1928, at Kirriemuir Lenoma met with one of those deadly accidents to which so many of her female relatives had fallen prey. Trapped by her long skirt she was dragged under a wagon and her head crushed by its wheel. Death was instant. She was twenty-seven and mother of two little boys, Bennie and John James.

John Moncrieff, alias Bingo, a clown who had also travelled with the Ghost Show, wrote of his grief at the death of this kind-hearted woman. 'She spoke to me of the nice people Biddalls were and that I would not find many like them. She sent Ben to me with a lovely dinner on the Sunday and spoke to me of the good old days of the Biddall's Ghost Show and her father.' (*World's Fair*, 23rd June1928)

But, Biddalls being Biddalls, all that was gold did not glitter in the past. There were glories to come. Although James had now retired, Biddall Brothers' Circus continued to tour. In September 1933 after opening at Nairn it was billed to visit Hopeman with a programme that boasted a host of clowns, performing horses, and the youngest wire-walker in the country. This was Pauline, daughter of Henry Biddall (better known as the clown, Spuds) and sister of Marius, trapeze and riding performer. After giving up their own tenting show, the family began appearing with Sir Robert Fossett's Circus and forged close links with this dynasty after Pauline married Bob Fossett. When Spuds died in June 1961, he was survived by two sons and three daughters all renowned as circus performers.

Meanwhile the family of James Biddall's elder brother, Ben Freeman, had been making circus history too.

4

A Clown Is Born

Clowns come and clowns go, but I say without hesitation that it is Pimpo's originality that has won him the foremost place in the ranks of modern jesters.

World's Fair, 13th July 1929

Imagine a dozen organs, with twenty trumpet-power added to each, some worked by steam and some by hand, all playing at the same time, but different tunes; half a dozen bells or other instruments announcing that it is "just going to begin" at as many shows; two great steam roundabouts, with whistles as shrill as railway engines; a genuine train with four cars going round and round; a waltzing machine, where several persons stand on circles of wood in a huge upright birdcage sort of arrangement, with their arms round slight pillars (not at all like waists), and are twirled round separately, and yet all together; a dozen or more shooting-galleries, from whence come the snapping sharp sound of guns and smashed bottles; machines (like pile-drivers) for trying your strength, a weight going up with a mighty spring and coming down with a tremendous thud; other machines for punching; several bowling alleys; thirty or forty swings.

And all this under one roof! 'Dogberry', writing on 5th January 1888 in the *Islington Gazette*, added: 'If anyone wants to know how much the nervous system can stand without utterly breaking down, let him go to the World's Fair at the Agricultural Hall ... The thing I most distinctly recollect is that as I came out an organ which had got to the serious part of the barrel, was playing, *What must it be to be there*?'

One little chap, in no condition to appreciate the experience, was about to find out, for the following day whilst Ben Freeman was in the midst of his clowning act with Walter Scott's circus, his wife gave birth to a son in their living-wagon parked close by.

Ben Freeman had married Elizabeth, daughter of Samuel Mayne, at the parish church in Bermondsey in January 1883 and their family eventually grew to include eight boys and three girls. Many of these children entered the circus but none followed a more distinguished path than their second son, Jimmy, named for his great grandfather James Scott and born within yards of the sawdust ring at the Agricultural Hall.

Ben Freeman continued to clown in his Uncle Walter Scott's circus, taking his whole family with him when the show moved to Ireland. As soon as little Jimmy could toddle he started to pick up the craft and at six years old was ready to make his first appearance. Face made up and in costume, he cart-wheeled into the ring as part of *Charivari*, or what was then called *Tous les Clowns*.

Before long Jimmy was also doing a little throwing about with jockey riders, Bob and Jimmie Scott. Then came a shock. Ben suddenly left Scott's circus to seek work in England leaving his family behind, stranded in their wagon some twenty miles from Dublin. He joined Wirth's Circus at

20. World's Fair in the Agricultural Hall, 1882-83

21. Tous les Clowns preparing to enter the ring at the Agricultural Hall

22. Pat Collins' Show at Nottingham

Bootle, but it was not until he secured a longer contract with Pat Collins that he sent for Jimmy to join him.

In the months that followed, Jimmy 'lost' his tumbling but developed other skills. He paraded on the front of the Bioscope with Mrs Collins and took part in the old style ghost shows. As Little Jim or the Angel he often worked round the clock until at midnight, eyes refusing to stay open, he sleepwalked through his part.

During the years when Jimmy Freeman was growing up, another circus dynasty was developing from the union of Walter Scott's daughter, Elizabeth, and Edwin Hanneford. When he was about thirteen years old, Jimmy was invited by his 'Uncle' Ned to join the Hanneford Circus then at Blackpool preparing to go to Ireland. He leapt at the chance and was soon hard at work outside the ring as well as inside practising his old tumbling and learning what he called 'real' riding. He eventually succeeded well enough to fake for Poodles Hanneford when this young man did not feel like doing his single jockey act.

During the next ten years Jimmy apprenticed himself to every trade in the circus and mastered them all. His speciality was high vaulting, an act he developed to include vaulting over elephants and horses when he appeared with the Hanneford troupe in 'little' Frank Bostock's Circus at Curzon Hall, Birmingham, at Christmas 1911. Jimmy was now in his early twenties. Small in stature – only four feet eleven inches in his socks – but strong and muscular, he was growing anxious about his future.

For the past few years his father Ben Freeman, a brilliant clown and one of the best tumblers of his day, had been suffering from a septic bone in the knee. Refusing to quit he had hobbled about the circus, taking on menial tasks such as filling the paraffin flares which hung on quarter-poles around the ring, regulating the flow of oil by packing their tubes with hair-pins. But in July 1912 his worn-out body gave up its struggle and he died in Belfast, aged 51. His passing weakened young Jimmy's link with the Hanneford show at a time when it was going through troubles of its own. After Walter Scott's death in 1909 a bitter dispute had arisen between Ned Hanneford and his Scott in-laws about ownership of the circus and now Ned was in two minds whether to continue. Jimmy tackled him on the question.

'Uncle,' he asked, 'are you giving up tenting?'

'I don't know. Why do you ask?'

'Well, I can't settle down and I have had an offer from Sanger.'

'My boy,' said Ned, 'if you think you can better yourself, then accept the offer. Don't imagine for a moment that I will do anything to prevent you progressing in your career.'[1]

Accepting this advice, Jimmy joined the Lord John Sanger Circus at their headquarters in Smallfield, near Horley.

The Hannefords continued with a tour of the West Country that proved very successful until they reached Penzance where Ned suddenly took ill and died. Without his direction the show foundered. His children – Poodles, Georgie and Lizzie – struggled on but were eventually tempted abroad. After the whole of their rolling stock, minus tent and six horses, was sold by auction at Stockton-on-Tees on 30th November 1916 the family left for America to seek fame and fortune – both of which they found in good measure.

23. Poodles Hanneford (right) with Tom Mix in America

24. Pimpo takes a trunk call

Meanwhile Jimmy was too busy to regret missed opportunities. His first night at Smallfield was difficult. The place was three miles from anywhere and he felt lonely and miserable, but next morning he was up and ready to begin his first practice at nine o'clock sharp. Undeterred by the group of girls who stood giggling at his efforts, he persisted in his routine: riding in the morning, elephant in the afternoon, trampoline after tea, and 'backs' for what seemed like all eternity.

His obvious talent and dedication were impressive and it was not long before he was taken on to the Sanger staff at the Farm. Apart from those belonging to the Brothers Austin, there were no ring horses in the show at that time, but the following year Jimmy helped to break in five fine animals.

One of the stars of Lord John Sanger's Circus was the clown Pimpo created by Bert Sanger and now understudied by Jimmy. When war broke out in 1914 the two athletic young men went along to enlist only to find themselves rejected as physically unfit. They carried on tenting until 1916 when both were again called up and again rejected. Together they carried out their energetic careers until a third call-up. This time, having passed their fitness tests (grade B2!) they were enrolled for military service. Which left Sangers in a fix because they had just booked a riding-act and elephants into Blackpool Tower Circus.

Three months' exemption for both men was secured, and Jimmy threw himself into a vigorous practising schedule. However, his mind – or rather his heart – was troubled. Military service meant being drafted overseas and leaving behind the girl he loved. With no certainty that he would return, what he wanted more than anything was to marry her so that they might enjoy some life together before having to part. The trouble was, the girl he loved happened to be the boss's daughter.

Victoria Florence Sanger was born on 28th September 1895 at York Road near Waterloo Station. No one had richer Sanger blood in their veins, because when her father George married his cousin Georgina he had united the streams of Lord George and his brother John. Vicky spent much of her earliest years in Tottenham where the Lord John Circus had its headquarters in Braemar Road. It was here that the animals were stabled. New elephants were purchased from Hagenbecks or Myers in Germany, Indian breeds preferred, being deemed more sensitive than African. On one occasion Vicky's grandfather went to collect his latest acquisition from the local railway station and transported it home in a handsome cab. That elephant was ever after known as *Tiny.*

One of Vicky's early memories concerned the terrible episode when another of their animals, a bull elephant called *Palm*, went mad and savaged her father. It happened at Bakewell in 1904. *Palm* stabbed its tusk into George Sanger's groin and George escaped only by rolling under a wagon out of the elephant's way. The animal's keeper looked on helplessly as *Palm* continued to rage and kept the injured man pinned under the wagon. As a last resort the Militia were called in to shoot the beast. George was carried away to recuperate in a hotel where part of *Palm*'s tusk was brought to him as a souvenir – as if he needed any reminder of his ordeal.

Soon after this episode Vicky was sent as a weekly boarder to a private school in Brighton. Her mother, called the Dark Beauty because of her startling looks, had chosen the school primarily for its family atmosphere and Vicky was happy there. Came time to leave, there was no need for her to rack her brains about what to do. Her father immediately set her to work in the ring. Nor did she question his decision. What George Sanger said, went. Not that he was unkind. Vicky judged her father and mother to have been excellent, if forceful, parents. Hence the problem that faced her and Jimmy in February 1917. Their courtship had been so secret that on one occasion in a local cinema, having spotted Vicky's father in the row immediately in front, Jimmy had crept away under the seats to avoid notice. How then could they say that they wanted to marry, knowing that if George Sanger opposed the match there could be no defying his wishes? With typical Sanger determination Vicky decided on a clandestine marriage.

She and Jimmy went to see the local vicar and immediately hit a snag. If he followed usual procedure and called banns, the Sanger name would attract attention and news travel back to the Farm. So, they bought a special licence.

24th February, the great day dawned. Mother and Father were away. The young couple got out their bikes and cycled to Burstow church where the vicar prevailed upon his wife and a stranger off the street to stand as witnesses. Throughout the ceremony Vicky was painfully aware that she still had on her old farm boots.

25. Vicky Freeman, 1938

Back at the Farm the newly weds stowed their bicycles in a shed and, growing nervous with anticipation, set off on foot to meet Mr and Mrs Sanger. They broke the news as they returned home with them in their pony trap. The fond parents took it well, although George quickly pointed out that his new son-in-law had no time to honeymoon in view of his practising schedule for Blackpool.[2]

That season proved unusually challenging. Bert Sanger decided to join up before his period of exemption had elapsed. Jimmy stayed on to see the programme through and took Bert's place in the riding and comedy elephant acts for the last two weeks.

After his return to Horley Jimmy was drafted into the RNAS stationed at Crystal Palace and then sent to France where he survived horrendous ordeals before being brought home to Epsom hospital on a stretcher suffering from gas-poisoning. He spent the last months of the war entertaining troops at camp-shows.

Demobilisation was followed by a short respite at the Farm where he threw himself into preparation for the new tenting season only three months away. Bert Sanger, alias Pimpo the Clown, had been demobbed two or three days before and had already set to work. Practising one morning without the 'Mechanic' riding machine, he attempted the Garters. His knee had been playing him up for some time and now, as he leapt over the ribbons, somehow the holder caught his foot and pulled him off the horse. He fell and broke his hip.

Three weeks to go and their chief performer out of action! What was Sanger's Circus without Pimpo? 'The performance of the elephants, as well as the turns all through, is considerably enhanced by Pimpo, a screamingly funny clown who seems able to turn his agility and ability to almost anything,' a reporter had written before the war.[3] George Sanger saw one solution. Turning to Jimmy, he said:

'Now's your chance to make a name. You're going to take over as Pimpo.'

Three weeks to go and Jimmy had to practise the low wire, learn to play a tune on the bells and do all Bert's other tricks. He succeeded so well that no one guessed that a substitution had taken place and fans of Pimpo continued to cheer the clown they had come to adore.

When in 1921 the Lord John Sanger Circus celebrated its centenary, it was acknowledged that: 'The King of the Castle is Pimpo who has the reputation of being the greatest living clown. He has all the buffoonery of the good old stagers of the ring, but there is genius in his fooling – especially that with the remains of a once tall hat. He is also a clown who is an expert in all circus accomplishments – trick-riding, balancing, acrobatics, gymnastics and all the rest.'

(*World's Fair*, 7th May 1921)

This incredible versatility never ceased to amaze.

> Pimpo, the perfectly ideal circus clown, who excels in every branch from lather boy to bareback riding, wire-walking, and flying-trapeze, establishes himself as a huge success from the moment of his first appearance; he seems to be associated with every turn and gives to each an enhanced value. His versatilities and all-round capabilities called forth spontaneous applause of the heartiest; one envies him his happy knack of infecting vast audiences with such unfeigned delight. (*World's Fair*, 29th October 1921)

> Out of a programme of eighteen events, Pimpo is the mainspring. In Circusland today there is no other clown so versatile as he. He is the one and only Pimpo, and has no equal in this or any other country. Pimpo excels in everything. (*World's Fair*, 14th June 1924)

As if this were not praise enough, the following year Pimpo was hailed in the *Daily Mail* as: 'the world's most marvellous man … There is surely nothing he cannot do.'

By now Jimmy was a family man. The birth of his only child was registered at Barnet in June 1920. Named George James Patrick Freeman, the little lad was always called Pat after his father's life-long friend, Pat Collins, junior. (Jimmy had been best man when Patrick Collins married Eliza Fossett at Chester in 1908.)

Jimmy also worked closely with his brother Sam who had proved a wizard at lighting up the circus ring. Both were stunned when they heard of their brother Bobby's death in October 1925. Together with a fourth brother, George, he had been appearing at the Croydon Empire with the Royal Italian Circus when he threw himself from a fourth floor window. He was twenty-nine years old.

Despite this tragedy and a run of painful accidents Jimmy continued to be heart and soul of the show. When he appeared at Hastings in August 1927 one reporter found it hard to find anything new to say about a performer who was such a consummate artiste in every branch of circus work:

> Be it wire-walking, riding, acrobatism, aerial work or comedy, it must suffice to say that in all he is *facile princeps* and at every appearance draws thunderous applause or shrieks of laughter from the onlookers. His *entrée* as a taxi driver of an extraordinary 'Tin Lizzie' is possibly the funniest thing that has ever been done in a circus ring, but it is run very close by his performance as a knight in shining armour mounted on a horse of weird aspect … Last but not least Mr Sam Freeman, the electrician, is responsible for the brilliant and effective lighting which very materially enhances the whole performance. (*World's Fair*, 27th August 1927)

After Hastings the circus visited Rye and Hythe before moving round the South East Coast into Essex and Suffolk, reaching Norfolk by November. Despite dreadful weather they had kept strictly to their planned route and dates, losing not a single performance. With a programme made up of seventeen items, most of which included Pimpo, it was a punishing schedule and he was glad of his new assistant – the young lady who rode the giant elephant and appeared as an Indian girl in the

Pimpo's Brothers:

26. Above – Freddie Freeman (left) with Otto Griebling

27. Left – Bobby Freeman (1896-1925)

28. Right – Wee Georgie Freeman, father of Ella and Adene

dashing bare-back riding act, impatient passenger in Pimpo's 'Tin Lizzie' and one of the death-defying duo on the high trapeze. The 'lady' was in fact Mr George Knight whose make-up and impersonations duped even his friends.

Six weeks at Glasgow's Kelvin Hall and then Sangers set out on a tour of Scotland in March 1928 via Dundee, Aberdeen and Inverness before turning south and heading towards '*Home, boys, home, to happy Horley*.' Everywhere they went their clown won favour. At Ballater the old people spoke of Pimpo as 'something handed in to delight the world.' (*World's Fair*, 21st July1928)

'Pimpo – the one and only – he, a nasty pinprick to the comatose, is the mainspring of the fun. In the humorous sketch *Pimpo's Joy Ride in the Magical Tin Lizzie* it is doubtful if any funnier or more laughter-provoking scene could be imagined. In Circusland today there is no other artiste who is so hard-worked, nor so versatile as he. Pimpo excels in everything he does, and over-excels in everything he tries to do.' (*World's Fair*, 16th June 1928)

Sangers' success was repeated the following year when they toured Wales and the West Country with Pimpo hailed as 'the world-famous clown and the cleverest most likely.'

At Taunton in June J.S. Fisher declared of Pimpo, 'Surely this man so indefatigable can do everything, and even do it backwards.' (*World's Fair*, 15th June 1929) Bridgwater, Burnham, Weston and

Wellington followed. They opened at Tiverton (Devon) on 10th June. 'Pegasus', describing Sanger's tour of the West, wrote: 'There is only one Pimpo, and small though he is, he is a "handful". Clowns come and clowns go, but I say without hesitation that it is Pimpo's originality that has won him the unchallenged title of Prince of Clowns.' (*World's Fair*, 13th July 1929)

When Vicky's uncle, 'Lord' John Sanger (nephew of 'Lord' George) died in August 1929 the circus that bore his name was in the midst of one of the most successful seasons in its long history. Returning east along the Sussex seaboard it opened at Chichester on 15th August, then Bognor, Littlehampton, Worthing, Seaford and Lewes before reaching Hythe on the 29th where, after a twenty-mile journey, the company gave performances at 3 p.m. and 8 p.m. A further series of one-night stands took them through Kent into Essex where they opened at Halstead on 21st October, then Braintree, Chelmsford, Romford, Bexley Heath. After reaching Dartford on the 26th they went into winter-quarters at Horley breathing, one imagines, hefty sighs of relief.

1930 saw Lord John Sanger's New Wonder Circus at Oxford in May before heading down to the south coast for the summer season. 'Pimpo is an easy favourite,' reported 'Southdown' who saw the show at Hove. (World's Fair, 7th June 1930) By the time they reached Folkestone in September Pimpo had added yet another item to his repertoire – high stilts. In this, as in everything else, he excelled. Writing about *Clowns & Clowning* the following month, 'Pegasus' declared, 'If asked to name the brightest star in last season's firmament I should unhesitatingly answer – PIMPO! In this clever little gent we have personality, originality and versatility combined [with] that most valuable of all assets viz. *energy!*' (*World's Fair*, 4th October 1930)

Starting the 1931 season at Uxbridge, Pimpo took a nasty tumble at the opening show but pluckily carried on. May found the circus at Wolverhampton en route for Rhyl where Pimpo met 'Rexe' who had performed as a contortionist with Biddall's show in Scotland more than twenty years before. Now mother of four, she had left to go on the halls where she said life was much easier. Amen to that, Pimpo must have thought, for not only was he undisputed star of the show, he still took on his full share of physical labour. An old friend spotted him that season heaving a rope and barking orders in a 'foreign' language. 'It was Welsh, anyway, Jimmy,' he conceded.

While Jimmy was eulogised wherever he went, his brothers were attracting attention too. Sam Freeman for his lighting skills; George, after a broken knee-cap put paid to his trick-riding, as a talking clown. At Sittingbourne in June 1932 George together with Jack Cooke, James Scott and 'Spider' was providing comedy for the Royal Italian Circus. Another brother, Freddie, was touring Australia with Wirth's circus.

During the winter of 1932/3 Pimpo toured variety theatres with Lord John Sanger's circus, arriving at the old-established Royal Artillery Theatre, Woolwich, in April, where he was photographed encoiled by huge live serpents.

The following winter Sangers played twice nightly plus matinees to packed houses at Birmingham Hippodrome. C.H. Lea took advantage of Pimpo's rare spare moments to chat with him in the wings. Afterwards he reported:

> It is Jimmy Freeman who has made the name of Pimpo synonymous with all that is best in the circus. It is not merely that his diminutive form strolling on to the stage convulses the audience or that his famous shrill voice crying: "Let's have another one" remains in the memory of anyone who has ever seen him. It is not only that he can ride, wire walk, stilt walk, tumble, somersault, train animals, do a trapeze act, and in fact do almost anything in a ring. It is not only that he is a handyman if ever there was one, being able to repair tents as well as a tent-maker, being able to shoe horses in a manner which many smiths could not excel, making his own boots for the big boot act, and being able to do any ordinary or extraordinary job that comes along. No, all these help to make

29. Pimpo with reptile friends

him a memorable figure, but what endears him most to those who have the good fortune to make his acquaintance is that he is above all a Man. With his many gifts there would be excuses for him to be conceited, overbearing, or bad company, but he is the contrary, a most delightful companion and conversationalist.

Many years ago Jimmy used to take part in high jumping acts, involving vaulting, and he declares that the last time in England this was done over animals was in Birmingham where he and others vaulted over three elephants and two camels.

His circus life has not been all honey for he has had his fair share of accidents. In fact, he showed me scars and lumps galore caused by accidents on the trapeze and horseback, and recently he fell from the trapeze and was unable to walk the stilts as he intended …

In addition to his other activities Pimpo has trained the elephant, the dogs, and some of the horses appearing now with Sanger's Circus.

Pimpo! You're a king without crown,
I foresee your immortal renown.
Many hearts may you thrill
Pimpo, with your skill!
O Pimpo, you adorable clown!

(*World's Fair*, 26th January 1935)

In the same year William Bosworth published a lively description of Irrepressible Pimpo of Sanger's Circus:

He is amusing in speech and gesture, versatile with his hands and feet, he carries off feats of acrobatics with an air of bungling incompetence, he knows how to be ridiculous in a becoming manner, and he can do a big-boot dance like Little Tich …

He is now about 45, smaller than the average, but beautifully muscular. He can ride, tumble, somersault, wire-walk, stilt-walk, train animals, show horses, mend tents like a sail-maker, cobble his big boots, make his own properties, and has numerous scars as souvenirs of the accidents of his lifetime in the ring. His shrill voice beseeching the ring-master to let him 'have a go' and his grotesquely clad, diminutive form, remain in the memory of all who have ever seen him in the ring. He was the first clown to use a comic motor car and he still works an act called 'Modern Transport', driving a freak car which sprays water from its radiator, has a door that will not close, and finally collapses.

His efforts as gymnast and conjuror show him in a new light, for his act requires a tremendous physical fitness. The first time he has 'a go' he fails, ludicrously, but he somehow seems to get the hang of the trick and then, as it seems, by accident, does it as well as the original performer. He trained Jumbo, the John Sanger Circus dancing elephant and puts it through its paces in the ring. They swing on a seesaw and then he leaps high into the air, landing on the elephant's forehead. His galaxy of talents would make many men conceited, but Pimpo is a choice companion and pleasant talker, as energetic as ever.

(*Wagon Wheels: The Romance of the Circus*)[4]

From Birmingham Hippodrome in 1935 Sanger's Circus travelled via Wolverhampton to North Wales where Jimmy was photographed with his old friend Pat Collins, junior, in Colwyn Bay in July.

30. Jimmy out for a stroll with Pat Collins, Junr, 1935

Returning home at the end of the season, Jimmy's sail-making skills were put to good use when he personally repaired the big tent after it blew down in a storm at Saffron Walden.

In 1936 Lord John Sanger's circus toured Scotland. The comic genius of Pimpo, now at the peak of his powers, was well portrayed by M. Willson Disher in *Greatest Show on Earth*:[5]

When the canvas flap lifts ... a stage whisper runs electrically round the benches: "Here he comes." He is Pimpo. In case this is your first circus, the name is printed for you in big letters right across the back of his black coat whose tails dust his heels. He has a large white collar, and large white spats on his tiny feet. His little figure is crowned with a large top hat; under this is a large mop of hair, nearly as red as his tie. He joins the others on the tightrope as bold as brass. But when his turn comes to step on it he is frightened to death. His knee shakes and his balancing-pole trembles. He slips. He falls – but only on the place meant for falls. He gets up and rides a bicycle on the wire ...

That Pimpo was a wire-walker was but the start of the story. When the skewbalds galloped round the ring, after floundering on their bare backs and being sent flying into the sawdust, he picked himself up, took off his coat and braced himself for the run and single bound which landed him on the croup. Next came the trapeze where, after being restrained from certain death, he flung himself into full flight.

After that Pimpo began to show his pupil, Bee Bee, a few tricks – falling over chairs and tables, decapitating an assistant who ran away leaving his head behind him – providing all the fun of *humpsti-bumpsti*. Then they stood on a double swing and while Pimpo looped the loop one way, Bee Bee circled round and under and above him in the opposite direction. The finale was *Dick Turpin's Ride to York* with Pimpo among those in hot pursuit. Exhibiting all the gestures of a man riding post-haste on a horse slower than a hearse, he is inevitably left behind.

"Who are you?" demanded the toll-keeper.

"I'm one of those men who have just gone through," squeaked Pimpo.

The Lord John Sanger Circus visited Southampton on Saturday, 7th August 1937, having been at Lymington the previous day and going on to Fareham for Monday – one-day tenting still being the rule. It opened on the Stadium car park with its large white two-pole tent (high enough for the Ansons' flying act), small canvas front and about thirty vehicles in green and yellow diagonal livery with SANGER outlined in red. A menagerie of seven beast-wagons plus horse and elephant tents made up the imposing show.

The programme included Clem Merk's lions, Captain Barth's liberties, Pedersen's giant sea lion, Jumbo the football elephant, and of course Pimpo, who joined the Ansons on the flying trapeze and introduced his hundred horsepower Rolls (Model T Ford).

When the show toured the south-west in 1938 one act much applauded was the Finandos, an equestrian troupe featuring Pimpo (of course), Vicky, and their nephew, Sammy Freeman, who at twenty-one had developed into an accomplished rider. Sam (senior) with thirty years conscientious work with the show was in charge of transport and lighting. As for Pimpo, *The Mighty Atom*, he was hailed as 'the most remarkable circus performer of his age.' (*World's Fair*, 17th September 1938)

On the outbreak of War Jimmy's son Pat, now nineteen, had enrolled in the London Irish Rifles. Passing through West Africa on his way to India five years later, he was amazed to find a French comrade in possession of a copy of *Seventy Years A Showman,* the story of his own great-great-grandfather. The man had evidently got it from another Frenchman who had taken it off a German prisoner. At home, when animal food became scarce and the family decided to sell the Lord John Sanger Circus in 1941, Jimmy went into variety with *Pimpo's Pets*, but he was happy to join Vicky's brother, George Sanger, when he opened his own circus at Stoney Stratford the following April. The new company was registered on 4th December 1944 as Lord George Sanger's Circus Limited. Address: Ballantrae, Massetts Road, Horley. Nominal capital: £5000 in £1 shares. Directors: G. Sanger; Florence I. Sanger; Victoria F. Freeman; and J. Freeman. During a tour of the West Country which included eight days at Bristol George Sanger and Jimmy Freeman were congratulated on 'keeping the old name up to its high standard.' (*World's Fair*, 23rd September 1944)

In 1945 Lord George Sanger's Circus opened at Brighton on Easter Monday for a week. After visiting Worthing, Lewes, Uckfield, East Grinstead and Crawley, they were close to home when peace was announced.

Jimmy was now approaching sixty. A director of the company and still king-pin of the programme, he might have been forgiven for delegating manual tasks. But that was not his style. One miserable wet afternoon in the summer of 1945 Sangers was built up beside the London road into Sutton. During the matinee a rent in the canvas top was spotted which would have to be repaired immediately after the show. As soon as the canvas was dropped a little man with a determined look on his face and implements of a sail-maker in his hands stepped from his wagon. He walked to the canvas, squatted down, and oblivious of the persistent drizzle set about sewing up the tear. When it was done he took his part in getting the canvas up again.

That evening he was in the ring – the clown of all the talents, loved by all.[6]

Lord George Sanger's Circus toured along the South Coast in 1946. After visiting Folkestone, Hythe, Dymchurch, New Romney, they moved on through Sussex and Hampshire to arrive at Lyme Regis in July. Then they headed back east to open at Bexhill in August. At West Molesey the following month the company was entertained by Countess Du Mariette at Mole Abbey.

And now a new star was rising in Sanger's firmament. After his demobilisation, Pat Freeman entered the ring as 'Sandy' and quickly established himself as a talented bareback rider. A *Pathé* film – *A Day with Lord George Sanger's Circus* – made in 1947 featured Jimmy and Pat. In the same year Pat and his wife Muriel presented Jimmy with his first grandson, christened Michael. With the birth of their second son, Peter, in 1948 the dynasty was secure. It was just as well, for Vicky had just retired from the ring and Jimmy was far from well when they opened at Sutton in April, even if his act gave no hint.

At the beginning of 1949 Jimmy welcomed his brother Georgie (an Auguste), together with his equestrienne daughter Ella into the company. For a time Jimmy, Pat, Georgie and Ella formed a brilliant Freeman foursome.

31. Scene from the Pathé film (1947) Pat Freeman, Phil Williams, Pimpo and Ray, above

32. Pimpo and grandsons, Michael and Pip (future jockey act riders), right

Before the annual Reunion of Circus at Park Lane Hotel that year (with Victor Biddall among the guests) Jimmy was elected to give one of the two responses to the Chairman. The strange thing was, this man who had been entertaining the public for over fifty years persuaded Albert Bandbox Austin to deputise for him – because he was so shy!

Jimmy was back in fine fettle for the next season. Under a heading *Circus Best Life in the World* the *Evening Standard* (5th September) reported that '61 year old Jimmy Freeman ... is one clown who claims to be happy outside the ring. Last night, after the opening show at Parliament Hill Fields, Pimpo puffed contentedly at his pipe – a short stumpy man with whispy grey hair – "I was born in a circus caravan while the show was on. I went in the ring when I was six. I have done every circus act there is, and I would not change a day of it."'

At the beginning of the 1952 season Jimmy's health was poor and he had to make the hardest decision of his life – to retire from the ring as a performer. But belonging as he did to circus, circus still claimed him and he continued for as long as he could as the show's handy-man.

The Lord George Sanger circus still travelled under the personal direction of Mr and Mrs George Sanger, but Pat Freeman was now the dominating figure with his *Old Regnas* act. (Regnas being Sanger spelt backwards.) Also prominent in the programme were Georgie Freeman's two daughters, Ella and Adena, and Georgie had taken over *Pimpo's Pets.* By 1956 Jimmy's failing strength kept him at Horley, unable to leave the farm when the circus set out for its new season.

In his seventieth year Jimmy journeyed to Scotland where the circus was booked for a season at Edinburgh's Waverley Market. When a *World's Fair* reporter visited their quarters in Seafield Road he found him confined to bed with a bad chill. Unable to attend the 22nd Circus Reunion in London, a telegram was sent from Vicky, Jimmy Freeman and Mr and Mrs Regnas in Edinburgh with "Best wishes to all for a happy evening."

The following year Jimmy, again too ill to attend, wrote wishing all concerned a happy night. Among guests who heard the letter read out was his cousin, Henry 'Spuds' Biddall, son of James and Clara. For the next twelve months Jimmy fought for breath. At one time an oxygen cylinder made this easier but, unable to stomach hospital, he decided to die where his heart was – with the circus.

The 24th Annual Circus Reunion took place on Sunday, 22nd January 1961. Just fifteen minutes from its close George Sanger phoned with sad news from Edinburgh. Jimmy Freeman had just died.

In his tribute to the man 'known to the public throughout the length and breadth of the land as Pimpo,' Edward Graves listed Jimmy's skills as blacksmith, saddle-maker, groom, bareback rider, tumbler – 'at his zenith he performed the cushions over no fewer than nine men and even after that he went over seven at every performance' – high wire walker, trapeze artiste. Adding that 'this by no means exhausts the list – it is simpler to name what he couldn't do,' Graves continued,

> He was funny too – really so. In fact, he was the incarnation of circus in all its aspects ... In his own day he was easily an all-rounder without a superior – and I cannot even think of an equal. History cannot produce one greater from out of the past. Physically there wasn't very much of him, but what he lacked in inches either way was more than made up for in the manner he measured up to whatever circus required him to do.[7]

33. Pimpo clowning at the fair

5

Biddall's Ghost

The Cumberland Run ... Famous shows forty years ago included Biddall's Ghost Show with its magnificent front, all richly carved in spectres and gnomes.

World's Fair, 13th November 1937

After the death of Henry St Clair Freeman in 1866, his youngest son George was left at the age of eighteen with a patrimony laid up, not in property or gold, but training and talent. Like his brothers and sisters he had imbibed show business with his mother's milk and as soon as he could walk was assimilated into Biddall's company. Throughout the summer months he travelled the fairs, blowing a musical instrument and tumbling in his father's booth. In winter his family joined with that of the Smiths to run a show at small theatres such as Whitby's Theatre Royal. In September 1861 the working partnership between Biddalls and Smiths had been cemented by the marriage of Henry and Hannah's second son, Samuel, to Augusta, daughter of Joseph Smith. They married at Maldon, Essex, the groom giving his profession as 'musician' and his age (possibly an exaggeration) as twenty-one.

Smiths and Biddalls were together the following winter at Whitby, giving rise to a debate seventy years later after Whimsical Walker had risen to fame. Augusta's brother Joseph Smith, who by then had himself achieved renown as King Ohmy, Glittering Star of the Air, claimed that he had been the first to dress Whimsical as a clown. It took Whimsical himself to point out that Joseph had been just a tiny lad in 1862 and that the real honour was due to another performer with Biddalls – William Wallser who later married Henry and Hannah's daughter, Polly. Signora Wallser's Japanese Illusions were named as the principal attraction at Biddall's Grand Temple of Magic when it opened on the circus ground at Scarborough in December 1868.

It was inevitable that young people growing up in families that lived and worked together became romantically involved with one another. Samuel, having married Augusta Smith, acted as witness at the marriage of his youngest brother to Augusta's sister, Selina, a clever tightwire performer, at Darlington on 2nd May 1870. Like their brothers, they had married into showbusiness, their father-in-law being Joseph Smith, owner of the Sans Pareil Circus and himself descended from a line of strolling players. It was this tradition that had brought George and Selina together and such was their dedication that, their wedding day being fair day in Darlington, once the church ceremony was over they hurried straight back to their business.

Both George and Selina were ardent and ambitious. They had talent, discipline – and an extra mouth to feed in December 1871 when their first child was born. How best to provide for their family? A travelling show was what they needed. Not just the kind of old hanky-panky show

34. The Ohmy Family

35. King Ohmy's daughters

36. Joseph Smith, King Ohmy (1854-1931)

37. George Sinclair Freeman-Biddall

38. Biddall's Ghost – 'the grinning skull that slowly melted away'

39. Selina Freeman-Biddall (King Ohmy's sister)

established by George's parents. Something different. Something new. Something to satisfy people's appetite for sensation and melodrama. Casting around, George hit on just the thing. A ghost illusion show.

In February 1863 Professor Pepper had introduced his new 'Spectre Drama' to excited audiences at the Regent Street Polytechnic in London. Presented every day at half-past one and on Monday, Thursday and Saturday evenings, 'This astounding optical effect, in which a living being walks through the apparently solid image of another person, surpasses all the phantasy of the Spirit Rappers and Mediums.' (*Era*, 22nd February 1863)

An instant success, by May Professor Pepper had gained the permission of Charles Dickens to read an extract from his *Tale of the Haunted Man* during which the ghost appeared to walk across the stage. A few weeks later the exhibition went on tour, showing at the Assembly Rooms in Cheltenham before the Duke of Beaufort. By July the Ghost was being advertised at Edinburgh, Liverpool, Leeds and Nottingham.

The *Era* of 26th July reported on its appearance at the Canterbury:

> On Monday last the old Canterbury presented an appearance recalling the crowded nights of its early career ... The cause of such an unusual gathering was the advent of the wondrous scientific illusion called the Ghost, which has been introduced through the medium of Mr Alfred Silvester, the well-known photographer of New Bond Street ...
>
> The vocal and acting part of the entertainment consisted of the ghost scene in Hamlet and an improvised duo pantomime for the purpose of trying the effective working of the apparatus ... On examining the illusion, we find every portion of the solid living figure acting with perfect freedom. No person not acquainted with the subject can possibly imagine that the figure they see before them, with head, hands and feet moving, with the lips in motion; nay, even the very eyes and eye-lashes performing their ordinary functions, is nothing but the reflection of some unseen person below the stage. Mr Silvester has succeeded admirably in his delineation of optical science. There was one incident in the second picture that was capitally managed; and that was the transfer of a rose from the living actor on the stage to the hands of the spectre.
>
> Of course anyone at all conversant with such matters knows how it is done, but as a beautiful though very delicate operation, requiring to be most carefully performed to prevent failure, we leave the discovery of the *modus operandi* to our ingenious readers.

After this Ghosts sprang up all over the country. Professor Duvernay exhibited his 'Polytechnic Ghost' in Leicester at the same time as Mr King, photographer, was showing his at Bath and another was appearing in a Leeds music hall where dissolving scenes of the Rhine were explained in an unintelligible lecture, and there was a gigantic portrait of Queen Victoria in her coronation robes together with distorted images of the Prince and Princess of Wales.

Professor Pepper was not pleased. Refusing to tolerate substandard Ghosts, he placed an advert in the *Era*, 19th July 1863: 'Polytechnic Ghost Illusion – to Lecturers and Managers of Theatres – Professor Pepper is prepared to fit up proper apparatus, and give full instructions, including all recent improvements with permission to use his name, on moderate terms.'

Moderate? It seemed that one man's moderation was another's extortion! When the Manager of the Stamford Theatre applied to the patentee, he was told that the charge was fifty pounds a night. This, he remarked, was surely 'pepper with the acridity of cayenne.'

And what right had Professor Pepper to claim a monopoly on the spectral drama in any case? There were other contenders.

> The rival ghosts have now fallen out and are doing battle with each other. We understand that Professor Pepper whose spectre has been provisionally patented, has applied for a completion of his patent. Mr H.N. King who has also provisionally patented a spectral illusion, on Wednesday lodged an opposition in the Patent Office against Professor Pepper's application, on the ground that the invention is not new, as alleged, that the Professor's arrangements contain no novelty, and that he (Mr King) believes the Professor intends to include in his final specification part of Mr King's improvements. (*Bath Gazette*, 26th August 1863)

Mr Hughes from the Zoological Gardens, Liverpool, also claimed to be the original inventor. 'It is now some twelve years since I exhibited the same effect at Vauxhall Gardens under the management of Mr Robert Wardle; the following year at Cremorne Gardens under the management of Mr Simpson (both will corroborate).' In fact it could be said that the Ghost had been stalking the world for at least three centuries, the illusion having been described in John Baptista de Porta's *Natural Magick* in 1558. But Professor Pepper was not to be put off. He took to advertising 'his' Ghost with a list of those with permission to use it. Although his name does not appear in this list, it seems that George Biddall was one of the first showmen to take the Ghost Show on to the fairground.

40. George Biddall's famous ghost show

PHANTOSPECTRA BIDDALLS GHOSTODRAMAS

With these gold letters emblazoned across a magnificent show front, the name of George Biddall began to make its impact in the north. Winter quarters were often at Hartlepool, where the family stayed in the Market Yard and their employees boarded out while the show wagons and equipment were overhauled and redecorated at the premises of Howcroft's Carriage Works in Ouston Street. Fresh for paint and drawn by well-fed and well-groomed horses the long line of wagons would then take the road for Trimdon, Halt-whistle, Penrith, Kendal, Ayr, Hawick and all over Scotland. It was not unusual to be faced with a succession of one-night stands that meant pulling down late and, depending on the number of miles ahead, making ready for an early start. After such backbreaking work to find themselves in one place for several days was bliss.

Erecting the show was heavy work but took surprisingly little time, everything being so well planned and organised. First, the huge wagon that formed the stage was positioned broadside on. This side was then opened outwards in sections and the top pushed up in a triangle to carry the stays and long canvas top. Next, two sumptuous and roomy living wagons were lined up to form the entrance. On these three vehicles the whole structure was reared with its magnificent gilt, wood and plaster facade and brightly painted panels. A big drum and cymbals stood to one side of the platform that ran along the front. The broad wooden steps leading up to the show's pay box and entrance were flanked by two ornate pillars.

But no matter how impressive, Biddalls couldn't rely on their show front to draw in punters when they stood against competition such as the line up of shows at Alloa Fair in 1880. It was up to their parade to make the difference. An ear-splitting crash of cymbals and reverberation on drum would presage the appearance on the front of George Biddall with his neatly trimmed beard, smart jacket and leggings. As Master of Ceremonies he would try to 'tell the tale' despite the antics of the company's clown. In later years George's son, Funny Joey, played this latter role to perfection,

41. *Funny Joey*

42. *Victor and Lion, the dog used in comic routines. His collar said: 'I'm Vic Biddall's dog, whose dog are you?'*

mischievously shadowing his father and imitating his every move. Enter a barking dog which sank its teeth into the seat of Joey's trousers, forcing him to scramble up on to the top of the show squealing: "They're all afraid of the dog but me!"

Children loved it. And it was good showmanship, for – as George used to say: 'A little nonsense now and then is relished by the wisest of men.'

After the clowning came a 'big boot' dance, conjuring tricks, and part of the ghostly drama to be seen within. Admittance to the show was 3d for best seats. For the 'working man' there were seats at 2d, children 1d. But what was money in the face of such delights?

'Inside the fare provided was ever new, and the encounters of the black minstrels and the clowns with the ghostly apparitions which by some ingenious arrangement were made to appear and disappear, were greeted with loud laughter and sometimes with feelings of awe.'[1]

The programme might consist of a sketch such as *The Haunted House* in which two fellows, one with a banjo and the other with a set of bones, were maltreated by a ghost which mysteriously appeared and disappeared after clouting first one, then the other. Then a huge skeleton would appear on stage and horrifically discard an arm, a leg, a rib – ending up as nothing but a grinning skull that slowly melted away. When business was good, twenty or more such shows were given in a day. When business was bad and the stay had to be protracted a more varied repertoire was called on – *Uncle Tom's Cabin* perhaps – with angels appearing and disappearing to the bewilderment of all.

Unfortunately not all people were prepared to enjoy the Ghost Illusion as such. Some, viewing it far too seriously, became convinced that they were in the presence of a real Black Magician. On one occasion in Wales George, after a successful start to his tour, found himself suddenly accused of being an agent of the Devil. The slander spread quickly through the principality with the result that business dropped off and George was forced to turn tail and make for Blackburn.

The trouble was, with tolls to be paid at frequent intervals on the road, his funds ran out and he found it hard to convince toll-bar keepers that the owner of such a smart-looking show was penniless. After one lengthy argument the fellow agreed to accept a pair of boots as security for his tolls. With the help of similar articles, George eventually reached Blackburn where his luck turned. Meeting a man who owed him money enabled him to clear his debts and open Biddall's doors once more to prosperity.

In a photograph of Alloa Fair in 1880 the only riding devices seen are one large single boat and a few sets of swings and dobbies. Apart from a considerable number of small stalls, Alloa fairground is dominated by the line-up of shows amongst which Biddall's Phantospectra Ghostodramas holds its own with the best. One member of the company stands on top of the steps – perhaps George, but too far from the camera to be recognisable.

By 1880 he had arrived at a comfortable position in life. He had a show that was fast establishing itself as one of the best in the north. An enviable personal reputation: 'George Biddall was one of the finest men who ever travelled and one who, though well endowed with this world's goods, was never affected, but just a plain upright unassuming gentleman,' wrote a colleague in later years.[2] It was claimed that even children cheered as soon as he set foot on stage, 'for who didn't know the famous George Biddall?' asked T.W. Carrick, Wigton historian, writing in his Parish Magazine. And George took delight in his thriving young family.

Selina had given birth to a daughter, Eveline Sinclair, at North Wall, Whitehaven, in December 1871. Albert Sinclair, born in the wagon as it lumbered along the road between West Calder and Broxburn two years later, could boast of being the first of his clan to be born in Scotland. Joseph Sinclair was born at Market Place, Middlesbrough, in January 1875. Selina gave birth to another son, William Sinclair, at Redheugh Bridge Approach, Newcastle, in March 1877. 1878 opened sadly with news that George's brother, Samuel, was seriously ill. He died in Glasgow Royal Infirmary on 22nd February of phthisis, leaving his widow with several children and a new baby to rear on her own. Much as they wanted to support Augusta in her hour of need, George and Selina were immersed in troubles of their own. Selina was already pregnant again when their little son William contracted meningitis and died at Oldgate Street in Morpeth on 29th April. At Priestpopple, Hexham, on 12th December, she gave birth to twins, Victor Sinclair and Henry Sinclair. Caring for five children under seven must have been wearing, especially with one of the babies delicate. Little Henry died at Percy Street in Newcastle the following April.

Fortunately family life wasn't all sadness in these years. There had been cause for celebration when Mademoiselle Ariella, alias Elizabeth Smith, Selina and Augusta's sister, married Charlie Keith, 'the Roving Clown', at Stockport in July 1877. Their guests included the great P.T. Barnum who happened to be staying with his father-in-law, Mr Fish, in Portland Street. In a congratulatory speech he quoted Pope: 'Honour and fame from no condition rise, Act well your part, there all the honour lies.' After the nuptials, the groom took advantage of having his brother-in-law, King Ohmy, in Stockport to arrange for him a special benefit performance at which Keith himself promised to give his 'interesting and practical illustration on spirit rapping and to mesmerise the audience.'[3]

43. Biddall's Show at Alloa Fair, 1880

44. George Biddall, 'one of the finest men who ever travelled' – striding out with his show on the road

Further celebrations took place at Cockermouth in November 1879 when Augusta Freeman, Selina's widowed sister, married William Palmer, himself a widower, in a ceremony witnessed by James and Harriet Stokes, long-time performers with Biddalls.

With the birth of Selina Elizabeth at Sunderland Road, Gateshead, on 20th January 1881 George and Selina's family was complete. Her presence, however, seems to have been overlooked by the census enumerator who found the Biddalls at Durham's Elvet Racecourse in April. The race-course would have had special appeal for George Biddall. Horses were his passion, an essential part of his life. Top priority in any town they visited was to find good grazing. If the horses had to be put out to pasture on the outskirts, someone on the showground would be detailed to fill nosebags every morning, load them on a trap and take them down to the field. George had been known to refuse to open his show in a town that could not provide adequate accommodation for his horses.

One horse, Captain, held such a special place in his heart that, when it died, George had its tail cured to treasure as a keepsake. Recalling the incident in later years, William Merrick, one of Biddall's oldest retainers, penned this tribute:

One night in my wagon, while smoking my pipe,
The smoke from the same brought my past days to light,
My eyes, glancing upwards, saw hung on a nail,
A part of a favourite old horse's tail.

I thought of that horse, and the roads I had been
While driving the same, and the sights I had seen.
How well he had worked and taken his load,
Regardless of weather, regardless of road.

North, East, West and South, I have travelled around,
In England, but chiefly on old Scotia's ground,
Till at last by the Humane Society told
He was not fit to work, he was getting too old.

So at once put him down, or the law take its course,
Thus the warrant was signed for the death of the horse;
The spot being chosen, without any parley,
The grave then was dug out by Andy and Charley.

I will not condemn, but will credit the brave
Old Lively the Ostler, lent a hand to the grave,
Then, all being ready, he was led to the spot,
Condemned by the hand of James Stokes to be shot.

And true to the last, stood firmly and steady,
And held down his head, as if to say ready,
The trigger was pulled, the bullet flew fast,
Poor Captain fell, and that was his last.

On Whickham Thorn farm, where oft he has fed,
He now lies at peace in his cold clay bed;
Thought well of by master, thought well of by man,
But with horses, as Christians, life's but a span.[4]

Old William Merrick, writing in retirement, could afford to be sentimental. There would have been little time to express such emotion when Biddall's show was on the road – if one were to judge from the following disastrous day.

It happened when Biddall's Show was at Anstruther, breaking new ground beyond Fifeshire where they had never been seen before. A call came for an early start.

45. Horse section leaving Lockerbie. Front wagon: Victor Biddall stands with horses, his mother holds the reins

46. Engine section leaving Lockerbie. Left to right: Victor, Charlie Miller and Joey (in driver's seat)

At four o'clock next morning the company roused itself, only to find that a pony had gone missing and could not be found. Then a nerved horse needed a shoe and in the absence of a blacksmith, they had to do the job themselves, a tricky business with a horse of this nature.

47. Biddall's engine in trouble at Prestwick (Ayr)

Then they had problems leaving the field. Trying to turn into the narrow approach lane, the engine pulling their heaviest load broke into a drain and became stuck in the most awkward of places. With help this was righted and the loads got under way until, passing through a village, another of the horses dropped dead in front of the minister's door. Nothing for it but to wire for a knacker with instructions where to find the carcase.

The show proceeded on its way until it reached a hill where for some unknown reason the horses pulling the wagons took it into their heads to bolt. Risking life and limb, young Selina rushed in front of them, holding up her hands to try and check their breakneck pace. She was knocked down, happily falling clear of the wheels of the heavy wagon as it rolled over her – the one piece of luck on this disastrous day.

Eventually Biddall's arrived at Leven where they had arranged to stand at the dockside, except – there were already wagons there. Rivals had pinched their site. Not to worry. Another was found. Suitable, even if it did involve crossing a stretch of soft sand to reach it. No sooner had they accomplished this difficult task than an objection came from a local lady of some influence. Official permission, it seemed, was required for them to stay. Since there was no time to seek this, they were advised to move. Laborious back-tracking over the sand brought them to a safe pitch on the golf links. Sighs of relief all round.

Then George was handed a telegram. The knacker had sent word that he could not remove the dead horse left behind that morning. Another wire followed – from the village constable this time. The carcase was obstructing the queen's highway and must be shifted. Forthwith.

Pity the poor showman at the end of a hard day's travel which had landed him sixteen miles from the scene and nothing for it but to return along that same road. One of George's sons and an employee trudged back on foot. With much difficulty and expense – it cost them thirty shillings – they arranged for the disposal of the carcase before returning to Leven, thankful to see the end of such a day.[5]

6

Almost The First

> Monsieur Lumière was greatly interested in what I told him, taking notes of many of the features of the lanterns and adopting many of my suggestions in the contraption which evolved into the first cinematograph.
>
> *World's Fair*, 14th August 1937

In the 1890s the twice yearly 'Cumberland Run' of hiring fairs in June and November always featured Biddall's Ghost Show with its magnificent front richly carved with spectres and gnomes and the fun on the outside before each performance being created by Funny Joey Biddall, the children's idol. Like his brothers and sisters and their mother and father before them, Joey had been taught the essentials of showmanship from his cradle – how to dance, sing, tumble, do acrobatics, handle a crowd, raise people's spirits. The family worked as a team. If one artiste was unable to perform, there was always another ready to jump in.

48. Biddall's Show at Cockermouth

Albert, the eldest brother, was grateful for his background, claiming that it had given him all the joys he craved – colour, change and crowds. He was also proud of his own achievements.

'Don't imagine that because I was born son of a show proprietor I was allowed to step up to top place immediately,' he told an interviewer for *The People's Journal* in August 1937, 'for I had to go right through the mill from ground scavenger to advance man. Advance man was one of the plums of the business and there was always keen competition for the job, for it involved the interesting work of preparing a town for the arrival of the show. It was many years before I was honoured with this responsibility.'

Albert shared his family's passion for horses, learning to ride and do circus tricks as soon as he could walk. When Buffalo Bill made his appearance in show business, Albert added more tricks to his repertoire – sliding over and under and balancing in any position on a galloping horse. Taking advantage of travelling with Sanger's circus he watched their vets carefully until he had picked up the rudiments of veterinary care and these he put to good use when he acted as horse doctor for his father's show.

He was also happy to act as teacher to less endowed assistants who sat beside him on the dickey seat spelling out names on signposts as they passed along the road. Albert's father, George Biddall, had never been to school and could barely write his name, but he made sure that his children did not suffer the same limitation by leaving them at Gateshead every year until they were fully educated.

Biddall's show often linked up with Sanger's circus to tour all over Britain and as far afield as Germany, France and Belgium – experiences which Albert enjoyed despite the behaviour of some members of the public. 'As a lad one had to be very tough to hold one's own against crowds which often turned nasty. It was no uncommon thing to have drunken crowds trying to wreck the place, but a grand thing to see how the show folk stood solidly up for one another as soon as a bit of trouble blew up.'

In Ireland people were apt to stone travelling shows – not from malice, just for a little fun at visitors' expense. But for Albert one of the most worrying things about Irish audiences was that they never applauded, so performers had no idea what they thought of their act. Yet, as soon as they left the show, they formed little groups to laugh at what the funny man had said and exclaim at the wonderful tightrope walker.

On the Continent showmen faced different problems. 'In France we struck a snag in the gambling activities of many of the show folks who went off to the local casino as soon as they were off duty. The heads on their shoulders were too good for the croupiers and the bank was usually losing badly while they played. In one instance the bank was cleaned out, and next morning when we were about to move off to a pitch in another town we found the local gendarmerie there to hold us up. The proprietor of the casino was alleging that he had been cheated and we had rather a hectic time clearing the names of our gamblers before we could get away. After that incident the casinos were put out of bounds to the showfolks.'

Another less dramatic experience stayed in Albert's mind. It happened in Lyons where he found himself in conversation with the owner of a small chemist's shop who was particularly interested to learn that Albert was connected with the show then visiting town.

"Do you know anything about magic lanterns?" he asked.

Albert modestly explained that he had used every type then known, expounding on the virtues of his own favourite – a combination of three lanterns that threw upon the screen the image of a man swallowing rats.

The Frenchman listened attentively, taking up a pen to make notes, avid for detail. "I couldn't tell him enough," Albert declared, "and had a bit of a job getting away from his shop, he was so interested." The reason became clear some years later when the same chemist, Monsieur Lumière, worked with his brother to develop the first moving pictures. And, according to Albert, the contraption that evolved into the first cinematograph incorporated many of his own suggestions.[1]

Did the incident in the chemist's shop really happen? It is possible. The Biddalls could have been in the right place at the right time – it was in Lyons in March 1895 that the Lumière Brothers exhibited their cinematograph. But who can say? Albert, after all, had inherited a gift for 'telling the tale.' On the other hand, it is likely that Albert offered his father the chance to be the first travelling showman to present 'living pictures' on the fairground and if ever a man could have kicked himself for missing an opportunity it was George Biddall in 1897.

Early in the previous year Albert had gone to Paris with a showman novelty provider and had seen living pictures being shown in a basement by the Lumières. Since this was months before they were shown in England, Albert returned home full of the experience – only to find his father uninterested because he thought his show needed no further boost. The season went by. At back-end they returned to the Newcastle district and saw that the old Empire Music Hall was featuring living pictures as part of its programme. When Albert realised that it was being run by the same chap with whom he had gone to Paris, he persuaded him to bring his apparatus up to Biddall's show at Byker so that his father could see it. George enjoyed the demonstration and declared it a good novelty, but not worth the £100 asking price for the apparatus. So nothing was done.

In Spring Biddalls started their tour again and visited the Temperance Festival at Newcastle. While in Newcastle they noticed a waxwork show in a shop showing living pictures. Albert went in to see the owner who agreed to sell because he thought the public had already tired of it. Albert immediately bought the equipment – a R.W. Paul machine worked with ether light and first used in Biddall's show at Cullercoats. It was not an instant success. The films were very old, worn and jaggy. George was unimpressed. When one night the ether caught fire, he told his sons to pack it up before they burnt his show down. They never used it again.

49. Biddall's Show at Egremont, 1898

For the rest of that year they travelled Scotland, arriving at Ayr for the races in September where – what should they see, but a nice ground booth showing living pictures by acetylene gas light? It was owned by George Green, senior, and doing good business.

Naturally Albert had a dig at his father. But George, not to be worsted, growled that if theirs had been a set like that he wouldn't have minded.

Albert needed no further prompting. Off he shot to London and brought back to Castle Douglas a complete outfit from Hayden and Urrys with George Monte as operator – brother of Jimmy Monte, better known as Monte Williams who married Randall Williams's daughter. Thus George Biddall could still claim to be one of the first to show films in a fairground booth or on a linen sheet hung up on the sands. Among his earliest pictures were Queen Victoria's Diamond Jubilee procession, Mademoiselle Lou Fuller's serpentine dance and a comic snowballing scene. And what did Mr Biddall charge for this unique show in 1897? The handsome sum of 2d.

Soon Biddalls were travelling with their Illusion and Cinematograph Show incorporating their ever-popular ghostodramas, poignant recitations of *Little Jim* and *The Collier's Dying Child* accompanied by Victor on his newly-acquired secondhand organ, plus – to the amazement of all – the latest moving pictures. Though still often referred to as the Ghost Show, it was mentioned as Biddall's Living Pictures at Gateshead carnival in December 1899 in a line-up that included Mrs Johnson's Circus and George Payne's Storm-at-Sea.

At Annan fair where the space in front of the town hall every October was taken by the show which continued to be known as Biddall's Ghost Illusion, George was credited with being one of the first to bring living pictures to the town, and what people found especially appealing was his filming and reproduction of local scenes – even if they all appeared to have been taken during a heavy rain storm and showed carriage wheels revolving anti-clockwise.

As a nostalgic contributor recalled in the *Annandale Observer* (14th October 1938):

> At night the picture in the town with the various illuminations from the shows, ranging from paraffin lamps to electric arc lamps, and the gay crowds, was an animated and attractive one; music floated in the air from all quarters, the spirit of carnival was abroad and a gay time was had by all.

A similar picture is conveyed by the writer of *A Kilngreen Memory*, recalling the old fairs at Langholm.[2]

> The illumination was paraffin flares, which hissed and spluttered with fitful gusts of flame and the pungent smell of paraffin and the myriad specks of black soot pervaded the Kilngreen from the Sawmill Bridge to Jane Maggie's of the Tollbar. Needless to say the principal attraction was Biddall's Ghost Illusion. As youngsters we heard that "Biddall's is comin' in the morn" from the town bellman, Gesca Geordie and off we went down the Dean Banks to meet the Biddalls caravans. This was indeed a great entourage. No traction engines for Mr Biddall – all his caravans were hauled by beautiful grey horses – and we looked askance at one of the caravans, and no wonder, because we were told in bated breath that "That's the yin the ghost's in, cheened up." It was given a wide berth and incidentally the ghost served as a great boon to mothers in Langholm who told their young offspring not to stay out late at night as Biddall's Ghost had escaped from the caravan and was roaming the town. That was enough. There were no juveniles to be seen playing Jock Shine or any other nocturnal game when Biddall's Ghost was about.
>
> As to the show itself, many will still remember Mr Biddall's exhortations to "Step up ladies and gentlemen, the show is just about to commence."

George Biddall spoke with an attractive nasal twang and had a pleasant smile that made him an

50. The show is about to commence ...

ideal showman. As soon as he finished his announcement, the organ struck up with *God Save the Queen*, at the end of which he peeped in to see how the show was filling up. Not enough? He would provide some patter on the platform to gather another crowd. Another *God Save*. Another peep. This would be repeated three or four times before the final *God Save* presaged the start of the show.

In the semi-darkness the audience would hear the strains of Victor's harmonium accompanying his father as he intoned the opening lines of *The Miner's Dream of Home* which included the sentimental ballad:

I saw the old homestead and faces I loved
I saw England's valley and dells
I listened with joy, as I did when a boy
To the sound of the old village bells,
The lamps were burning brightly;
'Twas a night that could banish all sin
For the bells were ringing the old year out
And the New Year in.

Another famous Victorian tear-jerker was *The Collier's Dying Child* which began:

The cottage was a thatched one,
The outside old and mean.
Yet everything within that cot
Was wondrous neat and clean ...

And on it went until the angel appeared from the top of the tent and floated gently down to the cradle in the corner where a mother sat beside the death bed of her child.

As the drama reached its lugubrious end there wasn't a dry eye in the tent:

> Just moisten poor Jim's lips again,
> And, mother, don't you cry.

But tears were soon forgotten in the riotous laughter produced by the Ghost Illusion that followed. For this Victor and his brother Joey took up seats on a form and with banjo accompaniment started to sing:

> Get away from the window you naughty boy,
> Get away from the window don't you hear me say;
> There's going to be a fight in the middle of the night
> And the razors will be flying in the air.

Cue for entrance of the Ghost in flowing cloak and monk's cowl. Positioning itself behind the pair, who were quite oblivious of its presence, the Ghost lashed out with one hand and down fell one of the singers. Away went the Ghost. Inevitable argument between the pair on the bench till at last they recommenced their duet. Back came the Ghost, this time knocking the other vocalist off the form. On its third appearance the Ghost used both hands to knock both singers off the form and this time did not disappear but stood ghostly and wraith-like. Trembling and '*feert*', the pair clung to each other.

"Who-o-o are you?" they whispered.

"I am the remains of Uncle Joe. Out of this house you'd better go."

By now George and his Ghost Show had become a legend in the border country. Winlaton boasted one of the oldest fairs in the County Palatine, its principal day being 20th May when its streets were packed with amusements. Townspeople looked to the presence of George Biddall, who had not failed to attend once in forty years, to make their fair complete. Nor could they mistake the man himself, for his appearance was distinctive – with his neatly trimmed beard and cycle breeches, sometimes wearing leggings, at other times cycle stockings.

Biddall's show was often accompanied by smaller concerns such as that owned by his nephew, Sam Biddall, son of Samuel and Augusta, who travelled with a rifle range, bottle battery, and a curiosity show notable for its performing seals. Together at Newcastle's Easter Hoppings in 1899 amidst a dazzling galaxy of riding machines, they returned the next year to hold their own against such competition as Buff Bill's Wild Beast Show, Reader's Menagerie and Cottrell's Swimmers.

Good business was done in June 1900 at Carlisle Fair where apart from Biddall's Living Pictures and Reader's Scottish Menagerie, the big draw was Lord George Sanger's Circus. After Annan Fair in October, George Biddall travelled back over the border for the pleasure fair on 15th November at Whitehaven where the large gathering of shows included Murphy's galloping ostriches, Hassard's gallopers, Cross's roundabout, Buff Bill's menagerie, Biddall's Ghost Illusion and Electrophone, Paulo's circus, and Mr Lavin's boxing show. Despite poor weather, the fair was a success. The year was rounded off at Cockermouth Martinmas Fair where there were no less than four Cinematograph shows – Biddall's, Reader's, Manders' and Harris's, besides Manders' Menagerie, Reader's Wild Beasts, and Johnston's Circus.

51. Dalbeattie Fair, c1900. George Biddall (right) with John Manders, owner of the Royal Moving Waxworks

The new century dawned with Biddalls happily bearing The Ghost from the last. And there was no getting away from the past when George arrived at Newcastle-on-Tyne's Easter Hoppings to find his cousin, Tom Baker, visiting with his family circus. With Newcastle United playing at home on Good Friday and the fair situated on Castle Leazes right next to the football ground, business was exceptionally good. A reporter did the round of the shows: 'Next we pay honest George Biddall a visit and see his grand Ghost Entertainment and Living Picture Show (which is worked from back of stage) and draws crowded houses every time. Joseph, Albert and Victor Biddall work hard and are worthy of the large patronage they receive.' (*The Showman,* 12th April 1901)

After Newcastle it was but a short jump to Winlaton for its Annual Hoppings where one of the principal attractions that May was George Biddall's Varieties, Ghost and Electroscope, 'with electric organ and bioscope showing all the latest films, with a good company of variety artistes for parade and stage.' (*Showman,* 24th May 1901) Crossing the border in June, Biddalls made their way to Hawick for the Common Riding, a custom commemorating the defeat of English marauders at Hornshole Bridge in 1514 by the local *callants* or youths, their grown men having been wiped out at Flodden the year before. The chief event was the ceremony of appointing the 'Cornet', a post of honour for which any unmarried man of the town was eligible. Describing the fair in *The Showman* (14th June 1901) a reporter listed among its main attractions Murphy's rocking gondolas and flying ostriches, Johnston's circus and cinematograph, and George Biddall's ghost illusion and electroscope 'which is up-to-date in every way'. He also noted Testo's living pictures, Miller's grand variety company and cinematograph, and Baker's Continental circus 'which had the best of the pull amongst the shows'. The weather was beautiful.

By this time George was popularly known as Scotch Biddall. The Scottish Round (although it included several towns on the southern side of the border) differed from the annual round of English fairs in that it had no church anchorage in fast or festival.

Opening at Roxborough on the first Sunday after 5th March, the Scottish Round proceeded to Haddington and then as follows:

Govan, Lanark, Stirling, Dunfermline	Ayr September fair
(all in Easter holidays)	*(first of Autumn fairs)*
Kirkcoddie	Castle Douglas
Leven	Dumfries
Cupar of Fife	Hutchy-Mutchy
Bridge of Allan	Annan
Burntisland *(2nd May)*	Stranraer
Berwick on Tweed	Lanark
Cockermouth (coinciding with *Carlisle Spring Fair*)	Musselburgh
Maryport	Roxborough
Workington	Carlisle
Whitehaven	Dumbarton
Hawick Common Riding	Govan
Greenock	Partick
Glasgow	Portobello
Dundee *(18th July)*	Huddington, Sinclair Town, Cupar,
Stirling *(last week of July)*	Dunfermline *(all in same week)*
Porth Head	Port Glasgow
Aberdeen	Irving
Perth	Kilmarnock

– after which preparations began for Winter Carnivals at Edinburgh, Glasgow, Aberdeen, Dundee and Greenock.[3]

Naturally not all these fairs featured in George Biddall's annual round. After starting out from Quarry Show Grounds, his winter quarters in Gateshead, in 1902 he opened at Newcastle-on-Tyne for Easter, joining forces with Reader's Cinematograph and Testo's show. By the time he set out the following year a significant event had happened in the family.

> A pretty wedding took place at Gateshead when the marriage of Mr Charles Miller, son of the well-known Northumbrian showman, Tom Miller, and Selina Biddall, daughter of Mr George Biddall, of ghost illusion fame was duly solemnised. Mr Victor Biddall acted as best man and a large party which included many lights of showland were afterwards entertained at the Bewick Hall.
>
> (*The Showman,* 30th January 1903)

Marriage must have been in the air, for on 25th February George's niece, Evaline, daughter of Augusta and Samuel, married Albert Sedgwick in Oldham where the Menagerie owned by the groom's father was stationed every winter at the Ice Skating Rink in Union Street.

George Biddall's Ghost Show had been a regular visitor to Glasgow since the 1870s, but he made his mark anew in 1903 when he installed scenes showing the dreadful accident that killed fifteen people at St Enoch Station on 27th July that year. Using a mechanical scenic change, he showed pictures of the platform before the disaster, then as Joey told the tale his words were accompanied by sounds of crashing, banging, railway whistles and dreadful scenes of the railway station afterwards.

52. Joey Biddall and Jimmy Stokes, 1902. Biddall's Electrograph is featuring a film of the Coronation Procession

53. Selina Biddall, photographed at Bridlington, 1897

54. Charles Christopher Miller, 1895

In 1904, after attending Durham Easter fair in the company of Messrs Johnson's circus and Manders' fine art academy, George Biddall headed for Winlaton where his Bioscope headed a list of shows that included Payne's Cinematograph, similar entertainments by Messrs Miller and Johnson and Frank Gess with his boxers and athletes. Thence to Carlisle where that year the great hiring fair, a rallying ground for Scottish and English showmen, saw Chipperfield's Menagerie and Sahib Leo with his Egyptian Hall marvels.

Hawick Common Riding on 10th and 11th June included Randall-William's show, George Biddall's ghost illusions, Miller's Variety Theatre, and Sahib Leo's Egyptian Hall. The weather was remarkably fine and despite stall-holders' fears that trade would be poor, Messrs Murphy declared that excellent business was done.

After Selkirk in June, and in July Johnstone where Paulo's circus was the main attraction, Biddall's Electric Ghost Illusions and Cinematograph appeared at Kilmarnock in the company of Sedgwick's Menagerie, McIndoe's (Arthur Henderson's) electric theatre, and George Green's Cinematograph of local events. Good weather but only moderate business was enjoyed at Paisley Races and Fair Holidays which lasted from 6th to 15th August and had attracted some of the finest shows of the North – Biddall's, Sedgwick's, McIndoe's, Green's, and Sahib Leo's.

It must have been with some trepidation that George headed south from Paisley towards Ayr Fair which was being held that year for the first time in Newton Park with Peter Swallow acting as lessee for the British Roundabout Proprietors' & Showmen's Union. For generations Ayr Races had been the showmen's Mecca, but in 1903 tradition received a jolt when the Harbour Trust barred access to their time-honoured stance along South Quay. Although Ayr Town Council allocated ground for shows in Newton Park, many showmen considered this too far from the town centre and, backed by the Association, had boycotted the new venue. The shows that had attended, however, did good business, so in 1904 showmen came prepared to accept the change.

There were advantages. The park had good tough turf over a subsoil of sand which made it cleaner and ideal for lamping. Moreover, Buffalo Bill did much to advertise the new site when his Wild West show arrived in the early hours of Sunday morning, 11th August. Next day a continuous stream of people visited the ground and on Saturday night there were about seven thousand people in the park, crowding in front of shows such as Biddall's Ghost and Electrograph, Chipperfield's French Menagerie, Johnson's Circus of Varieties, George Green's Cinematograph (being managed by Mr Monte) and – a new idea in roundabouts – Messrs H. & R. McIndoe's electric figure of eight monorail cars, the invention of a Kilmarnock clergyman. Thus, despite the fact that Chipperfield's lost several valuable animals whilst there, Newton Park proved acceptable.

Dumfries Fair proper in 1904 was on 28th and 29th September, although business began on 21st. Prominent among shows which worked Thornhill and Castle Douglas in conjunction with Dumfries were 'Scotch' Biddall & Sons' Electric Ghostoscope, Mrs Sarah Johnson's Circus of Varieties, and Pinder-Ord's Continental Circus. Sunday evening at Dumfries allowed time for showmen to attend the annual tea provided by the British Women's Temperance Association, a 'very successful, and a very pleasant and profitable evening spent by all.' (*Era,* 1st October 1904) After Dumfries, George Biddall headed back over the border to Penrith and the great hiring fair at Cockermouth, held on 14th November in 1904, and then east to complete the circle at Gateshead where he overwintered in the Quarry Show Grounds.

In 1905 George and Selina celebrated their thirty-fifth wedding anniversary at Darlington, the town where they had married, and it must have been a proud couple who arrived at May Hirings with

55. Biddalls Show in Scotland, 1904

56. George Biddall and his Ghost Show at Bo'ness, 1904

their famous ghost show hailed as one of its principal attractions alongside William Murphy's Golden Venice Gondolas. Thence to Newcastle Hoppings where George heard that his friend, John Manders, owner of the Royal Waxwork Exhibition which had stood alongside his own show at many border fairs, had died of asthma on 23rd May, aged 68, and was being buried at New Brumby, near Scunthorpe.

After a brief stay at Crawcrook, Ryton-on-Tyne, where Walker Hoadley's centaurs excited interest, George Biddall's well-known Ghosta Spectra Exhibition was seen being drawn on to the ground at Hawick Common Riding by twenty splendid horses. At Ayr Race Week, now that Newton Park had been accepted, the Corporation Tramways served the showmen well by delivering vast crowds to them nightly. The Corporation had originally let the stance to a non-Union showman. Finding that he had insufficient following to meet the rent, he sublet to the Union and the shows came flooding in. The tober was arranged in a great circle, the centre occupied by roundabouts owned by Messrs Wilmot, Green, Swallow, and Wingate, whilst round the edge stood Sedgwick's Menagerie, Biddall's Ghost Illusion, Clark's Ghost Show, Johnson's Circus, Testo's Circus and Green's Cinematograph. Amongst the stalls were the shooting saloon and varieties travelled by George's nephew, Sam Biddall, who had married Polly Newsom at Ulverston Martinmas Hirings in 1894 and was now father of Samuel Sinclair Freeman, aged three.

Continuing his run of backend fairs which included Dumfries, Maryport on 10th November, and Penrith, George arrived at Cockermouth in November to find himself in competition with Leo's, Cottrell's, and Testo's. The author of 'Stray Leaves' in the *Cockermouth Free Press* (17th November 1905) conjured up a miserable scene:

> Cockermouth Fair on a wet Martinmas Monday is not the most ideal fete. When it has mizzled and drizzled just sufficient to turn the binding of the macadam into pea-soup ... the most enthusiastic fair-dayer has to acknowledge the moist condition of affairs to be something terrible ... I never saw more – we used to call them caravans, but now they are traction-shows – at a fair. The switchbacks, the ghost shows, the swimmery, the over-bridge cinematograph, etc. represented a large capital outlay, but when an affair like the switchback can take 15/- every three minutes from 11 till 10 at night, they can easily afford to give us the organ selections for nothing. Taken as a whole it was a poor fair. There was a marked absence of the spending class from the coast, and there was a good percentage of servants unhired. It was a new sensation for the folks of Market Place to have such a magnificent organ on their fronts, but from what I can learn they will not be sorry to have encore next Whitsuntide.

May 1906 saw George Biddall's Ghost Show and Cinematograph at Annan Fair, then at Carlisle Hirings in the company of his cousin James Biddall's Circus, Wilmot's cars and Chipperfield's Menagerie. Rejoicing in the best weather for years, most of the showfolk left for Cockermouth and Wigton on the Monday morning.

Biddall's Ghost Show, which had been coming to the town for over thirty years, was principal attraction at Bryce's ground, Larkie Fair, a month later, before moving on to Blairgowrie for the fair held on the Wellmeadow. After trekking back for the Bridge of Allan Games, George headed south to join the unusually large gathering of big shows at Dumfries Rood Fair. Enjoying brilliant weather, the town was *en fête* and the *Era* (6th October 1906) reported: 'At the bottom end was Biddall's famous ghost illusion and bioscope, which did capital business with a nice company and a clean little show.'

Unfortunately the period of fine weather did not stretch to Cockermouth where the *Free Press* (16th November 1906) printed an even sadder dirge than the year before:

57. Biddall's Show at Dumfries, 1905

58. 'Evening Star' – Fowler Road Locomotive No.10694, used with Biddall's No.2 Show

Cockermouth Fair-day was a wet day. It has been said before, but never with more truth than about last Monday. Main Street which on the Sunday had looked so well and promising for a pleasurable feast became a quagmire, the tents looked unutterably sodden and sad, the gaudy caravans ran tears of rain down their faces, the tattooed woman became limp and bedraggled, and the carnivorous Zulus lost their usual pluck and took to cigarettes.

The Eiffel-tower sort of erection called the *Helter Skelter* was a source of attraction, and unfortunately for many of its patrons the mats became water-logged, which did not increase the comfort of the already soaked persons enjoying *all the fun of the fair*.

I have seen Cockermouth Martinmas Fair with snow on the streets, I have seen it in a thorough down-pour of rain, lasting however for a short period, but for downright wretchedness and drabblement, for wet clothes, spoilt hats, furs and feathers, I think last Monday beat the record. It was unfortunate for the holiday-makers, it was a calamity for the shopkeepers and confectioners, and it was not a good thing for the publicans, paradoxical though it seems. On the thorough wet day like Monday, the public houses are thronged, but the customers spend ten times more time discussing a gill of Jennings or a bottle of the Cockermouth Aerated Water Company's horehound than they do on a fine day, when it's a matter of only a few minutes and out again for the fun.

After his usual attendance at Newton Park, Ayr, in September where he met up with Mrs Johnson's Variety Empire and Paulo's Circus, both families connected to him by marriage, George Biddall travelled to Dumfries and thence to Strachan's Park where his bioscope attracted much attention.

The splendid exterior of the show which was brilliantly illuminated and the costly orchestration (which is said to be the finest instrument of the kind ever seen in connection with any travelling establishment) had elicited the admiration of large assemblages. Moreover, there were miles of animated pictures of an interesting, humorous and thrilling nature whose quality was exceptionally clear. (*World's Fair*, 28th September 1907)

In October Biddall's show opened in the High Street, Kirriemuir, the proprietor and his staff earning three hearty cheers when they donated takings, which totalled £20, to the town. It was a proud moment for George, whose delight must have been crowned when he saw on the front page of *World's Fair* (19th October 1907) a photo of his son, Joseph, as a clown. The caption read: 'A member of one of the oldest families of travellers. The name of Biddall is universally known. Joe is at present delighting Scottish audiences.'

From Kirriemuir George travelled south again for Dumfries and Annan before crossing the border to arrive at Maryport Hirings in November. Albert as advance agent had already placed an advert in local newspapers announcing: 'Biddall's Exhibition will visit Cockermouth Saturday, Monday & Tuesday. Our Living Pictures include the Great Thaw Case.' And, according to Tom Rudd, author of 'Stray Leaves', for once the town was blessed with good weather:

It is a very long time since we had such a Martinmas term ... The air was balmy as April or May, the streets were clean, there was an absence of wind, the visitors to the fair were not inconvenienced with mackintoshes and leggings (except what they had bought during the day), and they evidently enjoyed their brief holiday. Taking stock of the servants, male and female, one cannot but be struck with the improved physical appearance of them, as compared with those who attended the hirings thirty years ago. Taking them all round they are taller and straighter, walk with a better gait, and have not that 'nurlt' look that used to be so noticeable in comparison with the bigness of the farmers ...

The arranging of the stands, stalls, and caravans by the Council's staff worked smoothly on this occasion, and I think that it was much better to allow the showfolks to put their places up after church hours than to prohibit them doing so until twelve o'clock. I cannot see there was any more sin in working than in drinking, and this is what happened on previous occasions. Besides it allowed the caravan people to secure a few hours of much-needed rest, instead of having to toil on from midnight until dawn.

The principal attraction seems to be the cinematographs, or living pictures. The American show in Market

Place had some good sketches, but the old favourite, Mr Biddall, had a set of superb pictures. He showed besides others, a snow-ball fight in Deer Orchard, and another that was a great favourite with children was dinner hour at Mr Armstrong's saw-mill, when the scholars of Fairfield schools mingled with the workmen, and prominent amongst the living throng was the well-known St Helen's Street pony *Tommy*.

Showmen and switchback proprietors had little to complain of in the way of business, but the keepers of shooting-galleries and saloons, cocoa-nut shies and the like were persistent in their complaints of there being nothing doing in their lines. And from what I could see there seemed to be some grounds for their complaints, but taken all round I fancy the fair was fully up to the average for Martinmas. The only thing I could find any complaint about was the double tin-tinnabulation accompaniment of the bells to the organ music at one of the shows. They ought to be silenced on the next occasion. (*Cockermouth Free Press*, 15th November 1907)

59. Biddall's No 2 Show, formerly travelled by Randall Williams & bought by George Biddall from Richard Monte in 1906

That winter George and his family stayed in the Dundee area where his Cinematograph Exhibition attracted large crowds of people in East Dock Street after Christmas and into the New Year. George was about to turn sixty – a fact celebrated by publication of his photo on the front page of *World's Fair* in May, captioned: 'One of the oldest names in the travelling world is that of Biddall, and Mr George Biddall is one of the heads of the profession. For many years he has travelled the Scotch district where his exhibition is always welcomed.' In fact, day-to-day running of the business had now passed to younger hands and it was his son Victor who was managing when Biddall's opened in the Old Cattlemarket, Dunfermline, that month. *Dellar* described it for *World's Fair* on 9th May 1909:

The show consists of a very large Cinematograph Pavilion, the inside of which is well seated and illuminated with electric light. The magnificent organ which is the finest that has yet been seen in the city of Carnegia, occupies the whole front of the massive structure and is beautifully illuminated by large numbers of different coloured dazzling electric lights. The electric plant is driven by a powerful compound traction engine. The programme of Saturday was of excellent character. Both machine and films are acknowledged to be the best seen in any travelling show that has paid a visit to the Old Cattlemarket. The whole has greatly proved to be satisfactory to the public and, owing to its success, the whole enterprise is remaining another week.

60. Albert, Victor and Joey in front of 'Evening Star'.
The engine's brass plate reads: George Biddall, London & Paris

61. Ghost Show with Victor standing in foreground, George at top of steps

Other attractions were Joseph Clark's Shooting Saloon, Emmas and his Big Boat 'The Pride of Glen City', although these met with only a small share of business.

After attending Carlisle Summer fair in early June George Biddall's cinematograph travelled to Penrith for 9th June together with Sam Biddall's freak show, swings and Winchester ranges. Then they headed north for St Andrews' annual fair, where business was pretty good despite unsettled weather.

At some point during back-end George called on Thomas Louden & Company at Airdrie to order the new wagon which was delivered to him at Annan towards the end of October.[4] Taking advantage of a lengthy stay he placed an advertisement in the *Bioscope*, (30th October 1908) repeated twice in subsequent weeks: 'Wanted, Monday, Bioscope Operator – Gas – Provide everything – £3 per week. Also Girl, sing and dance. Also Scotch Comedian, Charles Derrick write. Biddall, Post Office, Annan.'

From Workington in December Charlie and Selina Miller sent greetings to relatives at Newcastle-on-Tyne: 'Dear Brother and sister, hope you are all keeping well as it leaves us all at present.' Their message fell sadly short of truth. Selina's father, George Biddall, was far from well that winter.

On 12th February 1909 an advert in the *Cockermouth Free Press* must have brought joy to many:

Biddall's, Fairfield, Cockermouth
Afternoon Performance. Tomorrow (Sat) at 3.30
Children admitted to all parts for 1d each.
The Ghost Illusion will be introduced in the Programme.
The most remarkable views taken in connection with
the recent Earthquake will be shown next week.

A week later a second advert appeared:

Everyone Delighted with the Splendid programme
provided at Biddall's, Fairfield, Cockermouth.
Each evening, Twice Nightly at 7 and 8.40.
Afternoon performance Tomorrow (Sat) at 3.30
The local picture of Market Day will be shown
at each performance.

Third week and another advert:

Afternoon Performance at Biddall's
Tomorrow (Sat) at 3.30.
Children admitted to all parts for 1d each.
Splendid Programme

62. Charlie Miller, Christmas 1908

When Biddall's Show remained a fourth week, newspaper reports may have led locals to believe that their extended stay was prompted by full houses.

<u>Biddall's Exhibition</u>

During the week Biddall's Exhibition has continued to draw large crowds and this is not to be wondered at because splendid entertainment is provided for the nominal charge made. The cinematograph pictures are of a very high order, and in this respect the show is undoubtedly one of the most up-to-date. There are two performances nightly and afternoon on Saturdays and a very pleasant one and a half hours can be spent.

A fortnight later and Biddall's famous show was still stationed in the Fairground at Cockermouth.

Tonight one long Performance only at Biddall's at eight o'clock.
Afternoon performance on Saturday at 3.30. Children 1d to all parts.
Night performances at 7 and 8.40. Always a Grand Programme

'One long performance only' ... Sadly that performance was coming to an end. The reason for the family's long stay at Cockermouth was that George Biddall was suffering from a malignant stomach disease and he died in his caravan on 7th April.

The interment of the remains of this well-known showman, whose death occurred last week in the Fairfield took place at Cockermouth Cemetery on Wednesday afternoon. The funeral was one of the largest ever seen in Cockermouth, and the esteem in which Biddall was held was abundantly shown by the very large number of showpeople who gathered together at a busy time to pay their last tribute of respect. A considerable number of Cockermothians and people whom he had been associated with in other towns also attended, for Mr Biddall was a man whose kindly acts and estimable disposition gained him friends wherever he went.

The Main Street, through which the cortège passed, was lined with people, and further marks of respect were seen in the shuttered windows of many of the tradespeople and the drawn blinds of householders. Preceding the hearse was a carriage filled with beautiful floral tokens, and then followed a long procession of mourning coaches, which extended the length of Main Street, the vehicles numbering twenty-seven in all. The burial service was taken by the Reverend W.E. Dixon, vicar of Christ Church. The coffin was of polished oak with brass mountings and the funeral arrangements were carried out by Mr T. Armstrong.

Beautiful wreaths were sent by the following people:

'From his dear wife and family,' Mrs G. White (eldest daughter), Mr G. White (son-in-law), Mr and Mrs Ohmy (Blackpool), The Keiths (Stockport), Mr Harvey and Staff of Biddall's Famous Show (Kirriemuir), James Biddall (Circus, Durham), William Biddall and family (Hampstead Heath), Mr J. Henderson (Newcastle), Mr and Mrs G. Harrison (Newcastle), Mr and Mrs Silvester (Wallsend-on-Tyne), Mr and Mrs G. Green (Glasgow), 'From a Friend' (Cockermouth), Mrs Manders and family (Durham), Mr John Spencelavh (West Hartlepool) and many other well-known showmen too numerous to mention.

(*World's Fair*, 10th April 1909)

Later reports suggested that Buffalo Bill Cody was amongst those at the graveside.

The author of 'Stray Leaves' in the local newspaper added what he called his own

... humble tribute to the memory of George Biddall, a man worthy of respect, a hard-worker, with a true heart and a ready sympathy for sorrow and distress. Many times his money was freely given for deserving causes in this town, and in other towns too. On one occasion a strange sight was witnessed – I think it must have been at Whitsuntide, though I am not sure – when he lent the front platform of his Ghost Show for the use of the Methodists at an open-air service one evening. Nothing of the sort seems to be done now, at Fair-time, save by the "Army". (*Cockermouth Free Press*, 16th April 1909)

The same edition carried a dignified acknowledgement by George's family:

'Mrs Biddall and family wish to thank all Friends and the General Public of the District for the kind sympathy shown to them in their recent bereavement, and also wish to state that the great respect shown has indeed been a comfort to them in their sad trouble.'

The strange thing is, even today it is possible to witness that 'great respect' being shown, for was George Biddall not one of the country's chief bioscope owners? And was George Biddall not one of the country's leading showmen? Far be it from his sons to let the occasion go without making some record. Amidst all the turmoil of grief and flurry of funeral arrangements someone had the presence of mind to take up the camera and film the event, and the result may still be viewed.

The scene opens with George in the midst of life, walking his two dogs off the lead through a crowd of people at Maryport. He carries himself well, in appearance like King Edward VII, his presence commanding, movements purposeful. Clearly a man used to being in charge, he strides forward confidently, knowing that his dogs – companions even in the crowd – will follow him.

Suddenly, without warning, we are at his funeral. Outside the famous show in which his body has been lying in state we watch as pallbearers carry George's coffin down the open wooden steps under which some little boys have crouched for a worm's eye view. We can almost hear the hush of the large crowd that is being kept in check by two burly policemen.

As the coffin is placed inside an ornately carved horse-drawn hearse, Selina, supported by two male relatives, walks down the steps. She is weeping. Several women in large hats and full mourning follow, to be joined by their men folk as they enter their carriages. Men pick up wreaths from the ground in front of the show and place them in the hearse. The cortège leaves to make its way to the cemetery.

The film would be incorporated into the show and George Biddall would not be forgotten. In 1911 his grave was marked by a memorial designed by Magnus Kennedy of Dumfries from a block of silver Creetown granite standing fourteen feet high and weighing more than ten tons. It featured a female figure of Grief writing a text, with a scroll, harp, and wreath of victory alongside. And for many years somebody remembered George with enough affection to leave small tributes at his monument every Cockermouth Fair day: a sprig of holly at Martinmas, a flower at Whitsuntide.[5]

63. Portrait of George Biddall, 18th November 1905

68. Model of Biddall's Touring Picture Palace, 1912

Market Hall, Frizington.

Biddall's
Perfection Pictures.

Present this Ticket at the Pay Box, and on payment of 1d. a Ticket will be given for the Best Seat.

This Ticket is only available at the Second Performance any night during the week (except Saturdays).

Signed..

69. People's Palace, Frizington

Bought by George's widow, it must have proved a success for, after selling Biddall's No.2 show to Harry Dawson of Dundee, Selina purchased another picture house within the year. In August 1912 Biddall's Electric Picture Palace at Aspatria was presenting a bill which included recent films and a performance by the London comedian, Vincent Godfrey.

The new cinemas were furnished with equipment acquired from Workington's Theatre Royal, 'Home of Perfect Pictures and Vaudeville', whose owner (according to a receipt dated 8th January 1913) sold Selina a 'Crossley Gas Engine direct coupled to 1 – Holmes Dynamo complete with all accessories as Switchboard, Fittings, etc. for the sum of £60. Delivered Carriage Paid Arlecdon Station.'[3]

It was another three years before the Ghost Show itself was disbanded. Meanwhile Victor was travelling down hill on his way to Cleator Moor in June 1912 when a wheel ran over his leg, bursting the calf. For weeks he had to rely on a member of the company, Dave Lewis (alias 'The Galloping Hairpin') to bandage the wound. Recalling these pre-War years, Lewis later wrote: 'What days! Dear Ma Biddall always fresh as a daisy and on the tober all hours with the youngsters like me, Jimmie [Stokes], Boxer [Browell], Mac, Teddy, all the rest, not forgetting the dog, "Lion". What an appetite! I nearly forgot Bingo [John Moncrieff], Funny Joey [Joseph Biddall], and Charlie Millar.'[4]

70. *Bingo (John Moncrieff)*

71. *Jimmy Stokes (seated right) 1916*

BIDDALL'S
PEOPLE'S PALACE
FRIZINGTON
Manager: C. C. MILLER.

Dear Sirs,
Kindly note we have the Film

Booked for Exhibition here commencing

Please see to early dispatch of same, and oblige.

C. C. MILLER.

72. *Film Request Note, c1918*

73. *Joe Miller (Selina's brother-in-law)*

Charlie Miller, married to the younger Selina, ran the Cakewalk which accompanied the Ghost Show but during the war he took over the People's Palace at Frizington. When he died (of peritonitis) in August 1918 leaving Selina with seven young children, a grand concert was staged at the cinema, proceeds going to his widow 'for the many kindnesses of the deceased.' Artistes appeared from theatres all around and the film shown was *When It's One of Your Own*.

Selina Miller had now settled down, living in a house in Main Street, Frizington. When her mother died in January 1922, it was from here that the cortège set out through heavy snow for Cockermouth Cemetery so that she could be laid beside George.

74. Selina Miller feeding Paddy, one of George's beloved horses

Meanwhile Victor spent his winter months in Annan, where one inhabitant of the town later recalled seeing his first movies in Biddall's exhibition when it was parked outside the Town Hall. The film being shown was *The Relief of Lucknow* or *Jessie's Dream* – 'a remarkable picture, particularly when the pipers came in at the last minute.' In 1912 Victor started showing regular pictures in the Albert Hall in Annan and whilst screening *Scott's Expedition to the Pole* had cause to interrupt the film with the sad news that the explorer had perished.[5]

BIDDALL'S PICTURES
Albert Hall, Annan
Week Commencing December 21st Monday & Tuesday
SPECIAL WAR TOPICAL
THE BATTLE AROUND DIXMUDE, NIEUPORT, & YSER CANAL[6]

Until 1916, when Biddall's famous travelling show was finally disbanded, Victor still took to the road every summer, but in 1917, having joined the RASC, he was sent to work at the local Munitions Factory. The buildings of HM Factory Gretna stretched over nine miles from the outskirts of Annan across the border to Longtown, and the two secret townships that grew up around it were later described by Conan Doyle as Miracle Towns for their innovative design. The enormous factory produced a thousand tons of cordite per week, more than the total output from all existing plants in Britain, and Victor's job was to drive one of the steam-transport lorries fitted with thick rubber tyres to minimise the risk of explosion.

75. Victor Biddall in his steam-driven lorry at Gretna Village, 1918

In September 1917, whilst on active service, he married Mary Alice Howat, an Annan girl who had been brought up by her aunt, Miss Bell, owner of the corner shop on Port Street. After his discharge in 1919 the couple settled at the Old Mill Toll, New Cumnock, where Victor would continue to live for the next thirty years in a wagon because, as he said, "there is a loneliness about a house that you don't get in a caravan."[7] In due course he became proud father of a son, Victor, and proprietor of Gracie's Banking Cinema, Annan; the Regal Cinema, New Cumnock; and for a few years the Eskdale Cinema in Langholm.

These were exciting times for cinema even though audiences declined after the munitions workers from nearby Gretna Village started going home in 1919 and the Albert Hall closed for film-goers in 1921. A review of Christmas in Annan in 1928 shows us Victor providing entertainment for the town with characteristic zest and love of hard work.

> Taken all over, the Christmas season has maintained a good average. Post Office work has again been heavy, but extra hands have managed deliveries in good time. In the churches special Christmas praise and sermons marked Sunday. The shops have again done well with their Christmas lines, and by Monday night a pretty complete all-round clearance had been effected.
>
> The man who rose to the occasion was Mr Biddall of the Picture House. For the first half of the week he engaged the Wide Awakes, a vaudeville touring company ten strong, who put up a two hours' programme on scale and in execution a long way better than anything of the kind ever seen in the district.

The company embrace a giantess from Vienna, two dwarfs from Germany and other two from Poland; two beautifully clever instrumentalists who are English; one Home Scot and the manager, a Yorkshireman. A midget does a striking and genuine weight-lifting turn. The violin solos and dulcimer duets are delightful. The midget dance and the conjuring, and indeed all the items were of the best. Crowded houses applauded all. Next week Mr Biddall screens the famous *Huntingtower* picture of John Buchan's famous Bolshevik thriller, featuring Sir Harry Lauder. There you see the bold, bad Bolshies checked by the Gorbals Diehards and *Auld McCunn the Grocer* who is Harry himself.[8]

76. *'Talking' Movies, 1931*

77. *Christmas in Victor Biddall's Cinema at Gracie's Banking, Annan*

With the advent of 'talking pictures' in the 1930s the Kinema at Gracie's Banking was showing films six nights a week and there was a change of programme every two nights. Prices in 1936 were 3d and 9d.[9]

Victor's flair in running his cinemas owed much to lessons in showmanship learnt not only from his father but also from his Uncle 'King Ohmy' who had opened more than thirty wooden circus buildings in recent years. Visiting one of these at Preston, Victor had arrived in the middle of a performance. Glancing around the auditorium in the semi-darkness he decided that the building was packed out. Imagine his surprise when the lights went up to reveal walls that had been painted to resemble a large gallery filled with people!

During the war years Victor Biddall's name became associated with the many charities that profited from his shows. But from 1946 he took a less active part in the business, especially once his son was demobbed and took over the running of Gracie's Banking where, incidentally, the first film he saw on his return was: *This is the Army*. Suddenly, just when Victor senior might have thought of retiring, he found he had a new career on his hands as public lecturer and broadcaster. Besides being in demand as a speaker on showlife, in October 1948 he took part in *Scottish Life Fifty Years Ago* produced by playwright Andrew P. Wilson, enacting scenes from Biddall's Ghost Illusions. He recited *The Death of the Collier's Child* and accompanied it on the original harmonium. (*World's Fair*, 9th October 1948)

He also began to take an active part in the Cinema Veterans' Association. Harry Scard defined a 'veteran' as someone in the business before 1903 so Victor easily qualified and nothing delighted him more than meeting up with old pals like Dick Monte Williams at Association events. Seeing Queen Victoria's Jubilee at the *Fifty Years of Film* Exhibition in Dorland Hall in 1946 he had excitedly exclaimed, 'I showed that in 1897!' And he returned to London twice more to see the show, on one occasion recording an interview with Roy Rich for *Picture Parade*.

'Thanks to Victor Biddall and adventurous spirits like him,' it was reported in *World's Fair*, 10th August 1946, 'the cinema industry today is one of the greatest in the world.'

A photograph taken at the annual reunion of the Cinema Veterans' Association in London in 1948 shows Victor with some of the pioneers of the cinema industry – Douglas Bostock, son of the famous menagerie owner, Dicky Monte Williams who had supplied George Biddall with the first cinema over fifty years before, and James Styles, orator with Green's travelling cinematograph.

78. Cinema Veterans' Association, 1948
Victor Biddall on left of front row, next to Dicky Monte Williams.
On the extreme right is James Styles. Centre top row is Douglas Bostock

The following year the *Cumnock Chronicle* reported:

At an age when other men are sitting back and thinking of taking it easy Mr Victor Biddall, spry, go-ahead manager of New Cumnock's Regal Cinema, is nipping around the country signing agreements, booking films, and conducting his business with a vigour and insight which proves that old troupers, like old soldiers, never die ... Mr Biddall will be 71 next birthday yet he drives his own car, devotes his attentions between 'The Regal' and a picture house in Annan and finds time to attend Circus Reunions in various parts of the country. He has just returned from the birthday celebration which was a "show for showfolk" staged by the veteran member of the cinema trade, Albert Ernest Pickard of Pickard's Panoptican fame ... Among those present on this occasion were the great man himself, members of Glasgow Corporation, directors of 20th Century Fox Pictures, representatives of United Artists Corp and Columbia Pictures and a galaxy of names that spells Show Business in Scotland.

Mr Biddall had a grand time at this function then dashed off to London to attend a great circus reunion where he renewed friendships of long standing and greeted circus performers he hadn't seen for forty years. Among those present were Cyril and Bernard Mills, the Delbosqs, the Austins, Chipperfields, Paulos and Fossetts and many other names which are inseparably linked with the sawdust ring. Here a pleasant surprise was in store for Mr Biddall, who bumped into Pimpo, the famous clown of Lord George Sanger's Circus. Pimpo is a full cousin of Mr Biddall and for them the evening sped quickly as they discussed old times together ...

One thing is certain – wherever show folks meet and start talking of the "good old days" the conversation can't go on for more than fifteen minutes without the name of the Biddall family being mentioned.

(*Cumnock Chronicle*, 25th March 1949)

Sadly by 1949 that family had dwindled. After marrying Catherine, eldest daughter of William Codona, Albert Biddall had settled at Portobello where, besides running his own cakewalk and figure of eight, he managed John Evans' dragon scenic and eventually became proprietor of Fun City at the west end of the promenade. He and his wife also had an interest in the Prestonpans Picture House and it was while paying a visit to this town that Albert was injured in a motor accident from which he never fully recovered. A quiet man and ardent Freemason, he sold Fun City to Joe Leonards in 1945 and spent the last two years of his life an invalid but always happy to receive friends at his home in Inchview Terrace, Portobello. He died in January 1947 and was buried at Piershill Cemetery, Edinburgh. At the start of 1949 Albert's sister, Mrs George White (born Eveline Sinclair Freeman-Biddall), died at Aberdeen. His younger sister, Selina Miller, died at Frizington three months later.

Of George and Selina's three sons and two daughters, only Joseph and Victor now remained. Joey, well into his seventies, was still travelling the Scottish fairs with sidestuff in the summer months and clowning after back-end. 'Wanted for Winter Months by J. Biddall, Clown and Film Prologue Actor, Engagements with Circus, Carnivals or Pantomime. Five times engaged at the Kelvin Hall, Glasgow. Address this week: Aspatria, Cumberland; next week: Market Place, Maryport' ran his advert in *World's Fair*, 4th November 1933.

In 1937 it was reported that Joey Biddall had been more than thirty years in the business of clown

79. Joey Biddall shaking hands with fellow showman, Mr Wharton, at Jedburgh, 1932. In the background are Randall Emmerson, Mr Smith and an employee

80. John Evans' Dragon Scenic which Albert Biddall managed

81. Albert Biddall in deer-stalker, standing top right, with chaps who worked on the scenic

and prologue actor, amusing crowds of up to 70,000 strong at Thornton Highland Games and appearing at Kinross July Fair, Tillicoultry, Perth, and Buchan. Joey had also been leading clown at Kelvin Hall Circus for seven years. He was back at Kelvin Hall in his usual position in front of Joe Caddick's Mirror Maze in December, 1938, and appeared on Alloa Showground the following May. He was welcomed at Cockermouth fair in 1949 as someone who had been attending for half a century, but by the time he arrived at Dumfries for the Rood Fair in October he was ill and confined to his wagon.

82. Joey Biddall, keeper of the Crooked House at Kelvin Hall, 1935

83. Joey Biddall with his grandson, Joe Williams, at Stevenston Fair, 1938

Victor, meanwhile, was as active as ever that winter, visiting his Keith cousins at Exeter where they had settled in 1914. After that it was the Circus Reunion at London's Park Lane Hotel and another chance to chat to his cousin, Jimmy Freeman. Mention of the famous Pimpo would have gone down well at Annan Old Folks' Party in March when Victor entertained the company with a lively account of Biddall's Ghost Show before singing and playing the banjo and the little organ which his father had bought to accompany cine films fifty-one years before. He repeated the performance at Annan Rotary Club later that year, evoking Biddall's Ghost at a time when it was fast becoming the stuff of history, for Joey Biddall, the show's beloved clown, died at Annan Fair Ground that October. His body was taken to Hawkhead Cemetery, Paisley, for burial.

Only Victor left now. He still ran two cinemas fitted with the latest gadgets and an incredible 140,000 people went through the doors of Gracie's Banking in 1951. He was still ardent as ever and determined to please his public. In a letter to the Films Branch of the Board of Trade in 1952 he expressed trenchant criticism of the current quota system that required him to take a certain number of British films.

> Dear Sir
>
> For this last two years in an endeavour to fulfil our quota obligation I have had to put up with a lot of third rate stuff … Previous to the Quota period I built up a reputation for showing good pictures – I admit there are some good British pictures and personally I like British pictures But the position today is this. I have 4 changes a week. Now, if 30% meant showing 30 British in a year it would not be so bad but to maintain the present quota it means

60 to 70 British pictures and as I have opposition it means the quantity available has to be divided between 2 of us... and my local opposition having a circuit of about 12 small halls seems to get priority. I could have got an early date on the big success *The Quiet Man*, but on account of trying to keep my dates open for British Quota my opposition and other local halls cashed in on it. Now I find most Scottish audiences don't like British pictures unless they are very good... Often my audience get out of hand, when I have to show this second class stuff and on more than one occasion I have had to stop the show and put the lights up and bring the police in before we can get going. You know what this means we are losing our prestige and a good relations with our patrons. On nights when I generally draw £18 to £20 – if I have a poor British picture on, the drawing drops to £5 or £6 per night.

I think under these circumstances I should be excused from Quota or a big reduction so as I can give my public what they like.[10]

Although not in the best of health, Victor still had a real zest for living, his radiant personality and pawky humour impressing itself upon all who came in contact with him. Regarded as 'one of the most colourful personalities in show business today' he continued to be in demand as a lecturer. On stage at the Regal, Dumfries, on 3rd November 1953 he spoke of the old days. Earlier that year he had sailed on the s.s. Lord Warden en route for a holiday in Austria. In December he celebrated his 75th birthday.

84. Victor Biddall on holiday in Montreux

1954 saw no diminution of activity. He attended the Cinema Veterans' annual gathering on 10th May, travelling to London by train because his wife was suffering from arthritis. Accompanied by Thomas Murphy, General Secretary of the Showmen's Guild, they stayed on two extra days to witness a special demonstration of the new *Perspecta* Sound System staged by MGM. In a letter later that year, Victor wrote that as a result of 'doing his stuff' at the Cinema Club luncheon at the Piccadilly Club, Glasgow, he had landed a BBC contract to appear in a programme the following year.[11] In June 1955 it was reported that Victor Biddall had recently stirred memories when he appeared in the *From Me to You* series on Radio.

85. In 1954 Victor (left) visited Britain's smallest cinema, owned by Mr Frazer of Newcastle-on-Tyne

He still ran two cinemas. He still had his showlife. Keenly interested in circus, he became Vice-President of the British Circus Ring, of which he was one of the earliest members. So how – at three score years and ten plus five – did he keep up his phenomenal energy? He was, he said, a great believer in the adage: 'There's no fun like work!' (*World's Fair*, 19th November 1955)

In 1955 Victor moved out of his beloved wagon into a house – 40 North St, Annan – where his visitors that summer included his old friends, Mr & Mrs Caddick from Rhyl. By the end of the year he was confined to bed with internal trouble. When he died on 14th May 1958, mourned as a 'Showman and a Gentleman,' *World's Fair* recorded:

'Victor Biddall's passing severs the long association which the late Mr & Mrs George Biddall and their sons had with show business. The family gained the respect and esteem of the residents in every town throughout Scotland which they visited annually with their popular Ghost Show.'

The words sounded very final, but half a century on and Biddall's Show is still talked about in the Border Country where its ancient spectral mask and shroud, photographs, slides and magic lantern are all carefully preserved in museums. When not on display, the Ghost itself sleeps peacefully, wrapped in layers of tissue paper in a cardboard box at The Beacon, Whitehaven, but inspection reveals a fearsome-looking skull made from gesso-coated leather and large enough to fit over a man's head. Painted white, it has round dark holes for eyes, shaded hollows below both temples and big teeth outlined in black. If the linen cowl fixed round its top and neck lends the head a monkish aspect, its accompanying cotton shroud appears reassuringly homespun. Fashioned like some comfortable bed-gown, the material has been roughly tacked together, its wide bat-wing arms edged with some four inches of lace probably cut from one of Selina's old tablecloths or a pillow case. Time has left its mark in the form of small rust patches on the cotton, but outside in the streets, especially at fair time, George, his family, their horses and even Victor's dog *Lion* live on in folk memory and Biddall's Ghost has never been laid.

8

Cockney Nank

The Biddall family were good knife and axe-throwers and wonderful musicians. Billy, the elder, was one of the best Cockney Nanks I ever met, and he could put his stuff over beautifully.

World's Fair, 26th April 1941

When William Biddall, George's elder brother, married at Woodford District church on 30th December 1856 he described himself as a 'musician', aged nineteen. His bride, Mary Ann, was the eighteen year old daughter of John Fairweather. Although the profession of both fathers was given as 'actor', Mr Fairweather must have had more than one iron in the fire for he died a 'brazier' at Ipswich two years later!

86. Mary Ann (Rosie) Freeman, née Fairweather

Mary Ann (Rosie) had been born at Debenham in Suffolk and the couple spent their early years travelling the southern and eastern counties in summer and overwintering at Wivenhoe or in East London. Rose Hannah, their eldest child, was born in Essex in 1859 and a second daughter, Sarah, was born on 18th February 1861 in King Harry Yard, Mile End Road. When Rosie fell pregnant again the following year, she was able to swap symptoms with her brother-in-law's new wife Augusta who had married Samuel Freeman at Maldon the previous September. Moreover, when both women gave birth to daughters within two months of each other, the new arrivals were both named Augusta.

Sam's daughter was christened at Ipswich in August 1862 whilst William's daughter, born at Brockdish in Norfolk the following month, was taken along with her young sisters for a triple christening at Foxton church in Cambridge on 12th April 1863. Sadly neither little Augusta lived long. At Beccles on 9th June 1863 Sam's baby daughter died of inflammation of the throat and William's daughter Augusta died at Aston Clinton on 16th October 1865, weeks after her third birthday. Cause of death, inflammation of the lungs. The mother's distress was evident in the garbled entry in the official Register that recorded the death of Augustus, her four year old 'son'.

In fact Rosie had a four *month* old son who was destined to thrive. William, named for his father, had been born on 17th June 1864 at West Molesey where his parents had arrived for the Races. The fact that his father had evolved from 'musician' to 'showman' on the birth certificate suggests that since the birth of the three little girls, William and Rosie may have acquired their own show. What kind of show? Whilst William's name became associated with many different types of exhibition during his life-time, the earliest and most enduring was the Temple of Magic, more popularly known as a hanky-panky show involving conjuring, clairvoyancy and the inevitable 'clever pony'. Always on the look out for fresh talent, one of his regular haunts was Barnet Pony Fair on the first weekend of September even if – as in 1870 – the event proved a wash-out.

Three days of rain left roads and fields churned into mud and an atmosphere thick with naphtha, frying fish and sausages, but there were, according to the *Barnet Press*, 10th September 1870, 'the usual number of coconut proprietors who, for every nut they lost gained at least one shilling – plus the usual number of infatuated investors throwing three sticks a penny. His wife takes the money while he poises the coconuts on the sticks.'

87. His wife takes the money while he poises the coconuts on sticks'

What attracted most interest were the roundabouts worked by steam. When enough people were seated, the engine gave a shrill scream and the circle of wooden animals, three abreast, began to move round, slowly at first, but with increasing speed until those seated thereon assumed a scornful smile caused by their wishing to look as if quite accustomed to this kind of motion.

There was just one novelty – the Velocipede – 'a number of wheels being joined in a circle, and capped with seats, on which pleasure, or rather labour seekers – seated themselves, and paid a penny for the privilege of helping a number of other foolish ones to drive the machine round, substituting their own legs as a motive power in place of the steam engine employed to drive the other roundabouts.'

Four years later the same newspaper provides a bird's eye view from the top of Barnet Hill: 'On one side runs a long row of stalls for the sale of gingerbread, on which the "gold" is thickly laid and of which Montreil in his *Histoire des Françaix* says it was in vogue in France in the fourteenth century and introduced to England in the reign of Henry IV since which time no fair is complete without it. Booths for the sale of toys and glittering ornaments complete the line. Opposite is a row of shooting galleries and the lasses in charge of them are obtrusively importunate; and ground marked out for the popular sport of throwing at coconuts.' (*Barnet Press*, 12th September 1874) There were also shows, which in 1874 included Walker's Grand Ghost Illusions.

88. Pipe shooting saloon, c1895

By 1874 there had been four more additions to William and Rosie's family: George born at King's Lynn in 1868; Rebecca Augusta, a winter baby born in World's End Yard, Mile End, in 1869 and taken to St Dunstan's church, Stepney, to be christened; John born at Ipswich two years later and Charles, their youngest, at Norwich in 1873.

Still the family returned to East London every winter, finding after 1874 a profitable venue with the opening of what was to become the annual World's Fair at the Agricultural Hall, Islington. Built in 1861/62 by the Smithfield Society to hold its annual cattle shows, the Royal Agricultural Hall covered an area of three acres, later expanded to five, and its iron-and-glass roof with a span of 130 feet was regarded as an architectural triumph. Although the phrase 'World's Fair' had been used as early as 1873 as an alternative title for John Sharman's Christmas Fair and Bazaar, described as 'This extraordinary and unparalleled idea of bringing the shows under a glass roof, thereby securing the visitors from the effects of our changeable climate,' until 1880 the event was advertised as a Grand Christmas Fête.

The *Islington Gazette* of 29th December 1879 set the scene:

> AGRICULTURAL HALL
>
> This monster building was occupied by Bostock & Wombwell's menagerie, comprising fourteen caravans, and a heterogeneous collection of swings, merry-go-rounds, shooting saloons, fancy stalls, etc. Flanking the "tree" were a number of fruit stalls and two gigantic merry-go-rounds, which latter were an immense attraction on Boxing Day, as the steam whistles of the engines incessantly testified. Immediately beneath the galleries were shooting saloons which were also well patronised by amateur marksmen.

89. Royal Agricultural Hall, Islington, 1906

Among other attractions were Clicquoet, the wonderful six-legged horse from South America; a dog and monkey exhibition in which the latter acted as jockeys to the former in a well-contested hurdle race which provoked hearty laughter; a large booth, with a stage in front, on which pantaloon, harlequin, and other stage characters went through the familiar antics prior to the performance within; then came a theatre, on the panels of which were depicted in gaudy colours the principal scenes in a tragedy, wherein the ghost was the central figure.

At the western end of the hall was a fine elephant, who was kept constantly at work in picking up toothsome tit-bits. In the vicinity of the elephant was a waxwork exhibition, which contained among other personages, the ex-king Cetewayo, Kate Webster, Peace, and others. The proprietors of these various establishments informed the visitors that the usual charge for admission was one shilling, but in consideration of the festival which "comes but once a year," prices were reduced to a few coppers.

The western side of the hall was devoted to the menagerie ... Not least of the attractions were some waxwork marionettes, a mechanical show, and the performances of a Spanish bull.

The galleries were set apart for the swings, which were in a state of constant activity. There were also a few additional shooting saloons, where "wide of the mark" was the order of the day, lotteries in which one was invited to take his chance for the small fee of "a penny a dip", tables on which were heaped lots of "Yankee notions" going at a "ruinous sacrifice"; electrical machines; and lastly our old acquaintance, "Aunt Sally". Each of these attractions had its due share of votaries.

Such are the prominent attractions of the Agricultural Hall – and which are hardly likely to be surpassed in variety, at least anywhere in the metropolis.

Although there is no mention of William Biddall a family tradition puts him there on 28th December 1879 when William, proudly presenting his show in the Agricultural Hall, was also acting host to his brother Charles, down from Scotland and due to return by train that very day. Rosie, between demonstrations of clairvoyancy and legerdemain, was doing her best to make her brother-in-law feel welcome. Must he go back so soon? Would he not stay a little longer? Persuasion prevailed and he agreed to stay the extra day that caused him to miss his place on the train that plunged off the Tay Bridge.

And what was Charles doing in Scotland? He was touring with his own show. Thirty years on from his marriage to Charlotte Lincon, he was now the proud owner of Freeman's Circus of Varieties with his ten sons and daughters as its star performers. Whilst continuing to use the Freemans' base in Mile End Road, London, until the early 1860s, Charles and Charlotte had toured through the Eastern Counties most years. Between 1850 and 1865 five of their children were taken along to St Peter Parmentergate Church in Norwich to be christened, their father's occupation being described as 'musician'.

It is likely that Charles travelled with Manders for some of this time, because his son Robert's christening at Norwich in January 1860 coincided with a visit to that city by William Manders' 'Royal Menagerie and Portable Domicile of Animated Nature.' Links between the families of Freeman and Manders were strengthened when Charles and Charlotte's son, Henry, married Helen, daughter of William Manders, at Leeds in 1875 and his younger brother Robert later married Amelia Manders.

Charles may have cheated Death in December 1879, but he could not elude his last enemy for long. While his Circus of Varieties was open in Edinburgh in February 1881 he was admitted to the New Royal Infirmary suffering from tetanus and died three days' later. His family, though devastated, had no choice but to carry on with the tour that was to take them to Glasgow. A month later the Census Enumerator found them parked on the Old Theatre Ground in Bank Street, Old Monkland. Charlotte Freeman, a widow aged 49, was described as a 'Travelling Show Woman.' She was accompanied by her eldest son, Charles, and his wife Emily (neé Meers); two unmarried sons, John and Samuel; and three unmarried daughters, Rosina, Lavinia and ten-year-old Martha. Forming a separate 'household' on the same site were her son Henry Freeman, 'Travelling Showman', his wife Helen, and their children, William Henry, aged five, and Amelia, aged three. Living nearby in Bank Street were Robert Freeman, Ring Performer, his wife Amelia, and their baby daughter, Mary Ellen, born in Dalkeith five months before.

South of the Border the 1881 Census found William and Rosie Freeman's family in travelling vans parked at Bollo Bridge Road in Acton, Middlesex. All seven children, including Charles aged 8, were described as Showman's Assistants and the family was accompanied by Martha Denny, their seventeen-year-old servant. Also with them were George Brown and William Lester, horse keepers. How good they were at their job is not recorded – nor the words of their boss when, in July the following year, he was summoned at Horsham for allowing six horses to stray on the road at Adversane where his van had parked on the verge.[1]

What is known is that William Biddall was on his way to Mitcham for the great three days fair held on Three Kings Common every August. At the top of a map of the fair drawn that year appeared a sketch of his show built up in prime position and described as: 'Biddall's Performing Pony, Legerdemain by Miss Bedall, and Living Head shown in a Box concluded the entertainment.' Next to him was 'Scott's small Circus with Poneys and Tight Rope Dancing by Children'. Other shows included Manly's Performing Birds and Pony, Scott's Marionettes, Campbell's Trapeze Feats and Dancing, Bailey's Sea on Land – 'a new kind of roundabout with Boats and Sails and very fine organ all worked by Steam.' Steam-driven – but, it was pointed out, 'The Electric Light was introduced by Bailey to light up the Sea on Land Roundabout.'

At the World's Fair in the Agricultural Hall that winter the *Era* (30th December 1882) reported that 'Biddle's Variety Exhibition' included a highly intelligent pony who told the time of day and did other feats to attract such audiences as must have brought an enormous amount to the treasury. And well it might, for the family was about to shell out for nuptials. On 8th January 1883 William's

member of the public who had been leaning over the balcony rails to survey the shows when he was hit by a stray bullet in his right arm.[4]

The following year there was a fire in the Sedgwicks' wagon. Mary Ann, wife of William Sedgwick, saw the wick of a paraffin lamp burning down into the oil and rushed to extinguish it. Her clothing caught alight. Flames spread to the curtains, the cot where her children were sleeping, set fire to the whole van. Mrs Bushnell of Portsmouth rushed to save two chavvies but could not reach William, the Sedgwicks' five year old son, who died in the flames.[5]

91. Chittock's Troupe of Dogs & Monkeys standing next to Biddall's Show, c1895

A decade later tragedy befell Matilda, wife of James Chittock, proprietor of the troupe of trained dogs and monkeys that had been coming to the World's Fair for years. Whilst pulling down their show on the last evening she fell off the stage, struck her head and never regained consciousness. She died an hour later.[6]

Although Sarah's marriage had robbed the Biddall family of talent, compensation was found in the persons of two cousins who joined the show at this time. Polly and Venie were the teen-aged daughters of William's eldest brother, Benjamin (alias the clown, Monsieur Antonio) and Polly (the famous Female Blondin). Both had inherited aspects of their parents' skills – the younger Polly proving herself a genius on the tightrope, Venie a natural clown. In time they would become welcome additions to William's family in more ways than one. For the moment though, the girls had come to Uncle William to work and they melded into the troupe so well that outsiders assumed they were his daughters.

Fifty years later '*G.C.C.*' was writing about Barnet fair in the mid-eighties:

> One recalls the parading of such excellent family artistes as the famous Biddall family, with William, expert cornet soloist; John, trombonist; George, double drums; Charles, second cornet; and Rebecca Biddall, with a *pot-pourri* of musical juggling with bottles, knives and tomahawks, assisted by the Misses Polly and Venie Biddall in walking the silver thread. This well-known and popular show on the Southern Counties route had built up an excellent name with a first-class connection.

In 1887 Colonel Cody, more commonly known as Buffalo Bill, came to England and presented his show before the queen in her Jubilee Year. Suddenly Wild West was all the rage. Annie Oakely's marksmanship, lassoing by cowboys, hatchet hurling of Indians – these were what the public wanted to see. Following the example of his friend Billy Russell, young Billy Biddall, now aged twenty-three, decided to develop a knife-throwing act and prevailed upon his eighteen-year-old sister Becky to become his partner. Soon he had sufficient skill to outline Becky's body as she stood stock-still and smiling in front of a board. He could lodge a knife in the gap between each of her fingers and split the string on the (admittedly large) beads around her neck. Sometimes he attached wads of cottonwool soaked in meths to the hafts and outlined Becky's body in fire, or substituted tomahawks for knives to produce what was billed as 'a sensational impalement'. Such was his prowess that he was hailed as a champion knife-thrower and awarded medals. One was presented by Mr T. E. Read, lessee of the World's Fair, another by Mr J. Mouse of the Colebrook Club, and a third by Johnny Cottrell, swimming show proprietor.

And what did Becky get for her pains? Twice her tresses were set alight, and she had her hair cut into a fringe to cover the scar left by a blade which failed to miss – a mishap that caused the audience to run shrieking from the show.

'Hi! Hi! Walk up. Be in time! The Islington fair is now on. Here you are for the learned Pig and the Siamese Twins! The road is blocked, the gaslights are flaring, and the great main street of a decent suburb is blocked to every decent man and woman for six days. In other words the annual fair nuisance has broken out again,' screeched the *Islington Gazette,* 8th December 1887.

And a month later 'Dogberry' of the City Press was complaining that,

> If anyone wants to know how much the nervous system can stand without utterly breaking down, let him go to the World's Fair at the Agricultural Hall ... I went the other evening as a sort of exercise in mental athletics, and I came away with an awfully confused notion of what I had seen and heard ...
>
> How the people there, whose business is pleasure and whose pleasure is business, can stand it day after day I cannot imagine ... One thing particularly struck me before my senses became too much confused. Wombwell's Menagerie is there, and it contains a splendid group of lions. The beasts did not seem in the least degree disconcerted with what was going on – they were used to it. One noble fellow in particular, squatting on his haunches, surveyed the scene through his shaggy mane with the utmost indifference, though I noticed that every now and then, looking up to the gallery, his eyes sparkled and his whole countenance lit up for a moment. Perhaps it was the passing of a fine fat baby that drew his attention.
>
> (*Islington Gazette*, 5th January 1888)

William Biddall was there with his marionettes 'warranted lifelike in all their movements,' his trained ponies and shooting gallery. Just as he and his family would be back the following year, wintering in their yard at Stepney Green until it was time to pull into the Agricultural Hall for six weeks at Christmas.

During the course of the 1888-9 World's Fair they found themselves mixing with the good and the great. Having survived the onslaught of Mr George Smith of Coalville and his attempts to reform caravan life out of existence, showfolk were understandably wary when approached by do-gooders. But they had no fears about Miss Millington of York, the showmen's friend, who came with a group of Christian women to issue *The Caravan* and supervise efforts to educate and (as they said) improve the moral welfare of their children. Having gathered up the 'little wanderers' every morning, the good ladies shepherded them into Berner's Hall where, besides writing, geography and Bible classes, chavvies were taught Band of Hope songs such as:

Who'd be a drunkard with old tattered clothes,
Covered with shame, with derision and woes?
Warned by his fall, we are sober and wise,
We must be abstainers, for we all want to rise.

Break the pledge, never, no, no, no!
Not while the streams in the valleys do flow;
Dear are the treasures which temperance can tell,
Health and pleasure follow when we drink from the well.

(*Islington Gazette* 18th January 1889)

Blondin himself was there that season to perform on a rope sixty-four feet from the ground, and Ma'mselle Alcide Capitaine to make dramatic descents from the roof with lightning speed, suspended only by her teeth. Wombwell's Menagerie boasted nearly eight hundred exhibits and had engaged Captain Dudley Vane and Madame Salva to give frequent performances with the lions. Scott's circus, Reeves' Richardson's Show, Chittock's dog and monkey circus, John Parker's ghost show and Cottrell's swimming exhibition were all present together with what was described as 'Biddall's American Knife Throwing Exhibition, Great Mechanical Exhibition, Variety Exhibitions with immense parades and entertainments.'

92. William Biddall driving the band wagon – 'His four sons were excellent musicians'

William must have been a proud man when he drove up to the Hall in his ornately carved and gilded band carriage newly-refurbished by Bates of Mile End. Proud too as he watched his family perform. Rarely any need to hire outsiders. His four sons were excellent musicians. No sheet music required. Each had simply chosen an instrument and taught himself to play by ear. And the girls, emulating their mother's proficiency with a needle, made all the costumes for the show, sewing on thousands of beads and sequins. Writing nearly fifty years later, Monsieur Henri, the Strong Man who was one of the few extras engaged by Biddalls, recalled that the dresses worn by all the performers were of the best and 'would put to shame the costumes worn now in some of the circuses and music halls.'[7]

By now old William's showmanship – and wicked sense of humour – were legendary. When later that year Biddall's opened at Shepherd's Bush on a piece of ground next to the Salvation Army, he could not resist a joke at their expense when they sent their band to play on the tober. Telling his daughters to dress in Salvation Army uniform, he started his show's parade by sending the girls out clutching the *War Cry* and dancing to the *Hallelujah* being played on the organ. Pandemonium ensued.[8]

Newspapers provided many accounts of Biddall's public performances but rarely a glimpse of their private lives. One reporter, coming on the showfolk in early September 1889 as they waited to draw on for Barnet fair, could scarcely conceal his delight at securing a peep behind the scenes.

93 and 94. Showfolk's caravans, c1895

The long narrow strip of land to the left of the road when one faces towards the town, has during the earlier part of the week become dotted over with caravans, which from north, south, east and west have been crawling along towards this temporary stopping place. Here at an early hour of the morning may be seen the Queen of the Ring bathing her royal countenance in an iron pail full of pump water, and combing her pretty hair with never even "a cracked looking-glass" to see her face in. Here too are the Mexican knife-throwers clad in sober corduroy and eating bread and onions with pocketknives of ordinary dimensions. Outside the Metropolitan Caravan of Natural Curiosities the proprietor and his family are at breakfast sitting in a ring upon the grass eating huge slices of bread and jam, and drinking tea out of cups and mugs each of different pattern.

Would it be believed there is not a spotted boy or fat girl among them? The baby is guiltless of possessing two heads, and appears to be blessed with the usual number of extremities, although it might be possible, judging from the lusty way in which, like Oliver Twist, he asks for more – it might be possible that he is the possessor of an abnormal quantity of lungs.

The door of the caravan is open, too; but nothing more wonderful presents itself than a pair of impossible china-ware dogs on the chimney piece, and an old woman scouring out a frying pan ...

And what have we here? A group of strikingly marked ponies cropping the grass in prosaic fashion. This is the pony that waltzes to the music; that the fiery, untamed mustang which is ridden bare-backed by the howling Indian, whose terrific appearance at night frightens the smaller children, till they nearly fall from their seats. Why, there he is as sober as any, and dressed in corduroy trousers and a patched shirt, banging with a horse's nosebag another person whom we recognise "by the droop of his eye" as Mr Merriman.

But away! before all is discovered to be but illusion. See that gipsy woman standing with her flashing black eyes; how scornful of wasp waists! With only the heavy gold earrings to adorn her, and mark what a proud, what a striking beauty is there ...

Close by is the heavy road engine of Bailey's patent circular switchback, which appears in Barnet for the first time, and which on Monday steered, with two trucks behind it, into the field through the narrow gate at the foot of the hill in a way that, considering its cumbrous nature, was truly wonderful. There are several trucks belonging to this novelty, but in the early part of the week, when these lines were penned, they were still in chrysalis stage, and no man could prophecy with certainty as to what would be the plumage of the butterfly. Judging from advertisements, Bailey (there is a Bailey junior, in the firm) must be a big man, even among the upper ten, for we see displayed upon his illustrated posters the cars of the switchback teeming with popular representatives of the *beau monde*. In one car we see Mr Henry Irving and Miss Terry, in another General Boulanger and Mr J.L.Toole, associated with the shade of Benjamin Disraeli; while, horrible to relate, in a third, we find Mr Gladstone in the centre of a circle of giddy but admiring coryphées ...

Across the railway, in the field used for the horse fair, the long booths of the refreshment contractors had taken root, and were gradually extending, but not a horse could be seen. In the cattle field at the top of the hill, opposite the cottage hospital, which, before the week is out, will be a wild sea of mud, a drove of some four hundred splendid Devonshire cattle were browsing on the still green grass; whilst in the fields on the northern and western outskirts of the town were other herds, driven up from the North by tall, bony Scotchmen with a keen eye to the main chance. Such is the prelude, the overture to our *Beggars' Opera*.

(*Barnet Press*, 7th September 1889)

Expectations thus roused, he took himself along to the main performance, together with all the world, his sweetheart and his wife who flocked down the hill towards the pleasure fair, bright on the horizon, flaring with a thousand lights. As he approached, the first thing that caught his eye was the roley poley, a huge platform balanced in the centre and made to revolve as if being rolled round on its edge in a slanting position, although the rim never touched the ground. Upon the upper side seats were arranged, and the illusion of a steam boat was enhanced by a tiara of gas lights enclosed in shades of blue and yellow cut crystal which, when viewed from the road, looked very pretty.

95. Bank Holiday on Wanstead Flats, 1895

Turning from the roley poley to the trapeze railway, our reporter described how 'a male fairist' might hang by his arms from a travelling pulley and skim along an inclined wire till he found himself slammed against a sackful of mouldy shavings. Then there was the switchback, and what a trap that was – with young couples being seated together in one of those rolling, swaying cars until the damsel became distressed and had to be comforted by an arm about the waist!

The roundabout with the 'rocking horses' next, despite having to run the gauntlet of 'teasers' – metal tubes full of water which lads bought to squirt at the girls. 'Ah! how the plain girls sneer at that, and how the pretty ones simper, for truth to tell a good soaking with ditch water is a sort of vote of admiration, and when you see pretty looks hanging round the head in draggled rat tails, you must understand that you are in the presence of very resplendent beauty indeed.'

Thus wrote the 'male fairist' before continuing:

> And so mid the glare of lights, the howling of fog horns and steam whistles, the beating of drums and gongs, the clashing of cymbals, cries of "Three shics a penny", the clamour of the organs, the bawling of showmen, and merry peals of laughter, the fun waxes fast and furious, yet is withal more innocent of real evil than many things much more respectable. Walk down the long line of booths devoted to articles for sale, and you see gingerbread which looks better than it tastes; toys of every kind, from the penny wooden man with the stiff back who does the mangling, to the shilling doll with a complaisant smile upon its waxy countenance ... China teapots, you see, and glass milk jugs, quicksilvered vases and a horrible compound of sugar known as peppermint rock. Walk back again till you stand appalled before the show of the Zulu family, where a man with a white pot hat and an Irish brogue is lecturing on the gaudy diagrams which present a group of savages torturing one of their number.
>
> "That," he says, pointing to the victim with a long wand, "is the brother there, all alive, and as you see them

96. Switchback railway, c1895

depicted there, so you will see them all alive inside ... Come and see the wild, blood-thirsty savage!" And then the tale is taken up by a negro, also in a tall hat, to the tune of "Oh, it's horrible, it's terrible to *see* such a sight – a human being that has been put through such torture, and had his teeth pulled out one by one and his nails pulled off! Only a penny, and no waiting."

After a spell of gazing at the 'Roll, bowl or pitch' stalls where folk queued to throw rings on to a row of hooks in the hope of winning a twopenny walking stick, it was the photographer who caught this journalist's eye, causing him to wonder whether he really had taken the portraits of princes displayed outside and how he was able to obtain any photos at all by the light of his naphtha lamps. But enough was enough. It was now time for our reporter to:

Take a parting glimpse at the gaudy colouring of the shows, the glitter and sparkle and flare that vanish with the daylight, the swaying crowd, and the fluttering streamers of bunting. Take a last look, for the prompter's finger is upon the bell, and he waits to strike. Three times does this gaudy transformation scene unfold itself, and then hawker, higgler, and showman

Fold their tents like the Arabs,
And as silently steal away.

9

Sensational Impalements

> They stood a gal up and she held back her throat, and they chucked the knives all round it as thick as a swarm of bees.
>
> *Barnet Press*, 6th September 1890

The management of the Agricultural Hall went to special lengths at Christmas 1889 to counter the opposition posed by Barnum at the other end of town. They decorated the building with flags and banners and, coming in from the Upper Street, people were greeted by the glare of thousands of coloured lamps, a huge Christmas tree and miniature tableaux of *Babes in the Wood.*

Once inside the great hall, visitors found themselves surrounded by Bailey's circular switchback and roundabout, whilst high up in the roof two young ladies – the Sisters Ongar – flew through the air on their flying trapeze and the immortal Blondin performed his tricks on the high rope. And if these or the Star Menagerie or Scott's Circus did not provide excitement enough, there was always the exhibition of sensational impalements in Biddall's show.

97. At the Agricultural Hall, c1888. Rosie & daughters, Rebecca (bottom left) and Rose Hannah (top left)

Showmen's families loved the World's Fair. It meant six weeks of slog but takings were usually good and the companionship wonderful. Six weeks were long enough for friendships between the young to develop into something more. And after the punters had gone, time for older folks to chat and reminisce and – dare one say? – share a jug or two. Just to whet the whistle, mind, after hours of telling the tale but – and here was the rub – they must take care not to upset those intrepid good people who saw in the World's Fair a useful net to catch sinners. Under their banner *Travellers' National Total Abstainers' Union* they pounced on the showfolk determined to educate their children and teetotalise parents. With what success may be imagined. Suffice to say many travellers enjoyed the free tea that was provided one Sunday before repairing to a local pub to discuss the matter – happily overheard by a correspondent of the *Islington Gazette* (14th January 1890):

> "Wery kind on 'em, to be sure; and a very good tea they give us; but they must try their teetotalism on the young 'uns – I must have my drop o' rum for this 'ere asthma." And with this solace the lady with the big broad face, well-tanned by exposure, and surmounted by an immense hat, took another sip, and wiped her mouth with the back of her hand.

On the other hand, there were aspects of showfolk that could not fail to impress:

viz: if they are not educated, and do not come very much under religious influences, they are singularly free from the bad language so common amongst people of similar calibre in the towns. And there is an *esprit de corps* which makes quarrelling a rare thing indeed. The above free tea, which was given in the Myddelton Hall on Sunday night, brought together a combination of experiences perhaps never before included in those walls – several hundreds of people knowing every inch of the roads of the United Kingdom, and the peculiarities of the residents of every city, town, and hamlet. They can tell of the ups and downs of life, but through all are cheerful and hopeful, with as much pride in their shows or catch-pennies as Irving in the Lyceum or Harris in Drury Lane.

98. Agricultural Hall – showfolk relaxing

The final weekend at the World's Fair was a case of 'Saturday night and Sunday morning.' On the one hand, all was glitter, gaiety, and order; on the other disorder and mundane hard work. Even before the last show had closed, packing commenced. Performers stripped off their tinsel in favour of workaday clothes. In less than no time the clown's chalk and paint had given way to grime; the muslin and tights of the dancer to the oldest of frocks. Flags were torn down, roundabouts dismantled and packed in trucks. Incessant hammering was accompanied by howling and screeching from the menagerie. Heaps of broken glass showed where shooting galleries had stood. Mounds of straw were all that was left of the Aunt Sallies who had been disembowelled for packing. But amidst all this kerfuffle a fellow must eat, so all over the place women were manhandling huge kettles and saucepans whose savoury contents tickled the nose. Even Blondin, hero of Niagara and with a mansion to go home to, remained long enough personally to supervise the taking down of his ropes and tackle and see them properly stowed away. That was the hall-mark of a showman.

99. Agricultural Hall – pulling down

Young Billy Biddall had done well at the World's Fair that year. On 28th February he was presented with a medal at the Colebrook Club and he realised that his knife-throwing act had other possibilities. He could take it on stage and seek engagements in variety theatres, especially in winter months when, apart from the Agricultural Hall, there was little doing on the fairground. He was lucky enough to secure a theatre opposite the Hall to work out his show for next season. With Becky and his brother Johnny, now also proficient at throwing knives, he appeared at the Stratford Empire, the first to take such an act on stage.

100. Billy partnered by his sister, Rebecca, c1890

Barnet's three day fair in September was the largest in quantity of stock and visitors that had been seen for five or six years. In the guise of 'Bill' out for the day with his 'Betsy', the reporter for the *Barnet Press* (6th September 1890) gave what may be taken as an eyewitness account of a visit to Biddall's.

I edges my way up to one of the shows of the Mexican knife-throwers, where they was a turning a barrel organ outside, beating a big drum, blowing a foghorn, a trombone, and a cornet all at once, and two chaps and a gal was a throwing glass bottles about as if they was made of cast iron and could be broke no how. When the chaps sang out, "Walk up now, posertively just a going to begin," I hooks my arm in the missuses and walks in with the crowd ...

Wot we see in that show was something that I never see equalled. They was a throwing up a dozen balls one after the other, and then a catching 'em all as they came down, as fast as flakes in a snowstorm. But the knife throwing was the licker; they stood one chap up and chucked knives at him so close that they shook his hair as they stuck in the wooden board agin which he was standing, and when he walked out there was his figger, as neat as a drawing, all lined out by the knives a sticking in the board. Then they stood a gal up, and she held back her throat, and they chucked the knives all round it as thick as a swarm of bees and never scratched her skin. The next performance was wery thrilling. One chap stood up again the board and the other chucked knives at him, the handles of which was all ablaze and there they smoked and flared and fizzled round his body, and him as cool as a cowcumber all the time. Then a performing pony came on, which his name was William, and a nodding his head when spoke to, by way of answering yes and no.

"Pick me out," says his master, "the biggest rogue in the company and get as nigh him you can." You should have heard the laugh when the pony poked his nose into his master's hand.

"Find me out," says the guv'nor again, "the lady wot likes a good cup o' tea and a leetle drop o' gin in it by way o' flavouring." Round the ring the pony comes, and blessed if he didn't stop right again the old woman.

"Bill," she says, very faint and a leanin' hard up agin me, "I know'd there was something wrong; I didn't have the usual seasoning in my tea, and I feels wery bad."

I tumbled to what the old lady was a driving at and, when we came out of the show, we went off to a booth to wet our whistles.

Later 'Bill and Betsy' approached the sidestalls where

... a handsome gal at a shooting gallery as we was a passing by, ses to me, "Now then my dear, have a shot, only a penny." And so I would too – just to oblige the pretty dear, but gazing at the missus out of one corner of my eye, I see the winegar getting agitated, so walked on sharp. Then both me and the missus had a cockshy with inji rubber balls at a chap with a black face, that poked his head through a painted board and got his living by being shied at three times for a penny. He was artful and had a way of working his neck round so that you couldn't hit him no how.

What a row there was a going on to be sure, bells a ringing, foghorns blowing, steam whistles nearly startling you into a fit, wooden rattles a clacking, and organs a blowin' fit to bust. *Rule Britannia* a going in at one ear, and *We won't go home till morning* in at the other, with a perwading atmosphere of naphtha, bad cigars and dirty water. Them squirts was a nuisance, if you stopped a moment to look at the fighting men a lounging outside their shows, or to see the gals a dancing outside the circus, or if you was a gazing promiscuous up at the people hanging over the railings of the roadway and staring down at the fair, you was sure to get some of the ditch water right in your eye and, as the missus observed, it was mostly hussies wot done it.

Every year the family's return to the Agricultural Hall revived memories of the dreadful shooting accident that had happened to Rose Hannah even if, despite being disfigured and left blind in one eye, she had made a remarkable recovery. In 1891 she found herself being courted by Tom Ridley, a young man from another family of showfolk whose pedigree stretched back generations. Now aged thirty-two, Rose Hannah accepted Tom's proposal and became engaged to be married. All seemed set fair for a happy future.

Most years the family spent Easter at Wanstead Flats and then travelled through the eastern counties aiming to reach Doncaster Races in June. On Sunday, 21st June 1891, Rosie was driving one of the wagons up Gringely Hill, near Gainsborough, when Rose Hannah jumped off to chock the wheels, tripped in her long skirt and was crushed. When William Brown, a groom driving the wagon behind, ran to pick her up blood spurted from her mouth and nose. They rushed her to Wiseton, hoping to find a doctor but there was none available. Instead a Mrs Myers examined poor Rose Hannah and pronounced her dead. A broken rib had penetrated her lung and she had died within minutes.

The family was devastated. Her mother inconsolable. She fell ill and her hair dropped out, growing again into tight black curls. When less than ten months later she was lying in bed in the wagon at Canning Town fairground, Becky heard her sadly singing *Silver Threads Among the Gold.* Rosie died the following day and was buried at Manor Park. A certificate cited apoplexy as cause of death. The family knew it was a broken heart.

Ten days later, on 3rd May 1892, whilst still parked on the Marsh at Canning Town, young Billy got married. His bride was Polly, twenty-one year old daughter of his father's eldest brother, and the ceremony at Holy Trinity Church, Barking Road, was witnessed by J. and Annie Smart. Monsieur Henri, was there too, able to recall the event over forty years later.

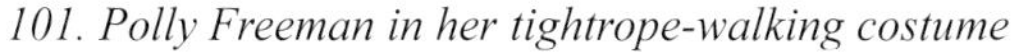

101. Polly Freeman in her tightrope-walking costume

102. Billy Biddall with his medals for knife-throwing

103. Harris's gallopers on Wanstead Flats, 1895

Life, like the show, went on. They attended Barnet fair as usual in September and this year William must have found it more comforting than ever to meet up with his eldest daughter there. Her marriage to Abraham Harris had apparently worked well. By 1892 they were proud parents of three children – Rosanna, Mary (Polly) and William – and Sarah was expecting a fourth. Business had prospered too and the couple was now travelling the eastern counties with their own set of steam-driven gallopers, based at Biggleswade. Thither went William and his family in October. 'Biddall's Exhibition of Varieties was located on the Market Place on Friday and Saturday of last week and attracted large numbers of people,' reported the *Biggleswade Chronicle* (15th October 1892).

Maybe some of the fire had gone out of William's belly but with seven young people dependent on the show there was no time to brood so it was off to the World's Fair again at Christmas.

'I did the fun of the fair one night last week and met many old friends. There were the knife-throwing Mexicans from Stepney Green in the old corner over against the giant whelk stall,' wrote a reporter from the *Islington Gazette* (5th January 1893). The following year too there was special mention of the 'sensational hatchet-throwing' being staged at the Agricultural Hall.

Although on the surface things proceeded as before, there must have been a question mark over the family's future. For much of the year young Billy was working on his own account, accepting engagements for his knife-throwing exhibition. But it wasn't earning him enough, not now that he and Polly had started a family and there were extra mouths to feed. The show must expand and develop, but in what direction? Should their branch of the Biddalls start a circus like that travelled by cousin James Biddall, brother of Polly and Venie? They certainly had the manpower and talent, if they wanted to pull together. Or should they split up and join existing enterprises as individual performers, as cousins Benny Biddall and Bob Freeman were doing with some success? This possibility lacked appeal to young men brought up to be their own masters.

The *Era,* 13th January 1894, carried an advertisement: 'Wanted to Sell, Shooting Gallery, Tubes, Rifles, Front Complete; also Truck, suitable for Circus or Galloping Horses; nearly new, by Bedford, London. On view. Biddall, Agricultural Hall, London.'

The shooting gallery, with its painful memories of Rose Hannah, was sold together with the van that might have been suitable for circus or gallopers. None of these were relevant to the big new idea forming in the minds of William and his sons with an urgency all the more pressing once Becky announced her marriage plans. On 13th December 1894 she walked up the aisle of St Paul's in Old Brentford with John Francis Stroud, who made his living from coconut shies on the fairground. Witnesses were William Freeman and Becky's cousin Lavinia (Venie) Freeman. The bride, giving her occupation as 'theatrical profession,' made such an impression in her red velvet dress and large red hat that locals still recalled the event over twenty years later.

104. John Stroud who married Rebecca in 1894

105. Rebecca Biddall

106. Rebecca's 'chavvies' – Jack, Nell and Lilian Stroud, c1898

That Christmas the World's Fair eclipsed all previous shows in excellence and attendance. It was calculated that between midday and half-past ten on Boxing Day 66,789 people passed through its doors. (*Islington Gazette*, 28th December 1894)

A month later a sardonic reporter added his weight to the numbers:

> Feeling in need of quiet, with a longing for a peace which would assist meditation, I turned the other night out of the hum of Upper Street into the World's Fair. With nothing to disturb my thoughts but three brass bands, ten steam organs, four or five drums, a railway whistle, and a gong or two, I meandered amongst the habitations of giants, fat women, dwarfs, and monstrosities.
>
> The World's Fair this year is so much like the World's Fair any other year, that at first glance one does not see any novelty in it. There is the same ghost show, the same Chittock with the dogs and monkeys, the same merry-go-rounds, and the same wild beast show ...
>
> The same Channel Tunnel railway puffs and whistles in a corner; but in another corner there is a distinctly new and novel show called *The Haunted Swing*. If you want to know how you would feel if the world were upside down try the haunted swing; it is the funniest experience ever given to man for the small charge of twopence. The swing is suspended in a small room on an artful axle, and when it is put in motion you appear to go over and over in a continual whirligig, but, as a matter of fact, you do nothing of the sort, for the room goes round; you are almost stationary. The illusion, however, is perfect.
>
> Another novelty is the Kinetoscope of the wondrous Edison. Such a peepshow as that would have made your grandmother sit up. Living, acting, almost speaking photographs, is the only description I can give of this marvel. I look and see a boxing match. There are men fighting in earnest while a crowd surges and bellows its encouragements to the boxers. The referee walks round and round the combatants, every movement is the movement of life reproduced with marvellous accuracy. Talk of the invention of the steam-engine! That was a tinpot performance to this fearful and wonderful record of animate life.
>
> Going from the Kinetoscope into the boxing booth, where the champion light weight of somewhere or other was engaged in dabbing the face of another champion, I was able to test the accuracy of the picture ... When one has done a round of the side shows, there is yet the intrepid Blondin and the Flying Eugenes to make a splendid show. (*Islington Gazette*, 24th January 1895)

There was no mention of the knife-throwers. Perhaps because Billy and his brothers were already busying themselves with their new venture. The *Era*, 2nd March 1895, carried an advertisement: 'Wanted to Purchase, Two Performing Male lions; also Four Wolves, Performers, and Two Bears and Two Hyenas. Biddalls & Son's Exhibition, Ivy Street, Hoxton.'

Lions, wolves, bears and hyenas – what were they up to now? The explanation came the following week: 'Wanted to Purchase, 2 Male Lions (Performers), also Wolves, Bears, Hyenas, or anything suitable for Wild Beast Show. Biddall's Exhibition, Ivy Street, Hoxton.'

There was no mention of father and sons in this advertisement. An oversight perhaps, or sad acknowledgement of the fact that William was ill and not expected to recover. The same disease that had killed his brothers, phthisis exhaustion, now had him in its grip. He died in the presence of his family on 4th April 1895 at 52a Ivy Street, Hoxton, and was buried with his wife Rosie in Manor Park cemetery. The inscription on their headstone reads:

> Two faithful friends lie buried here
> A father and a mother dear
> We hope their souls have gone to rest
> In Christ to be beloved and blest.

And above these words is carved one of their beloved performing ponies.

10

Wanted, A Lion Tamer

The attack was an absolute surprise to the keeper as well as to the manager, as Viola had performed with the same lion for two years and without any fear of danger whatever.

Dorset County Chronicle, 14th October 1897

The Biddall's show that set out for its first season in 1895 was more than just a menagerie. It combined all the talents of the family – rope-walking, juggling, knife-throwing, vaulting, clowning. With all this – and animals too – how could it fail? Years later Monsieur Henri penned a description of Biddall's Wild Beast and Mexican Exhibition.

Polly did a first-class rope act. Vieni was not only a fine jester but also did a nice snake-charming act and worked a den of beasts mixed. George and John were great jugglers, and all of them were first-class performers on brass and no one could stand against them on the parade. Billy and his sister Beccy did a knife and tomahawks throwing act. Charly was a good vaulter (I know, I taught him) and was also a splendid lion performer and one of the best at working the bouncing lion act. Altogether they had one of the best travelling beast shows on the road. They were all Freemans, and I am sure if such a show was again on the road, nothing would please the public better. My wife, Madame Elise, the strong lady, and I with my bits and pieces as a gymnast, tumbles and vaults, were the only strangers with the show.

107. Monsieur Henri, strong man and acrobat

108. Madame Elise, 1896

109. Mander's Royal Moving Waxworks at Lewes, c1896 – standing alongside Biddall Bros (see 110) just as it would stand next to George Biddall's show at Dalbeattie, c1900 (see 51)

I may say that we all worked well together and had a happy time. Some little trouble such as the tamer getting mauled and rescued by the strong man Henri, and a big python escaping from its box in our living van and getting into our bed one night, helped to make up our life.

The shows were made up as follows: nine wagons of beasts and wagon group of performing lions by Captain Charly; snakes by Vieni; untamable lioness by Charly; juggling act by John and George Biddall; Mexican knife and battle-axe by Billy and Beccy Biddall; rope act by Polly Biddall; jester Vieni; flying trapeze, Mons Henri; vaulting, Charly and Henri; and Mddle Elise, champion strong lady – ten first class acts and the wild beast show, and all for the low charge of 2d. The same show would be a gold mine at 6d. I may add that the dresses worn by all the performers were of the best ... I worked for Biddalls times out of number when they had the tumbling show, when they had the wild beast show and when they had the wild beasts and circus at the back.[1]

Monsieur Henri's wife, Madame Elise, was an extraordinary character. Allegedly born at Neuilly, near Paris, one of her greatest feats had been to lift eight men weighing a total of 1700 lbs. Moreover, whilst travelling with a circus in Cornwall some years before, she had been sitting in a caravan with five other artistes when the horse pulling them had come to a halt halfway up a steep hill. What with passengers and circus paraphernalia, the poor beast was quite overcome and nothing could persuade him to proceed. Grabbing a bit of rope, Madame Elise harnessed herself to the wagon and dragged it in triumph to the brow of the hill.[2]

Despite Monsieur Henri's words, he and his wife were not the only 'strangers' with Biddalls' show. What he meant was that they were the only outsiders to stay long enough to travel as part of the family. Other performers came and went. Especially lion-tamers.

110. Biddall's Circus & Menagerie at Lewes, c1896 – Advertising special engagement of Zaio and Mdlle Elise. Billy Biddall is leaning on big drum (right)

'Wanted, Useful Act in Ring. Will J. Clack write in? Month's engagement. Address: Biddall, Drill Hall, Alfred Road, Portsmouth,' it was announced in the *Era*, 23rd November 1895.

Another advert on the same page read: 'Wanted, Lion Tamer, for Menagerie. Perrino, Animal Trainer, write in. Join at once. Address: Biddall, Drill Hall, Alfred Road, Portsmouth.' A fortnight later it was 'Wanted, Known that Messrs Biddall Brothers thank all Artists that wrote in answer to their Advertisement. We have engaged.'

With regard to the lion-tamer, they were pleased with their choice. Captain Marco, a black man, had shown that he could keep a cool head when a lion escaped from the menagerie for which he was working earlier that year. The lion took refuge in an outhouse at Queen Camel and Marco calmly lined up a van with the door and enticed the beast into the vehicle. In the same week another menagerie travelling a few miles away at Martock came off less well when one of their lions escaped, attacked an elephant and was shot by its trainer, Captain Rowland. (*Era,* 16th November 1895)

As can be seen from their advertisements Biddall Brothers were spending Christmas 1895 at Portsmouth where under the management of Mr T.R. Gannon the Volunteer Drill Hall had been converted for the holidays into a World's Fair. It was nowhere near as big as that in Islington, of course, but Biddall's was the only Menagerie, whereas in the Agricultural Hall Wombwell's held sway that Christmas with their lions, tigers, elephants, leopard, camels, dromedaries, monkeys, and birds. 'In fact,' wrote a columnist for the *Islington Gazette*, 'a most interesting sight for old as well as young; though there is the probability that the (to our mind) superfluous exhibition with the lion tamer will be omitted.' The reason for this omission became clear two days later when the same newspaper reported:

> TERRIBLE AFFAIR AT THE AGRICULTURAL HALL – A LION-TAMER KILLED
>
> A coloured man, named Alexander Beaumont, died at St Bartholomew's hospital on Monday, from injuries inflicted by a performing lion at the World's Fair, Agricultural Hall, on Christmas Eve. The deceased was a lion-tamer of repute, and on the night of the 24th ult. entered a cage containing three full-grown lions to take them through their tricks. The animals – Victor, Brutus and Nero – were the property of Mr Frank Bostock, and had performed together for the last two years. The Hall was crowded with spectators when the cage was placed in the centre of the circus arena, and Beaumont was loudly applauded on entering the animals' den.
>
> He had hardly closed the door behind him, however, when Brutus advanced towards him and laid hold of his right arm with his teeth, at the same time growling fiercely. Beaumont, being taken unawares, was knocked down. However, he quickly recovered himself, and hastily left the cage, which was then drawn out of the arena. Very few of the audience realised that an accident had occurred ... Death, which occurred early on Monday morning, was due to blood poisoning, arising from the wounds.
>
> (*Islington Gazette,* 1st January 1896)

111. The cage in which Beaumont was mauled, photographed six months later when Ricardo had taken over as Bostock's lion-trainer

The tragedy must have been still fresh in the minds of those attending the showmen's annual supper on 30th January in the Agricultural Hall. Introduced two years earlier as an opportunity for people to cement friendships and enjoy each other's company away from the noise and competition of their shows, the event had quickly assumed the proportions of a banquet.

At midnight on the last day of the World's Fair, once lights and sounds were turned off, the show people rushed back to their wagons to prepare. In 1896 more than four hundred sat down to an excellent meal, after which there was a dance and entertainment by the Mohawk Minstrels.

One eyewitness was impressed by the formal dress of the show folk as they emerged from their cramped wagons.

> Take one lady, for example. Hair nicely curled over the forehead and rolled behind, and a spray of flowers deftly introduced. White satin blouse and streamers over a black satin skirt with a flowered flounce. Add to this a healthy, animated face, and there was a very creditable picture for ball or supper-room.
>
> And now let us take a gent's toilet. Not a swallow-tail coat to be seen, but a mixed array of arts and fashions. Take an example. A light brown tweed suit, with open vest. An expanse of pink shirt front with an immense carbuncle, surrounded by brilliants, as the "dress stud"; a white dress bow, and a big stand-up collar and tall hat.
>
> These are but examples. There were other pretty dresses and tasty coiffures and an abundance of freshly cut flowers, in all a healthy and wholesome appearance, and a subdued excitement which made the scene most exhilarating.

112. Showfolk formally dressed, c1882. Madame Crecraft, famous show-proprietor, is sitting front row, far right

113. Showmen photographed on same occasion

Chairing the supper was Randall Williams, ghost show proprietor, supported by Messrs H. & T. Read, Mr Fowler, and a number of showmen wearing smart tri-coloured badges saying *steward*.

> And who were the diners?
>
> Not only the men who shout at the outside of the shows and exhibit inside, but the actual exhibits themselves. The strong man and the strong woman, the fat girl and the living skeleton, the midgets, the circus people – clowns, riders, etc. – Professor Beckwith, the swimmer, Chittock, of dog and monkey fame, and others, mixed with each other with no restraint; and were as zealous for each other's comfort (and perhaps a little more so) as at ordinary table.
>
> And that there is a frugality amongst these people was apparent from the quality and quantity of their drinks. They did not order bottles of wine for appearance sake. They quaffed from the "foaming tankard" and eschewed the conventional toasting of each other. Indeed, when it came to toasting time, the Chairman beat the record. Never before in a long experience have we seen a toast run through with such rapidity. The Chairman rose and addressing his audience as "Ladies and gentlemen and fellow-showmen" proposed "Her Most Gracious Majesty the Queen" and said he was sure she and her widowed daughter had the heartfelt sympathy of the nation in their sad bereavement. Without sitting down, the Chairman said he would pass on to the toast of "Messrs Read and Bailey, and success to the World's Fair". These gentlemen, he said, were most creditable managers of that great World's Fair, and he knew that all before him would like to acknowledge this, and to join him in hoping Messrs Read and Bailey would long live to continue operations as lessees of the World's Fair [Applause.]
>
> (*Islington Gazette*, 31st January 1896)

The guest-list probably included Biddalls, possibly some of the late William Biddall's family even if – according to the following advertisements – their menagerie and show were still based at Portsmouth. 'Wanted, Two Acts in Ring, Wire Show and Contortionist preferred. Must be Good and Cheap. Fortnight sure. Address: Biddall, Drill Hall, Portsmouth.' (*Era*, 21st December 1895)

'Wanted, Cornet Player, used to Fair Business. Single man preferred. Reasonable terms. Biddall Menagerie, Portsmouth, Hants.' (*Era*, 1st February 1896)

After leaving Portsmouth, they worked their way up through Surrey into Essex where an alarming incident happened on 10th April while they were performing at Becontree. A woman trying to enter the menagerie through the back without paying passed too close to the lions. A lioness stuck out her paw and tore open the woman's face, ripping her upper lip away and nearly removing one eye. Only the intervention of Monsieur Henri, strong man, who beat the animal off, saved the intruder from being torn to pieces.

Their route that summer can be traced through their endless efforts to secure musicians for the band. Not just any musicians, mind. But young, single men who were 'Used to Fair Business' – able to cope with the rigours of a travelling life, building up and pulling down for one-night stands, not fazed by the odd escaped beast or overturned wagon. 'Wanted, good Cornet Player, that Plays by Book or Ear. Single and used to Fair Business. Wire terms. BIDDALLS, Menagerie, Saturday, Reading; Monday, Swallowfield; Tuesday, Odiham' appeared in the *Era* on 2nd May 1896, to be repeated a week later from Godalming and Dorking together with an advert for a 'Respectable Young Man as Agent in Advance for Menagerie. Must Thoroughly Understand the Business.'

Lest applicants should be in doubt, an advert the following week spelt out the kind of punishing schedule involved: 'Wanted, Good Cornet and Bass Players, With or without Music. BIDDALL'S Menagerie, Saturday, Mitcham; Monday, Hornchurch; Tuesday, Orsett; Wednesday, Stanford-le-Hope; Thursday, Pitsea; Friday, Hadleigh; Saturday and Whitsun Week, Southend-on-Sea.' (*Era*, 16th May 1896) They were also advertising for a 'Useful Act for Centre of Menagerie, Wire or Tight Rope preferred. Long engagement for suitable Act.'

After the welcome respite of Whitsun week at Southend the Menagerie headed east for Rochford, Rayleigh and Wickford with another problem on its hands. Or several. For the wolves had done what animals do in spring and produced a plethora of young. Tiny cubs were an attraction that soon outgrew their charm, so to keep the wolf from the door, so to speak, the Menagerie had to dispose of surplus stock. 'Wanted, to Sell, Four Wolves, Eleven Weeks old; Performing Wolf, three years old. Biddall's Menagerie, Saturday, Rochford; Monday, Rayleigh; Tuesday, Wickford, Essex.' (*Era,* 30th May 1896)

114. Rare photograph of female trainer with wolves

There being no immediate takers, they tried again a fortnight later. 'Wanted, to Sell, four Wolves Twelve weeks old, three males, one female; or Will Exchange other animals. Also one Full-Grown Female Wolf. Biddall's Menagerie, Saturday, Dunton Green; Monday, Watersham, Kent.'

July found Biddall's Menagerie at Battle in Sussex, still advertising for an Advance Agent presumably because Percival Dixon, who had been with them since February, was announcing his imminent departure. In the event, he stayed on till the end of the season. Ninfield, Arundel, then Boxgrove – but still no good cornet player had been found, despite the thirty shillings a week on offer and part fare paid. At the end of August, now on their way to Barnet Fair via Northfleet and Walthamstow, Biddalls were still advertising for that elusive commodity, as well as a 'Smart Boy or Girl for Wire Walking and Balancing.' Moreover, there was still the matter of those prolific wolves.

'Wanted, to Sell, Mother of Six Young Wolves. Mother good Performer; also Four Young Wolves, ready for breaking in. Quite Tame. Or would exchange for other animals. Biddall, Menagerie, Saturday and Monday, Barnet; Tuesday and Wednesday, Tottenham; Thursday and Friday, Ponder's End; Saturday, Waltham Abbey.' (*Era,* 5th September 1896)

After eight months as their agent, Percival Dixon took his leave in mid-September and Biddall Brothers appealed to a young man called Lucas to write in at Enfield or Southgate for his job but to state his lowest terms. (*Era,* 12th September 1896)

During a back-end run through Buckinghamshire taking in Princess Risborough, Watlington and Wallingford, they were on the look-out for circus talent for the winter season: 'Wanted, a Useful Act or Two, Suitable for Ring. Tight or Slack Wire Preferred. Male or Female. Used to Fair Business.' (*Era,* 26th September 1896) On to Deanshanger, Towcester and Foster's Booth in Northamptonshire, still advertising for 'Useful Acts for Centre of Menagerie, Stage or Aerial, Must be Good and

Cheap.' (*Era,* 17th October 1896) They then travelled through Wiltshire, at Swindon in November putting in yet another plea for a good cornet player and two useful ring acts before heading south towards their main winter venue in Portsmouth. Here, as lessees of the Drill Hall where they would stay for over a month, they were responsible not just for the Menagerie but for providing a wide range of amusements for the local population: 'Wanted, Good Novelties, to open at once, on Share or Rental. Good Business. Wire, Biddall Bros, Menagerie, Drill Hall, Portsmouth.' (*Era,* 9th January 1897)

Nor was political correctness any bar to advertisement. 'Wanted, Novelties, Fat Women, Midgets Preferred, or anything suitable for side-show. Half shares,' they announced a week later. But once on the road heading towards Basingstoke, it was back to more basic requirements: 'Wanted, Good Cornet Player, to join at once; steady, and know his business. Wire lowest terms. Six months sure, if suitable.' (*Era*, 6th March 1897) If only!

The quest for a good musician – this time an E flat Bass Player, with or without his own instrument – continued to exercise minds at Amersham where the Menagerie opened at the end of April before heading for Reading. Here at the Register Office on 3rd May George Biddall squared the family circle by marrying his cousin (and sister-in-law's sister) Venie.

'*Now we shan't be long*' cried the cryptic slogan at the end of their advertisement for a horse-keeper and 'describer' to join them at Newbury or Kintbury, Berkshire. Perhaps it was a call to the West Country, for thither they were bound the following month, reaching Newquay via St Austell and Roche by 10th July. Returning through Buckfastleigh, Ashburton, and Brixham they arrived in Newton Abbott at the beginning of August. For weeks they had been looking for a 'Good Agent. One that Understands his Business. Single Man preferred.' (*Era,* 31st July 1897) They were still looking when they arrived at Dartmouth en route for Teignmouth and Dawlish at the end of the month. September was spent travelling through East Devon and Somerset, taking in Middlezoy and Martock in early October, managing as best they could while still short-staffed. One of the family suggested an old friend who might be available to help. Monsieur Henri had been put out of action earlier that summer after being knocked down by a runaway horse. By now he should be fit. The Brothers placed an advert:

'Wanted, Good Agent. One that Understands his Business. W. Lucas write in; same time state terms. Henri, Zaio write in. Known as the Strong People. Saturday, Biddall, Middlesey; Monday, Martock. Bridport Fair follows.' (*Era,* 2nd October 1897)

Fortunately Monsieur Henri responded and was on hand to help Charlie in one of the most dangerous encounters of his life. Charlie Biddall had developed a 'Bouncing Lion Act' where thrills were generated by a carefully trained 'untameable' lion that apparently objected to its trainer entering its cage or forcibly tried to prevent him leaving it. At Bridport Fair the act got out of hand. Witness the *Dorset County Chronicle*, 14th October 1897:

> Bridport, West Dorset.
>
> An incident which caused a great deal of excitement happened at Biddall Brothers' circus and menagerie in the Fair Field on Friday.
>
> Mons Viola, the lion-tamer, had just finished a thrilling performance with a couple of lions, and was about to make his exit from the den, when one of the brutes sprang upon him and brought him to the ground. The attack was an absolute surprise to the keeper as well as to the manager, as Viola had performed with the same lion for two years and without any fear of danger whatever. Indeed, it was only a short time ago that an inhabitant of the town in which they were staying, taking up a challenge, entered the same den, smoked a cigar, and patted the lion.

The animal had clenched the man by the shoulder while on the floor of the cage, but the tamer threw him off and beat the brute round the den and then made his escape. Meanwhile blood was oozing from Viola's right shoulder. The wildest excitement prevailed and shrieks were uttered by the females present.

It is supposed that the new garment that the trainer was wearing caused the lion to suddenly attack him.

The incident, although – or, because – shocking, did nothing to hinder business and people flocked to see the show at Stalbridge the following week. Moreover, Charlie, knowing that it would not do for the animals to sense that he had lost his nerve, quickly got back in the cage. It was a decision that nearly cost him his life when, at Winfrith a few days later, a lioness leapt on him, seized his right leg and tore it apart. Only the intervention of Henri, strong man, who beat off the beast, saved him. Charlie was rushed to Dorchester Hospital where he remained for weeks in a critical condition.

It was a sad end to an otherwise successful third season for the Menagerie. It was also the end of Charlie's career as lion-trainer. An advertisement in the *Era* (13th November 1897) signalled the change. 'Wanted, Coloured Lion Tamer, Can Join at Once. Comfortable Engagement to Steady Man. Send Lowest Terms and Full Particulars in first instance. Biddall, Menagerie, Dorchester, till Monday.'

If applicants knew what had happened to the previous man, that emphasis on 'comfortable engagement' might have rung a little hollow. But the vacancy was filled and Biddall Brothers' Menagerie finished its touring season as it had begun, still searching for that elusive musician: 'Wanted, a Good Cornet or Bass Player; must be used to Show Business; a good shop. Biddall's Menagerie, Glastonbury, Somerset.' (*Era,* 27th November 1897)

After spending Christmas season at Portsmouth's Drill Hall, Biddall's Menagerie set out in early March 1898 for a provincial tour which took in Kingswood, near Bristol, Epsom and Hampton in Surrey, Acock's Green, near Birmingham, and Walsall. July found them in Suffolk where, although it was height of summer, the Brothers were clearly thinking ahead. When advertising for the inevitable 'Good Cornet Player' to join their Band, they added as an inducement that there was a 'Winter's Engagement to follow.' What was more, the show was about to expand into an exciting new area of entertainment. The Wild Beasts would stay – at least for the moment – but, in the light of recent developments on the fairground, the Biddall Brothers had decided to copy their Uncle George in the north by acquiring a bioscope. The *Era,* 2nd July, carried their request: 'Wanted, to Buy, Cinematograph, with Films; also Maker's Name, Cheap. Biddall's Menagerie, Saturday, Clare; Monday, Cavendish; Tuesday, Glensford, Suffolk.'

With their proud new acquisition they headed back south for Barnet fair in September and a back-end tour. When Biddall Brothers opened at Aylesbury on 7th and 8th October, the *Era* reported that 'The animals, though not numerous, were choice specimens, and apparently in the best of health. The Boxing Kangaroo was a great favourite, and Manico obtained prolonged applause for his performance in the lion's cage. The Wrestling Bear attracted universal attention and performances were gone through with trained wolves, hyenas etc. The cinematograph was also good.'

Marlow and Wokingham followed. In November they visited Petworth, Midhurst, Harting, East Liss, Petersfield and Horndean. By the time they arrived at Portsmouth's Drill Hall for the Christmas season their cinematograph had proved so successful that they decided that the Menagerie would have to go. There were other reasons for the decision. Although the brothers appeared to be working well together, below the surface simmered tensions inevitable when several young families travelled as a group.

Early in the New Year an advert announced:

> For Sale by private treaty – To Circus and Menagerie Proprietors and others – the well-known Menagerie of Biddall Brothers, consisting of seven waggons of beasts etc. together with two waggon show-front, band-carriage, etc. The whole of the show in first-class condition. Reason for selling, the Brothers separating. Can be seen daily between 2 and 9pm until January 30th 1899 at the World's Fair, Portsmouth, to where address all communications. (*Era*, 14th January 1899)

Almost immediately the decision was reversed, a new opportunity bringing change of heart. Now it was announced: 'Wanted known, owing to Menagerie having to fulfil another engagement at Southampton, the sale is postponed.' (*Era*, 28th January 1899) As if to emphasise the point, this was followed by: 'Wanted – lion tamer, male or female, black or white. Write or wire, Biddall Brothers' Menagerie, Skating Rink, Southampton.' (*Era*, 25th February 1899) Whoever they found did not last long, for a similar advert appeared four months later: 'Wanted – lion tamer, male or female. Good shop to suitable people. Money sure. State terms in first letter. Biddall's Menagerie, Maidstone, Kent, all next week.' (*Era*, 17th June 1899)

At Maidstone *Ye Ancynte Fayre* still attracted people from near and far to see the shows. Nor were they disappointed in 1899 for a big array was gathered. 'In the front rank were the Brothers Biddall's Menagerie and Circus, two capital concerns; Prof A. Ball's electric diagraph *Pictures of life from day to day*; Hastings & Whayman's switchback; Pettigrove's gallopers; Penfold's steam roundabouts, etc.' (*Era*, 8th July 1899)

Journeying on through Kent the Brothers tried to slim down the menagerie by selling off a group of Russian wolves and the 'Untameable' lioness seen working at Strood Fair in August. Once again their thoughts must have turned early towards winter. George Baker, organiser of Christmas festivities at Southampton's Drill Hall, urged them to contact him before the end of the month and in adverts for a 'First class Cornet, Tenor Horn and Bass' Biddall's stressed 'Sobriety Indispensable' whilst promising 'a Good Winter Shop to Steady People.' (*Era*, 26th August 1899) They were still advertising for that elusive Cornet Player after Barnet Fair when the Menagerie embarked on a tour of Hertfordshire taking in Redbourn, Hemel Hempstead and Berkhamstead.

Travelling on into Buckinghamshire, they advertised again in the Era, 23rd September: 'Wanted, Good Cornet Player. Must be Good Reader. Can join at once. 30s. per week. Comfortable Shop for suitable man. Biddall's Menagerie, Beaconsfield, Saturday; High Wycombe, Monday & Tuesday.'

After a busy October that included opening at Buckingham, Brackley and Deddington Biddall Brothers proceeded to Southampton where they advertised for other showmen to join them. 'Wanted to let, prominent position in World's Fair for good novelty, midgets, or stalls. Commencing Monday next for nine days. Wire: Biddall Bros, Skating Rink, Southampton.' (*Era*, 18th November 1899)

Here the last days of the old century found the Biddalls poised on the brink of another big adventure, having arrived in Southampton not only with their menagerie but also equipment for showing what everyone now wanted to see – moving pictures.

11

Bioscope Days

His cinematograph machine ... although one of the first sent over from America, was a thoroughly reliable instrument. Not so showy as more recent models, perhaps, but Biddalls had carried it for hundreds of miles and it had always worked well and did not flicker.

The Showman, 31st January 1902

A reviewer of the Christmas Pleasure fairs in 1899 wrote, 'There is no sign of the modern showman's life more marked than the facility with which he adapts himself to rapidly changing circumstances.' Following Messrs Read & Bailey's lead at the Royal Agricultural Hall, by the end of the century World's Fairs and winter carnivals had been established in Manchester, Liverpool, Birmingham, Portsmouth, Southampton, Plymouth, Newcastle, Sheffield, Edinburgh, Glasgow, Greenock, Aberdeen, Dundee, and Belfast. (*Era*, 23rd December 1899) Portsmouth's World's Fair opened that year at the Drill Hall under the management of William Symonds with his switchback, steam swings and gallopers. On leaving Southampton, Biddall Brothers' Menagerie and Cinematograph arrived as chief attraction and did well despite bad weather. Such success seems to have breathed new life into the old firm who, having moved back to London, were soon announcing that they 'Wanted, all Friends to know Biddall Brothers' Menagerie is to be seen at Goldsmith Road, Peckham.' (*Era*, 20th January 1900) Moreover, lions once more loomed large in their lives as they advertised: 'Wanted to buy, Lion and Lioness. Must be about three years old, and sound and perfect. For cash. Apply, Biddall, Menagerie, Goldsmith Road, Peckham.' (*Era,* 3rd February 1900)

Getting ready for the touring season meant lining up new staff, preferably those used to the business. At Southall in April Biddall's was advertising for a cornet player (of course) as well as an Agent and Good Knockabouts who could join in time for Easter at Wormwood Scrubs. After that they travelled to Colnbrook, Staines, and Reading, unable to move too far from London with a court case pending, for the previous Whitsun they had opened at the Riddlesdown pleasure resort in Surrey and their organ had caused annoyance to a Mr Gardner who lived only four hundred yards away. An action was brought against them in the Court of Queen's Bench in May 1900. Despite the Defence's explanation that, since proceedings were taken, the steam organ had been replaced by a piano organ covered with material to deaden the sound, the verdict went against them.

Biddalls were not alone in fighting battles about noise. Indeed, the question of music with roundabouts and shows had become so vexed that when Scarborough's Town Council voted that year to suppress all machine-made music, a local roundabout proprietor simply unhitched the belt connecting the organ to his steam engine and set a man to turn the handle instead. The noise was the same; his legal position a conundrum.

115. Trumpet organ, c1900

That music in some form was a prime necessity on a fair ground was obvious but, as the *Era*, 22nd September 1900, explained: 'Showmen are not wedded to one kind of music. We have no desire to force steam organs on an unwilling public. In the palmy days of George Wombwell, William Manders, etc. both brass and reed bands were the delight and attraction of our fairs. In those days almost every showman was a musician and had to take his place in the band.' And there was the rub! Not only did steam and electricity represent 'progress' but you couldn't get the musicians ... Witness: 'Wanted, Cornet, Tenor Horn, and Bass, to open Monday. Wire: Biddall's Menagerie. Saturday: Eastville, Bristol; Monday-Tuesday, Post Office, Eastville, Bristol.' (*Era,* 23rd June 1900)

By the time Biddall's Menagerie arrived at Woking in July after a tour of Somerset they had hired a good advance agent in the person of Jim Westray but were still looking for a 'Cornet Player who can be heard *and* Read at sight.'

After their usual visit to Barnet Fair in September Biddall Brothers' Menagerie opened at Southgate, Enfield, Biggleswade and Potton. Together with Thurston's switchback and Harris's steam horses they were among the main attractions at Bedford fair on 12th October. All backend Biddalls had been advertising for a good cornet player. 'Wages, 30s. a week. Money sure. Amateurs save stamps.' As they moved back towards London they made a one night stand in a meadow at Harlington which led to another day in court.

'In the Queen's Bench Division on Thursday before Mr Justice Ridley, sitting without a jury, the trial of the action of Sanders v. Goodwin and Others was concluded,' reported the *Era,* 22nd December 1900. The 'Others' were the Biddall Brothers who, together with John Goodwin, owner of the meadow, were being sued by Alfred St George Sanders of Harlington Lodge for damages to cover injuries to himself, his house, his horse and his dog-cart caused by the 'noxious odours proceeding from the menagerie of wild animals included in the show' and he claimed an injunction to restrain the nuisance. Naturally the Biddall Brothers denied the charge, insisting that there were no dreadful odours, no steam organ or any noisy musical instruments. And (sadly, perhaps?) they denied the presence in the meadow of large crowds of people. Arguing that the plaintiff could not maintain any action of nuisance or an injunction against them because they were merely on their co-defendant's land as temporary licensees, they won the day and were granted costs.

There was little time to celebrate their victory. Early in the new year, whilst open at the Exhibition Ground in Deptford High Street their latest lion-tamer, the renowned Captain Bartlett, was severely mauled when one of the animals knocked him down, clawed his shoulder and tore away the fleshy part of his thigh. The lion was driven off and Bartlett taken to the Miller Hospital in Greenwich where, after a stay of three weeks, he made a good recovery. The lion was less fortunate. It died a few weeks later at Brixton.

Meanwhile the nation had been plunged into mourning by the death of Queen Victoria. On the evening of Tuesday, 22nd January, the news was relayed to stunned crowds at the World's Fair, Islington. After being given admission tickets for another night, eight thousand people left quietly and the Royal Agricultural Hall closed. The Showman's Annual Supper and Ball arranged for the following night was abandoned.

With the death of the queen and dawn of a new century, everything was saying that it was time for change. When the Biddall Brothers turned up at Tom Norman's auction of Harvey's circus at Kensal Road in February they may have been interested in the horses and ponies or were merely there to test the market. A week later they were offering their own menagerie for sale, specifying five wagons of best lions, wolves, bears, hyenas, monkeys, birds and other small animals. 'Also Two Front Waggons. Front 40ft. One Horse Loads. To be seen from February 16th till the 23rd. Biddall's Menagerie, High Street, Stratford, Essex.' (*Era*, 16th February 1901)

In the absence of serious takers, they advertised the beasts again a week later, with or without wagons and giving their address as Brixton. No sale ensued and with Easter coming they could not afford to wait about, so they started to marshal staff and prepare for the road. Once more the hunt was on for a cornet player and an agent: 'Wanted, Cornet and Euphonium and Bass to Join Others; also an Agent-in-Advance. Young man preferred. State terms in first letter to: Biddall's Menagerie, Brixton.' (*Era*, 2nd March 1901) 'Wanted, Agent-in-Advance. Must be Sober and Reliable. Young Man Preferred. State terms in first letter. Biddall's Menagerie, Brixton.' (*Era,* 9th March 1901) 'Wanted, Agent-in-Advance, Good Cornet Player & Euphonium. Write in and send Lowest Terms in First Letter. Young Men Preferred. Biddall's Menagerie, Saturday, Brixton; Monday, Fulham Pal. Road, Hammersmith.' (*Era*, 23rd March 1901)

One of the young men taken on was J. Simpson who later recalled his time with Biddalls as one of the happiest in his travelling life: 'And what a clean show it was. Mrs Biddall saw that you had a clean bed and there was always plenty of eats.' As for Billy Biddall,

> I have never seen a knife-thrower to equal him. His brother Johnny used to do a juggling turn and Mrs Biddall and the two daughters used to parade on the front, and what a parade they put over! One girl impersonated Vesta Tilley. What a showman Billy was! I have seen him hold hundreds spellbound while he had one of the girls balanced on a bush shaft (mock mesmerised) as Little Red Riding Hood. I remember once at Grantham Fair we had very strong opposition; one show which stood opposite to us had a brand new front all carved gilt work. There were hundreds of people standing with their backs to us, but Biddall was not beaten. Out of a hole in the parade floor came a long fishing rod all covered with white muslin with something hanging on the end of the line. When the people saw this hanging over their heads they turned to see where it came from. Then Biddall's parade started and he packed the house and did good business all the time.[1]

William Biddall had no need to use any such tricks at Blackheath on Easter Monday 1901. Opening at ten o'clock in the morning, his show did not close till nearly midnight. Mr Simpson recollected: 'That was one of the quickest money-takers I have ever seen. There was no knife-throwing or juggling. We just showed two pictures, *Queen Victoria's Funeral* and *The Attack on the Dispatch Bearer in the Boer War.*'

With business buzzing the Biddalls had to rely more on their staff. There is a tone of mounting exasperation at the type of men coming forward. 'Dummies need not apply' their advert for musicians declared when the Menagerie moved on via Chelmsford and Dunmow to Braintree. 'Wanted, Young Man as Agent, one that understands his business. Sober and reliable', they stressed in May as they pulled on to Wanstead Flats for Whitsun. (*Era,* 25th May 1901)

116. Donkey boys on Wanstead Flats, Whitsun 1900

> At Wanstead Flats on Monday the usual Bank-holiday fair was held. The first show on the Dames Road Ground was Crighton's Cinematograph, with a fine display of animated photography. Next was Biddall's Menagerie and Circus of Varieties, which is one of the finest exhibitions travelling. The programme was long and varied, including a splendid impalement act by the Brothers Biddall, giving a thrilling exposition of North American life. Following this was a clever snake-charming show by Madame Biddall. Captain Hunter then entered a den of wolves, placing them through different feats, concluding by putting his face and hands in one of their mouths, and leaving the cage by feeding them with his naked hands.
>
> Similar performances took place in a den containing a hyena and a bear, and another den containing two educated lions; the performance concluding with an African lion hunt. A good display of living pictures was given, including many realistic and grotesque subjects. The audience then prepared themselves for the *pièce de résistance*, viz. Victor, the untameable lion, introduced by Captain Hunter, who is undoubtedly one of the smartest men in the business. The noble animal hurled itself to and fro in its steel-latticed lair, vainly attempting to prevent the aforesaid gentleman from effecting an entry. A partition was placed through the middle of the cage, separating the Captain and Victor; it was then suddenly taken away, and the sport commenced; and after a few minutes Captain Hunter left the den amid the cheers of the audience, who shouted themselves hoarse.
>
> A word of praise is due to the daring performance of an Arab gymnast, who gives a splendid show without the aid of a net, and to the excellent management of Mr Biddall, senior, who in addition to a splendid organ, has provided a good brass band. Next to this is Biddall's Novelty Museum, where for a penny you can see a petrified woman, a giant rat, and two midget kangaroos. Adjoining this is Alf Ball's boxing booth, who caters for the fistic fraternity of that neighhourhood. Bennett's double child and Johnson's merman conclude the list of sideshows. The usual spot joints, Mollies, and throwing games are here; and in the centre of the ground is Mr Davies' magnificent riding machine. (*Showman,* 31st May 1901)

William Hunter may well have been 'one of the smartest men in the business' but he bit off more than he could easily chew when he staged a little sensation at Southend-on-Sea a fortnight later. Hearing that a local resident, Sidney Milles, had made a bet with another that he would enter a cage full of lions, Hunter accompanied him into the den where the visitor enjoyed a cigar and a bottle of champagne while the beasts looked mildly on. It was only after he left the cage that the lions pounced on their trainer, tearing at his arm and it was left to Mr Milles to return and help beat the animals off. Four months later the Biddall Brothers presented him with a large lion's claw, handsomely mounted in gold and suitably inscribed, for his bravery.

A good cornet player was being requested to join Biddall's Menagerie at Mildenhall, Barrow, Bury St Edmunds or Woodbridge that summer with thirty shillings a week on offer and half his fare paid. Biddall's was also seeking two horsekeepers, two inside men and other musicians.

By mid-August they reached the cathedral city of Ely where not a little excitement was caused when a Mr R. Cranwell, a well-known local man, was persuaded to enter the den of lions, smoke a cigar and drink champagne with the keeper. This time the 'sensation' worked to plan and both men left the cage unhurt.

E. Bert Jarvis, the bright young business-manager of Biddall Brothers' Menagerie and Circus was not so lucky. Driving his pony and trap through Cambridge that week he met a speeding motorcar whose driver had lost control. The resulting crash left the trap smashed, pony seriously injured, and Bert Jarvis with a sprained ankle that kept him off work for over a week. It could hardly have been worse timed. With Barnet Fair coming up, the show had to be at its best. They were already advertising for fresh talent: 'Wanted, Good Artist, to Work Traps, Swinging Perch, and Monkey Rope. Lady doing Two Acts preferred. Long contract given if suitable. No Fancy Price Paid. Also Two Inside men for Menagerie, used to the Business. Apply, Biddall's Menagerie, Ely, Monday; Soham, Tuesday; and Cambridge, Wednesday.' (*Era*, 10th August 1901) 'Wanted, Artistes, Traps, Swinging Perch, or Monkey Rope, Male or Female; also, other Acts suitable for Menagerie. Lengthy Engagements suitable turns, but no fancy prices paid. Particulars to E. Bert Jarvis, Manager, Poste Restante, Chipping Barnet.' (*Era*, 24th August 1901)

After Barnet Fair on the first weekend of September the Menagerie travelled to Hemel Hempstead Fair on 16th in company with Holmes's Wild Beasts, Matthews's Fine Art show, and Bailey's steam horses. Langford and Sandy in Bedfordshire followed, and Biddall's Double Menagerie together with Alf Ball's Bioscope were numbered among the best shows on the south Midland round when they appeared at Banbury Mop in mid October. Marlow towards the end of the month saw further attempts to persuade a local landowner, General Owen Williams, to relinquish the Charter allowing the statute fair to be held in the town's main streets. Although these attempts failed, Alf Ball was fined £1 plus costs for driving stakes into the highway and the showmen were antagonised.

Marlow was not alone in showing hostility towards travelling showmen. In a year of general depression private speculators and corporations had seized the opportunity to exploit ground rents all over the country, and what made resultant conflicts worse was lack of unity among showmen – as an interview with the veteran, James Chittock, made clear. Explaining why he confined himself to working the southern counties, he said that ground rents for shows at fairs had increased so much that it was nearly impossible for him to take the big jumps.

"Places in the Midlands that used to welcome us showfolk twenty years or more ago with open arms – aye, and even write to me, begging me to come, ground free, and make the fair worth visiting, or to have ground for a mere acknowledgement – now make such exorbitant demands that it is impossible to work them at a profit."

"What do you blame for this altered state of things?"

"Well, in the main, I attribute it to the senseless competition of the large riding-masters, one competing against another for the option of taking the whole of the fair ground, and after selecting for their own use the best position sub-letting to the smaller concerns the remainder of the land at a profit." (*Era,* 9th November 1901)

By late November the Biddalls must have been glad to pull into Major Road, Bermondsey, to prepare for the Christmas season which would be spent at Deptford showground under the management of Mrs Weatherhead. One of the first things they did at Bermondsey was place an advert for musicians, a good E Flat Bass and Cornet. After which they concentrated on freshening up the show. No longer able to rely on their trusty strong lady, Madame Elise, who had dislocated her kneecap, they placed another advert: 'Wanted, Trapeze, Swinging Perch or Good Clairvoyant Show, open Monday, Show Ground, Deptford. Double turn preferred. No fancy prices. Amateurs save stamps. Wire, lowest terms, Biddall's Menagerie, Major Road, Bermondsey.' (*Era,* 14th December 1901)

A reporter for the *Showman* (10th January 1902) visited Biddall's show that Christmas:

> At Deptford Messrs Biddall Brothers' American Menagerie and Cinematograph holds the premier position. The first item is the North American Indian impalement act by the Bros Biddall. The next number is Captain Hunter, the clever animal subjugator, who enters a den containing a pack of Siberian wolves and places them through a clever performance, concluding by placing his face in one of their mouths and feeding the pack from the naked hands. His next performance is with two educated lions who behave themselves and work very well. The "star" item is Captain Hunter and Brutus, the untameable lion. The excitement caused by this turn was marvellous, the audience were perfectly silent whilst Hunter was in the den, but as soon as he sprang out, the audience let itself go and gave him three terrific cheers, after which several made a rush to shake hands with him.

As well they might if they remembered the dire state in which he had been taken from this very ground to Miller's Hospital just twelve months before!

From Deptford the Biddall Brothers moved to Bow Common Lane, near Mile End, whence they attended the Ninth Annual Showmen's Supper held in the Banqueting Suite at the Royal Agricultural Hall on 22nd January 1902. Tickets were priced 3/6d. Supper was served at 11.45pm sharp. A Dance followed. Among other guests were Frank Bostock and Francis Ferrari[2], principals of the Bostock and Ferrari Midway Carnival Company in America, who were in England for a short stay

117. Alphonso, Intrepid Lion Tamer who survived severe maulings by lions and bears. Alias Richard Sedgwick, his brother Albert would marry Evaline Freeman

118. Evaline Sedgwick, née Freeman, daughter of Samuel and Augusta

before returning for the inauguration of their latest venture, the Elks Carnival. Also present were Albert and Victor Biddall; and Albert Sedgwick of Menagerie fame who would the following year marry their cousin, Evaline Freeman.

Calling in at Bow Common Lane later that week, a reporter met the Menagerie's indefatigable manager, Mr E. Bert Jarvis. Discovering the twenty-year old to be not only a conjuror and exponent of 'Black Art' but also an old Pressman and former correspondent of the *Era*, he fell to chatting.

Jarvis explained how he performed his magic routines during summer tours when the menagerie gave provincial audiences a two hours' entertainment consisting of an exhibition of knife throwing, balancing and juggling, the ever popular and indispensable cinematograph, lion taming by Captain Hunter, performing wolves and a description of the various caged animals. The show concluded with these being fed upon their appropriate viands, much to the delight of spectators. The star turn was the pelican that strutted around as if he were the proprietor until he saw his bucket of fish, whereupon he cast dignity to the wind to indulge his appetite. After that it was a case of comic pursuit and struggle before he returned to his cage. But the most thrilling turn was provided by two lionesses apt to quarrel over their food, the one who finished first trying to steal from the other.

Continuing their conversation, Bert Jarvis turned to praising his cinematograph machine which, although one of the first sent over from America, was a thoroughly reliable instrument. Not so showy as more recent models, perhaps, but Biddalls had carried it for hundreds of miles and it had always worked well and did not flicker.

"You've a fine lot of films," said the reporter.

"Oh, yes. Just now we are showing *The Road to Ruin*, *The Prodigal Son*, and *Scrooge*, which, of course, is appropriate to the season, and you would be surprised how the public like it. Some of the remarks they make about them are very droll. It is quite an education to hear them."

"You are giving very few shows just now."

"Oh, yes, we are really resting and using the time for painting up and getting things ship-shape for the spring. We go round during the best part of the year to all the principal fairs. At Cambridge last year we gave thirty-two performances in one day, and had the enclosure crowded each time, but, of course, that was exceptional. It is when we are visiting ordinary towns that we give the longer shows and less performances, but at a higher charge for admission." (*Showman,* 31st January 1902)

While this conversation was taking place the keepers had been busy bedding down the animals. Taking this as his cue, the reporter exchanged a cheery good-night with Mr Biddall and Bert Jarvis, both of whom wished success to the journal.

Biddall Brothers spent the rest of that winter in and around London – Goldsmith Road, Peckham, in February; York Road, Battersea and High Street, Deptford in March. From Peckham they advertised for a young man to act as agent and doorsman for their cinematograph show, a good sober horsekeeper and inside men for the menagerie, and the usual musicians – cornet, euphonium, trombone, bass and tenor horn players. At Battersea they advertised for a lion tamer, a week later extending their request: 'Wanted, Lion Tamer, Black or White; also Good Doorsman that understands working Living Pictures, and Two Knockabouts. Must be strictly sober and attentive to business. Young men only of good appearance. Biddall's Animated Pictures, Deptford.' (*Era*, 15th March 1902)

Before going on tour they also announced: 'Wanted, Wire walker, Swinging Perch, Trapeze. Lady preferred, must do Two Acts, to open Good Friday. Six months contract if suitable. Will L. Vera write? Lowest Terms First Letter to: Manager, Menagerie and Cinematograph, Deptford.'

(*Era*, 22nd March 1902)

At Addlestone, Surrey, in April they were advertising for yet more musicians as well as 'Wire, Trapeze, and Second-Sight Show, Double Turns preferred.' The reason for all these extra artistes? Biddall Brothers were now operating two separate shows. Travelling via Uxbridge, Seven Stars, Knowl Hill, and Twyford they arrived at Reading fair in May 1902 with the Menagerie and Living Picture Exhibition as well as their new Number 2 concern, Biddall's Royal Electric Bioscope, ready to exhibit the Sheffield United versus Southampton Cup Final, pictures of Lord Methuen's great fight, and scenes of a recent fire in which seven lives were saved. A thrilling programme – which it needed to be if it was to compete with Professor Alf Ball's animated picture show with its wonderful parade and sensational offer of £1000 'to any person that can show a picture as good as the Bioscope.'

And Alf Ball had more tricks up his sleeve. Taking his camera, he had travelled into Reading in the front of a tram to film the journey along main street and Messrs Huntley and Palmer's employees leaving the biscuit factory at lunch time. The audience's shouts as they recognised familiar scenes and faces testified to the popularity of such experiments. Moreover, he had thought up a smart dodge for disposing of old films. During the entertainment he sent a midget round the audience to sell packets of 'living pictures' at a penny a time, each containing a dozen negatives cut from an old reel.

Reading fair in 1902 was a great success. Among big machines present were Gale's switchback, Wilson's gallopers, Wall's roundabout, the Excelsior hunting ponies and Venetian gondolas, Bailey's switchback gondolas and Forrest's Caledonian skyscrapers. There were cup-breaking saloons (smash a cup with a penny ball and you won a coconut), shooting galleries, a peepshow and 'fine art' exhibition. For one penny you could see a rat and eel fight, giant lizard, two-headed pig and a live badger. Whilst automatic machines read characters from hands and heads, itinerant vendors hawked pirate music, hymnbooks, Bible texts, gingerbread, and ice-cream. What made it all the sweeter for smaller concerns was that the market inspector had controlled the letting of the ground. Frontages cost only sixpence a foot instead of the two to five shillings usually charged when the fairground was taken by one man and sublet. (*Showman*, 9th May 1902)

119. Hokey-pokey, c1900 (ice-cream stall)

From Reading the Biddalls moved back to Wormwood Scrubs where, despite cold wind and pouring rain, hundreds turned out on Whit Monday to amuse themselves on Daniel Cooper's flying ostriches or the three riding machines owned by the Beach Brothers. Nor did the wet weather dampen enthusiasm for Biddall's Menagerie and the family's thrilling exposition of North American life, including their famous 'impalement' act, after which Bartlett Lindo made a show of risking life and limb with his wild animals. Biddall's Bioscope, a completely separate show, did good business and nearby Madame Rendoff's Home of Mystery and novelty show offered a strange exhibition of the 'Earth People,' elephant man, and Aztec skeleton.

120. Madame Rendoff's Home of Mystery, c1900

A tour of Sussex by Biddall's Menagerie got as far as Horsham and Billingshurst in May but, though advertised to give two performances in mid-June next to the Crown Hotel, Heathfield, it failed to appear. Perhaps its owners had hied back to London to prepare for the Royal Coronation Fair to be held on forty-eight acres at Kensal Green in a kind of revival of Bartholomew fair. On 5th July the *Era* reported that in Southern England entertainers like the Chipperfields, Baileys, Biddalls, Buckleys, Thurstons, and a hundred others had been at work preparing for Coronation Week and thrown into consternation by news that the king was ill.

That same month they visited Grays, Stanford-le-Hope and Rayleigh where their enterprising manager worked up local excitement to a degree even higher than that being registered by thermometers in the current heatwave. Having announced that a well-known local gentleman would enter the lions' den and drink to the health of Rayleigh, there was an extra large audience on Wednesday, 16th July, to witness this feat. Punctually at nine o'clock Charles Biddall, who rarely performed with lions since being mauled, stepped on the platform to introduce the daring volunteer who (surprise, surprise!) turned out to be the same Mr Sidney Milles who had come forward at Southend the year before. Expertly working on the emotions of the audience by describing his own experiences in the lions' den, Charlie made the beasts plunge round the cage. Then Mr Milles stepped into their midst, opened a bottle of wine, poured himself a glass and proposed the toast. All this while the lions remained quiet, but no sooner had their visitor reached the safe side of the bars than they flew ferociously at the door. Whereupon Mr Milles was loudly cheered – and, being a local cigar agent, proceeded to take advantage of the situation by distributing samples to his new fans.

After Rayleigh, Biddalls took advantage of the glorious weather to push on from town to town, commanding full houses at every show. The pace was hectic. There was no room for passengers. When advertising for useful men and knockabouts to join them at Sudbury at the end of July, they minced no words: 'those that come to learn need not apply.' Returning south via Braintree the following month they were still appealing for: 'two men that can make themselves generally useful; also a Good Horse Keeper and Doorsman.' (*Era,* 9th August 1902)

In September, after visiting Dunstable and Stevenage, Biddalls opened at Hemel Hempstead in the company of Chittock's Circus and Cinematograph, both firms doing good business. There followed Peterborough Bridge Fair and Irchester. But as they were entering Earl's Barton in Northamptonshire on 10th October one of the wagons containing a bear, two wolves, one hyena and a puma overturned into someone's garden, demolished their wall and railings, causing damage amounting to £3. Fortunately the animals escaped with nothing worse than a severe shaking and the manager, E.Bert Jarvis, assisted by the keepers and a number of Northants cobblers (jokingly addressed as 'balls of wax') were soon on the spot to right the wagon and set it back on the road.

Less fortunate that week was their old friend William H. Davies of Forest Gate whose roundabout was severely damaged by fire at Matching Green Fair in Essex. A spark from the engine which had smouldered most of the night destroyed all the top centre carvings, glass boards and drops, tilt, rounding cloths, figures, truck, entire electric plant and organ. £1200 worth of damage and no insurance – it was every showman's nightmare.

For Biddall's Menagerie and Cinematograph, continuing their back-end run through South Bucks, Princes Risborough presented another opportunity for their favourite publicity stunt. Arriving there on a Saturday in mid-November, by Monday evening they had arranged for Jim House of the aptly named White Lion pub to enter the lions' den accompanied by their trainer – a deed which attracted a capacity audience.

Now it was time to think about Christmas. Bert Jarvis, describing himself as 'Undoubtedly England's greatest agent, Lecturer, Operator and Manager' announced from Princess Risborough that he would shortly be at liberty to represent a first-class concern as he was just concluding a third season with Biddall's. And Biddall Brothers had already made it known that they were free to accept an engagement for either five or seven wagons of wild beasts for the forthcoming winter season. They needn't have worried about having no takers, for they eventually found themselves double-booked.

First, though, they pulled into their Major Road showground to refurbish and reorganize. Again they advertised for sale the double wagon which opened out to provide a forty foot front, with or without its underworks. A week later more details appeared: 'Wanted, to Sell, Double Waggon. Carved and Gilded Show Front, opens out 40'. Complete with Sliding Doors, Steps, etc. Ready for Opening. Will Suit any class of Show. Can be seen open at Biddall's Show Ground, Major Road, Bermondsey.' (*Era*, 6th December 1902) Also on offer were a truck and set of six swing boats, good as new.

By the second week of December it was clear that they had a problem. While the Electric Bioscope, their No.2 Concern, opened at Kensal New Town, the Menagerie proceeded to Deptford, which promised to be more profitable. They decided to try to re-let the ground at Kensal. 'Wanted, to Let, owing to prior Engagement, Show Ground, East row, Kensal New town, now occupied by Electric

121. W.H. Davies's Gallopers, Wanstead Flats, 1900

Cinematograph. Suit Roundabout and Swings for Christmas. Terms moderate. Apply, Biddall's, lessees, as above; Saturday, Monday, Deptford.' (*Era,* 13th December 1902)

Although the advert was repeated the following week, the two concerns remained apart over Christmas. The Electric Bioscope opened at Kensal New Town while Biddall Brothers' American Circus and Menagerie occupied its usual site at Mrs Weatherhead's fairground in Deptford High Street where it caught the eye of a reporter for *The Music Hall & Theatre Review* (19th December 1902):

> The show is remarkably "up-to-date" both outside and in. The usual mechanical band is dispensed with, in its place being a very vigorous human one, which is most successful in inducing the public to patronise the exhibition. The first item on the programme is a thrilling exposition of North American Indian sports and pastimes by the Biddall Family, introducing their celebrated impalement act. Following this, Captain Marco introduces a very clever pack of performing wolves, and poses them in some exciting tableaux. The audience's attention is then directed to the educated lions, who give a capital show. Brutus, the untameable lion, defies Marco to the last, but is eventually caught unawares, and before you can realise it Marco has entered, and is driving the recalcitrant round the den amid the burning of much red fire, the clanging of a Javain gong, and the deafening applause of an excited audience.

12

Join At Barnet Fair

> Wanted, Useful ladies that can do Cake Walk in Style for Outside Parade, also one or two Good Knockabouts.
>
> *Era*, 29th August 1903

Early in 1903 William and Polly moved with Biddall's Electric Bioscope to Pott's Fairground in Lillie Road, Fulham, where they reported excellent business. At Deptford meanwhile Biddall Brothers' American Menagerie had engaged extra talent in the persons of the Great Blondon (sic) who nightly walked from one end of the ground to the other on a rope forty foot high, and Crypto, the strong boy who performed remarkable feats of lifting and pulling.

The Biddall Brothers put in their usual appearance at the Showmen's Annual Supper and Ball at the Agricultural Hall and Charles Biddall was recorded among those present at the thirteenth AGM of the United Kingdom Showmen and Van Dwellers' Association held there on the same day with its President, Lord George Sanger, in the Chair.

One week later and the Great Blondon had given way to Montano on the high mast at Deptford – or perhaps Blondon had assumed a less provocative pseudonym, knowing how touchy Blondin was about people poaching his name as well as his tricks. In addition to the usual programme Biddalls had hired the Mystos, experts in second-sight.

On the lookout for talent they inserted the following adverts in the *Era:* 'Wanted, Lion Tamer, Coloured Man preferred; also a Young Man to make himself generally useful and to Describe Pictures; also Two Knockabouts. No Fancy Price; money sure. Address: W.Biddall, Goldsmith Road, Peckham, London.' (*Era,* 28th February 1903) 'Wanted: Four Inside Men, to make themselves useful. Those who have been with this Show can write in, Biddall's Menagerie, Saturday, Deptford; Kensal New Town, Monday and rest of week.' (*Era,* 28th March 1903) 'Wanted, Young Man to Work Trapeze and Wire and make himself generally useful. No fancy salary; money sure. Trombone, Cornet, and Bass write. Biddall's Menagerie, Kensal New Town (till next Wednesday).' (*Era,* 4th April 1903)

They must have been pleased with the response, for by Easter Biddall's had assembled a thoroughly good company. Captain Montano had left the rope and assumed the mantle of daring animal trainer, Monsieur Viola also appeared in a den of forest-bred lions, Mademoiselle Silvana featured as a snake-charmer, there were performing bears and other beasts, and of course their marvellous exhibition of animated pictures.

At Hampstead 'Holiday makers stared with saucer-eyes at Messrs Biddall Brothers' magnificent shows. Probably the Heath has never seen such an electrically illuminated show before. Certainly the majority of the visitors had not. Each show boasted a capital parade of mummers, who shone to full advantage in the glare of numerous arc-lamps. It puzzled the 'Arries to know whence came the current. One solemnly assured his 'Arriet that wires must have been laid under the Heath to London. Messrs Biddall's well-stocked menagerie and their "Electric Empire" animated picture show rivalled each other in popularity, both doing such business that we shall doubtless see them on the same ground at Whitsun.'

Not that Biddalls had it all their own way. Chittock's Queen Cinematograph Exhibition was also doing excellent business, a full house waiting to 'walk up' as fast as the show could be emptied, notwithstanding the fact that it could accommodate five or six hundred people. Such was the hold that the bioscope had on the fair-going public.

Despite occasional snowstorms Hampstead Heath enjoyed pleasant weather that Easter and the return of the kind of bigger shows which had been absent for some years did much to revive the ancient glories of this fair. (*Music Hall & Theatre Review*, 17th April 1903)

The Biddall Brothers split up after Easter. The Electric Bioscope travelled south into Hampshire, opening at Alton and Bishop's Waltham in June. The Menagerie headed west via Amersham, Stokenchurch and Watlington on a provincial tour which provided 'an excellent programme at its various halting places' – Monsieur Viola and Captain Montano with their wolves, bears and big cats, Mademoiselle Silvani with her astonishing snakes and crocodiles. What was dubbed the *Oxomotoscope* supplied an animated picture exhibition.

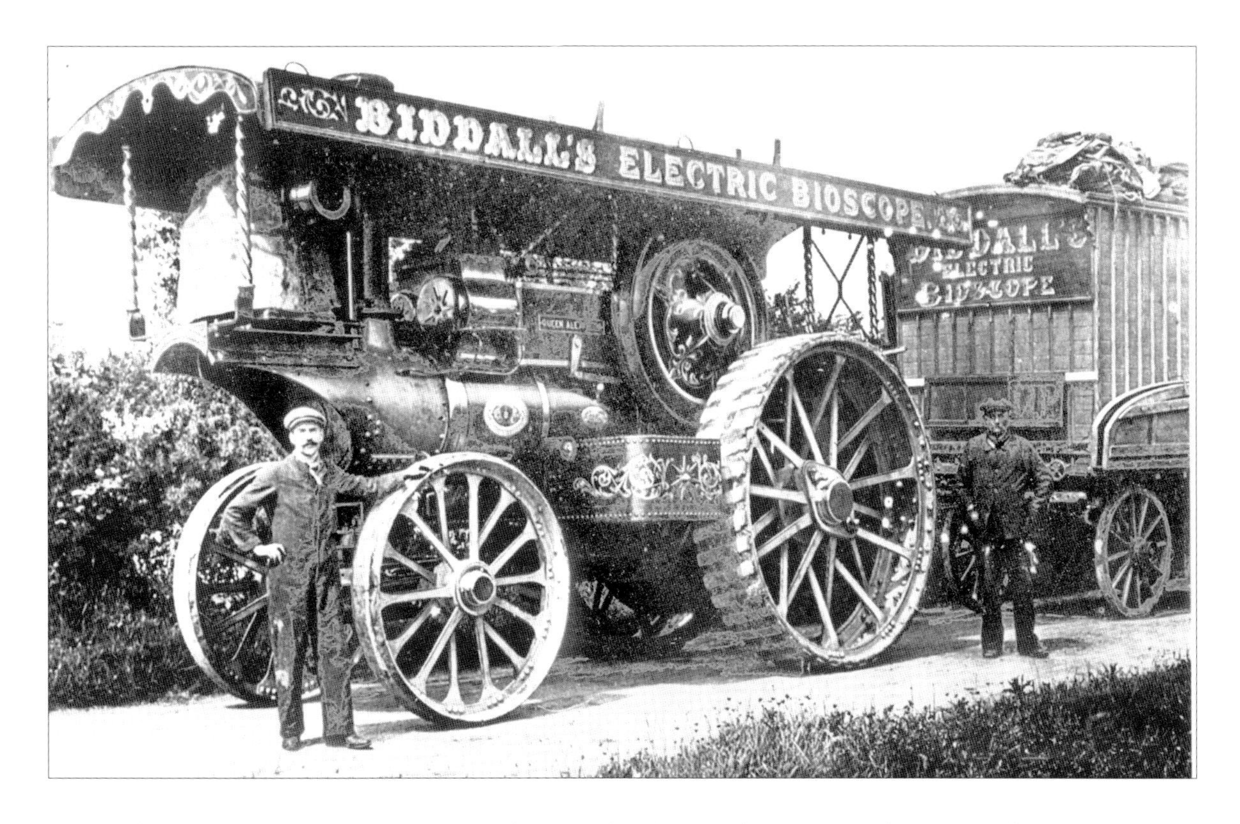

122. Biddall's Bioscope drawn by Queen Alexandra, a Fowler Class A5 Showman's Road Locomotive built in 1904 for Jacob Studt and sold to Biddall Bros in April 1905

After opening at Leominster Fair on 2nd May Biddall's American Menagerie was spotted doing good business at Hereford May Fair the following Wednesday together with Jacob and Henry Studt's riding machines and Wadbrook's Electrograph. Staying in the same company, it then journeyed into South Wales via Monmouth. Summer was opening up, the road beckoning, but life with a travelling show was hard. You were either born to it or bore with it for a limited (but oh! so memorable) time before returning to a more settled existence. The owner of a big show was therefore always on the lookout for 'Useful People'. Witness:

'Wanted: two Knockabouts; also Female Paraders used to Fair Business. Good salaries to Useful People. Those that can do an Act preferred. Biddall's Menagerie, Fairground, Monmouth, Saturday & Monday.' (*Era,* 9th May 1903)

Early in June they opened at Treorchy's four day fair in the company of Studts' magnificent riding machines, Wadbrook's Electrograph and Dooner and Haggar's shows. The weather was fine and business keen. At Biddall Brothers' American Menagerie Captain Bartlett Lindo put his numerous forest-bred lions through a sensational performance. The people flocking into the show were probably unaware of the slur on menageries recently cast in the national press. Praising forthcoming improvements at Regent's Park Zoo the *Daily Mail* said that it was previously deplorable, on a level with travelling menageries. If the reporter thought this, retorted the *Music Hall and Theatre Review*, 19th June 1903, 'Let him visit Bostock & Wombwell's, Purchase's, Biddall's, Sanger's, Chipperfield's or any other reputable concern on the road and he'll find the animals in an equal, if not superior, state as those of the Zoo.'

Another accolade for Biddall's had come in an advert for Morecambe Winter Gardens whose manager, William Holland, was seeking 'a High-class Menagerie and Zoo' to open on the site. 'A good show would take a large amount of money on this unique position. Rent or share.' He added, 'Will Biddall's Menagerie communicate?' (*Era,* 30th May 1903)

Whether they did or no, nothing came of it and it is hard to imagine William's sons, the London Biddalls, taking up residence so far north. That was their cousins' territory. The family of their Uncle George Biddall was established near the Border, Sam and Augusta's family travelled in the Gateshead area and most of Charles and Charlotte's family had settled in Scotland. An exception was Henry Freeman who had married Helen Manders. He had brought his family back south where both he and his son, William Henry, were making names for themselves on the fairgrounds of South Wales and along the Marches.[1] In the summer of 1903 George and Venie, travelling with Biddall's Menagerie, would certainly have met up with this branch of the family.

By mid-June, having attended the fête and gala at the Park, Pontypool, in the company of Danter's gallopers and Haggar's Bioscope, Biddall's Menagerie moved on to Pontypridd where it advertised again for men and musicians: 'Wanted, Three Useful Inside Men, also Bass, Cornet and Trombone. Biddall's Menagerie, Saturday, Pontypridd; Monday, Llantrissant, Glam.' *(Era,* 13th June 1903*)*

After Llantrissant it was time to head back to the border, taking in an additional fair at Chepstow on 22nd/23rd June arranged by Mr Simmonds and featuring a magnificent electric switchback and gallopers, Butlin's steam horses, and Brewer's Cinematograph. As they crossed Gloucestershire in one-day hops their music situation grew desperate: 'Wanted, a Band of Five, Can Open Monday. Two Cornets, Euphonium, Trombone and Bass. Young Men preferred. Small Hungarian Band may write in. Apply, Biddall's Menagerie, Saturday, Lydney; Monday, Blakeney; Tuesday, Newnham.' (*Era,* 27th June 1903)

123. Marriage of Mary Ann Freeman to Thomas Danter, 1922.
Back Row: Fanny Freeman; John Freeman; Bride & Groom; Alfred Davies; Betty Davies
Front Row: Ellen Freeman; W.H. Freeman (bride's father); Lilly Noble; Johnny Davies; Florence Freeman (bride's mother); W.A. Freeman (bride's brother).

In Wiltshire a month later and now short of a lion-tamer, Biddalls urged W. Hunter to write in to them at Trowbridge or Bradford. He was probably slow to respond, for as the Menagerie travelled on through Bath, Twerton, Calne, Wootton Bassett, Lechlade, Garrington, Bampton and Burford the position was still being advertised.

Meanwhile Biddalls' other half, the Electric Bioscope under the management of William and Polly, had opened at Epsom for three days in July before travelling to Kent for Dartford's Charter Fair held on Thursday, Friday and Saturday before the Bank Holiday. Despite threatening weather large crowds turned out to enjoy the rides and shows gathered in the field next to the Rifleman Inn. Charles Bailey's electric switchback, Sam Jones's gallopers, Wilson and Bailey's Coney Island wheel, and Forrest's overboats were all present. There were boxing booths owned by Elijah Ball, Sol Elliott, and James Purchase. Professor Alf Ball was showing some fine films in his Bioscope. At Ridley's Wonderland Madame Randolph presented interesting experiments in *legerdemain,* and Tom Knighton's 'fine art' show included an exhibition of Inquisition tortures. What excited most attention, however, was Biddall Brothers' electric picture show. Spectators standing outside were charmed by the splendid music of a giant gaviolaphone and a brass band while they watched an excellent variety show. Once inside, in addition to the long picture programme, they were thrilled by the Biddall family's celebrated North American impalement act.

After a rushed pull-down on Saturday night most of the shows including Biddall's Bioscope bustled up Watling Street to Blackheath Holiday Fair where fine weather brought in vast crowds. From Edenbridge the following week they advertised for 'two or three Good Knockabouts (Male or Female) for Parading. Good People and Lowest Terms. Dresses found if required.' (*Era,* 15th August 1903) They would open at Farnborough, Kent, on the Monday and Crayford after that.

Crayford Chartered Fair was held in a field opposite the Swan Inn, the ground being well laid out by Mr Clasper, lessee of this and other Kentish fairgrounds. In 1903 Biddall Brothers' Mexican & Electrical Exhibition, described as a branch of the American Menagerie, occupied a commanding position against the entrance and was commended for its excellent programme, both outside and in.

> On the front stage the public are provided with fine operatic selections by a giant Gaviolaphone, performances by the 'Fakir of Oulon', aerial suspension mystery, songs and dances by the Royal Midgets, living statuary, and the illuminated juggling act of the Biddall Brothers. The performance in the interior is opened by a thrilling exposition of North American Indian sports and pastimes, embracing the wonderful impalement act for which this family have become so justly famous. This is followed by a long series of animated photographs depicting the latest events. (*Music Hall & Theatre Review*, 28th August 1903)

Next to them stood Alf Ball's Royal Electric Bioscope with its wonderful parade led by Mesdames Lawrence and Manley, Chittock's Cinematograph whose programme included the Gordon-Bennett Motor Race, and boxing booths owned by James Purchase, Sol Elliott, and Elijah Ball. Tom Knighton's 'Art' Gallery sported a new set of top paintings by Alf Smith and the riding machines included Charles Bailey's Electric Switchback, Hill's Gallopers, Forrest's Overboats, Miniature Horses and Cockerels, and Wilson and Bailey's Coney Island Wheel.

124. Alf Ball's Coliseum with its 110 key Gavioli organ

The start of Strood's three-day fair the following Wednesday was a wash-out and even on Friday when the weather improved the town was depleted by the hordes who flocked to Chatham for Buffalo Bill's Wild West Show which had run a huge poster campaign in the district. Biddall's Electrical and Mexican Show responded by inviting any member of the public to hold a clay pipe in their mouth while a performer threw a knife with sufficient precision to cut the pipe's stem to the lips – a great publicity stunt, but it could not compete with the hype surrounding Colonel Cody.

Barnet fair was coming up and, to succeed against competition there, Biddall's would have to throw everything they had – and more – into their parade. Besides, it was important to cut a dash when they met up with their other half. 'Wanted, Useful ladies that can do Cake Walk in Style for Outside Parade, also one or two Good Knockabouts. A Good Bending, Hand-Balancing, or Wire Act write in. All for Parade. Join at Barnet Fair. Lowest terms to Biddall, Living Pictures, Galleyhill, Northfleet, Kent, Saturday and Monday; after, Barnet.' (*Era*, 29th August 1903)

Meanwhile, Biddall's Menagerie newly returned from its tour of South Wales opened on 17th August at Farringdon where a reporter observed: 'This concern is worthy of much praise for the excellence of its performance and the fine condition of the animals. The exposition of wild animal training by Captain Bartlett Lindo met with much approval, as did the fine display of animated photography projected by the Oxomotoscope.' (*Music Hall & Theatre Review*, 21st August 1903)

Filling in before Barnet Fair with stands at St Albans and London Colney, George, Venie and Charlie were equally keen to freshen up their parade and advertised for two young lady dancers, aged 15 to 16, and two good knockabouts for the outside show. They also appealed for Dick Sanders (Strong Man) to write in. Their efforts evidently paid off, for at Barnet where the Mexican and Electrical Exhibition reunited with Biddall Brothers' American Menagerie, it was the latter that attracted attention.

> The performances, both outside and in, were conducted in a style characteristic of this clever family. The various groups of animals look thoroughly healthy and well fed and go through their acts with great spirit. The first group, handled by that clever animal trainer, Captain Bartlett Lindo, are six Russian wolves, followed by an exciting scene with a pair of fine lionesses, which met with considerable applause. But it was evident that the audience were saving themselves up for the chief "thrill" of the performance – supplied by Monarch, "the Untameable Lion."
>
> That noble brute paced to and fro in its latticed den with an air of fierce expectancy, long before the previous act was concluded. Mr Biddall, rifle in hand, mounted the stage in front of the cage to give an elaborate speech on the danger of this performance. Then Captain Lindo walked up the steps and attempted to enter the den, but was rudely repulsed by his leonine majesty. Again and again, attempts were made with the same result. Red-hot bars, even, were introduced, which had but little effect.
>
> At last, with a swift movement, Lindo effected an entry, and drove his savage charge round and round the den at breakneck speed midst the burning of red fire and the harsh clanging of a Javain gong. Then, with marvellous alacrity, he opened the door and stepped out on to the stage. Up till then the audience had remained silent, but seeing the Captain's safety they gave a deafening cheer. (*Music Hall & Theatre Review*, 11th September 1903)

125. Jane Gray, née Elliott

From Barnet William and Polly Biddall travelled into Hertfordshire and were at Stevenage fairground when they heard tragic news about the Elliotts with whom they had often travelled. Edward, a member of the 'Fighting Elliott' clan, had taken his boxing booth to Nether Stowey, Somerset, for its Athletic Sports Day on 10th September, and afterwards parked his two wagons under an elm tree near the church. That night a gale brought the tree down, smashing both wagons. Edward, Hannah and their nineteen year old daughter, Susan, were killed outright. Their two younger children were injured. In the other wagon a married daughter, Jane Gray, her husband Alfred and their baby escaped unhurt.

The heart of every travelling showman went out to the orphans – Emily, aged eleven, and her nine year old brother, Henry. With the help of the *Era* newspaper, William Biddall and John Barker organised a subscription on their behalf. One of the first to respond was William's cousin, Eveline White.

> Sir,
>
> With ref. to the appeal in *The Era* on behalf of the children whose parents were killed by the tree. I am a daughter of Mr George Biddall (Ghost Illusion) and a cousin to Mr William Biddall who is taking an interest in the case. Of course I do not know your plans for the future of the children; but I have lost my own little girl and as you state the children are entirely destitute, if it would cause no offence I am quite willing to adopt the little girl. I have boys, but no girl. I am quite willing to put the girl to the same school as my own little boys and to give her a good education. I am enclosing PO for 10/- in aid of the fund. The little girl will have a really comfortable home, and I shall be happy to do my best for her welfare.
>
> Yours faithfully,
> Mrs George White
>
> (Switchback Gondolas), South Esplanade, Torry, Aberdeen, September 30th. (*Era,* 3rd October 1903)

George Biddall, Eveline's father, took a subscription sheet around Dumfries Fair and collected £7 for what he called 'a very deserving case.' The *Era* also received a letter from Lord George Sanger enclosing £20 for the Elliott family. By early December the fund stood at £55.18s. – an amount that by the end of the month had increased to £96.16.6d.

In November, nearing the end of its back-end run through Bedfordshire and Herts, William and Polly's Living Picture Exhibition advertised for 'a Good Clairvoyance Show (Lady and Gent of good appearance). Must thoroughly understand their business. Long Engagement to suitable people. State lowest terms and full particulars in first letter to W. Biddall, Saturday, Dunstable; Monday, Tuesday and Wednesday, London Colney; Nov 16th onwards, Show Ground, Plough Hotel, Tottenham. Mysto communicate.' (*Era,* 7th November 1903)

Meanwhile George, Venie and Charlie, returning to London from Buckinghamshire, were advertising for musicians: 'Wanted, Small Band of Four, Cornet, Trombone, Tenor Horn, and Bass. For particulars, apply Biddall Brothers, Menagerie, Great Missenden, Bucks (Monday) or call on Thursday, Show Ground, Lillie Road, Fulham, between 7.0 and 8.0, for a fortnight or longer if required. Those who were with this Show last winter may write or call.' (*Era,* 31st October 1903)

A fortnight later they still needed a trombone player to open at their show in Major Road, Bermondsey, but there were no advertisements for lion-tamers or animal keepers. Nor did Biddalls need a clairvoyant to see that the future of menageries was bleak. An article in the *Era* on 2nd January 1904 spelt it out. For the last three years public interest in travelling menageries had been waning, so much so that recent sales of wild animals had failed to realise more than a third of their original cost. In the same issue of the *Era* Biddall's Menagerie was advertising: 'Wanted, to Sell, 5 waggons of Wild Beasts, with or without waggons, including Two Lionesses (Performing), One Full-grown Lion (Finest Bouncer in the Business), Four Male Performing Wolves, One Striped Hyena, One Bear, and One Female Wolf (Performing Together), Ten Monkeys, and Variety of other Animals and Birds. The whole of the above are in the pink of condition. For price and particulars, address ... High Street, Deptford, where the above can be seen.'

Together with Biddall Brothers' Cinematograph the Menagerie remained as part of the amusements at Deptford Christmas Holiday Fair while the advertisement was repeated the following week. And the following week – being now extended to include eight sets of silver-plated red parade harness, one band carriage, a large trumpet organ, a ribbed living carriage, two lumber trucks, an agent's four wheeler, and one Cinematograph. Either no one was interested, or once more something happened to change the brothers' minds. When the next advert appeared a month later, all that remained on offer were the '6 or 8 Sets of Red Parading Harness in Good Condition.' (*Era,* 15th February 1904) Biddall Brothers' Menagerie had been reprieved again.

126. Venie and Rosie as 'Midgets', Barnet Fair, 1902

From Deptford William and Polly's Mexican Exhibition moved to the fairground at Burdett Road, Bow, where, prior to their knife-throwing act and display of animated photography, they provided an exciting parade featuring what was described as 'a talented midget duo'. And who were these 'midgets'? Little Venie and Rosie Biddall, young daughters of William and Polly, already treading the boards. Attractions at Bow fairground also included Le Neve and Sullivan's wrestling and boxing booth, Roberts' Eastern Exhibit, Forrest's Overboats, and a variety of throwing games and sidestuff.

At Easter 1904 Biddall Brothers' American Menagerie with its company of lion-tamers, snake charmers and variety performers opened on Hampstead Heath. Alongside them was Biddall's Electric Bioscope and Mexican Show presenting a fine programme of pictures followed by the Red Indian impalement act for which Billy Biddall and his brother John were famous. Their Bioscope, with its giant organ, beautifully carved proscenium and large seating capacity represented a load of nearly twenty tons, equivalent to a set of gallopers. To transport this and provide power and electric light, Biddall Brothers had recently taken possession of a new Road Locomotive, Fowler 9887, which they named *The Mexican*. In Reading at the end of April they advertised for a traction engine driver who could assist with electric lighting. The advert was repeated when they opened on Hampstead Heath for Whitsun before moving to the Welsh Harp, Hendon. Just down the road at Dudden Hill, Willesden, Biddall's Menagerie was wanting: 'One or Two Useful Young Men that can do Trapeze, Perch and Wire. Also make themselves Useful. No Fancy Prices, but Money Sure. Long engagement to suitable people.' (*Era,* 28th May 1904)

About to embark on a summer tour of Hampshire, George and Charlie also embarked on a hunt for that invaluable creature, a good lion tamer. After a month's tour that included Romsey, Eastleigh, Gosport, Fareham, Emsworth, the Menagerie crossed into Sussex and opened at Bognor on 5th and 6th July. Reaching Horsham in mid-July they were still short of a lion tamer 'through disappointment' and also appealing for a young man who could do trapeze and perch. In competition for a good trapeze artiste was Biddall's Bioscope which was also present at Horsham fair. Travelling on together, the two shows opened at Horley, Surrey, then made their way to Strood fair in Kent, calling in at Westerham, Farnborough and East Malling en route. Mindful of what lay ahead, both shows were advertising for knockabouts, lady paraders, perch and wire acts, and a good bender or contortionist, for after Strood Fair and a brief stop at Swanscombe it would be pell-mell for Barnet.

All day Saturday, 3rd September, strings of carts, caravans, swings and roundabouts arrived to take up positions in the half-mile between Barnet Hill and Underhill that held the pleasure fair. Dogs barked and babies cried. Women set about their washing while their menfolk built up, swearing and whistling all the while. By night time they had got fairly settled in an atmosphere heavy with fumes from flaring paraffin lamps mingled with the smell of fried fish and dank earth.

Next day there was a real feeling of Sunday as, their clothes now hanging out to air, the women engaged themselves in preparing vegetables and washing up. An observer coming on the showfolk at midday noticed that their camp had a tidied-up appearance.

> Women had done their hair in curls, donned bright blouses and clean white aprons, and spotless white tablecloths were spread in the open air and dinner duly laid for the family in quite the orthodox style. The baking had evidently been done in the town, and the male portion of the community for the most part were to be seen bringing home the steaming viands under clean white cloths. They seemed a careless, happy, healthy crowd, orderly and deeply appreciative of kindness, and fairly well off. At night one or two preachers found their way into camp, and they were given a quiet and orderly hearing.

The fair started early on Monday morning. As soon as it was light crowds began to arrive for the pleasure fair. One of the first sights to meet the eyes of this reporter from the *Barnet Press* (10th September 1904) was Biddall's:

> The outside show at Biddall's Menagerie was exciting. Boa constrictors were swelling about with ladies in tights, and large unsightly birds with Roman noses were helping the showman to beat his drum. A girl of eight summers was doing the twist to the music of a march, and with her was a mite speedily mastering the intricacies of the cake walk. The organ played the National Anthem, and in I marched. There was not time to look around; the show was at once commenced. I do not know how many times the anthem was played before I risked my twopence.
>
> A fire-eater having had a supper of flames and paraffin oil, a lady mounted steps leading to a den of wolves, smiled sweetly to the spectators, and stepped inside the cage. Having been instructed to jump over her head, the wolves did so, but as they did not obey instructions either willingly or gracefully, they each got a thump with a riding whip. This little performance over, the lady left the cage, again sweetly smiled to the spectators, and disappeared. In the caravan opposite were two lazy lions. The tamer went in, and after persuading them that a little healthy exercise would be to their advantage, they rose from their couches, walked once or twice round the cage, walked over a board – height, a foot-and-a-half – and then lay down again to sleep.
>
> The most sensational item on the agenda was the entrance into the cage of "Monarch, unquestionably the largest captive untamed lion," and of the tamer, several times disabled in days gone by in his efforts to persuade into submission this monster of the forest. There were two entrances to the cage wherein Monarch roamed about seeking whom he might devour. The lion positively declined to admit the tamer into its preserves without a struggle. At one entrance the tamer was met by the growling monster thirsting for blood. The tamer bolted like a shot to the other entrance, so did the lion, which gave utterance to repeated growls, shook its tail, and sprang at the gateway outside of which the tamer stood trying to effect an entrance. Away he bolted to the other door, where he was again met by Monarch, which had evidently made up its mind to wring the keeper's neck or die in the attempt. From door to door the keeper ran on the outside, yelling like a negro, and from door to door jumped the lion, exceedingly angry, and growling mightily. The wit of the tamer surpassed that of Monarch. After various ruses he effected an entrance into the cage, round which the lion jumped, raved, and howled like half-a-dozen elephants trapped in the jungle. The keeper seized the first opportunity and escaped from the cage, and while he was fixing the gate with bolts the lion came and licked his hand.
>
> There was also to be seen in this show for another penny the largest rat in the world. It must have changed hands frequently; every menagerie I have seen boasted of this self-same rat ... It is estimated that half-a-million people visit Barnet during the three days of the Fair.

After Barnet the Brothers travelled to Sandy in Bedfordshire where E.C. Cooper marvelled at their Show. 'They used knives, tomahawks and hatchets. They also had the Handcuff King [Carl Mysto] whom no handcuffs or bars could hold; also the pony with the human brain, that could tell the time and people's characters. Then one of the daughters did the Human Butterfly in the lion's cage. Outside they had their grand organ, one brother playing the cornet, the other the trombone, one clown on the big drum and cymbals, and another on the kettledrum.'[2]

On Wednesday 21st September they arrived at Potton where their collection of wild beasts, birds, reptiles, performing lions and the amusing pictures shown by the Oxomotoscope attracted attention from the *Biggleswade Chronicle* (23rd September 1904). Whilst in the area they would have heard about their eldest sister's recent troubles. Left widowed with eight children to bring up when Abraham Harris died in 1900, Sarah had taken over the running of her husband's travelling fair. In July 1904 she was summoned before the magistrates in Biggleswade for allowing a street organ to be played in contravention of a bye-law and fined ten shillings plus costs. It was another example of the firm stand being taken by municipal authorities against unwelcome noise.

The Biddalls were in Peterborough for the first Wednesday and Thursday in October when its ancient Bridge Fair was held in a field on the south side of the River Nene. In 1904 the ground was well set out by Mr J.W. Walshaw, City Surveyor, and being the most popular fair in the district it attracted visitors from all over the country. Barker and Thurston brought their Venetian gondolas, gallopers, and switchback, but the premier position was held by Biddall's Menagerie. William and Polly were there with Biddall's No. 2 concern, the Cinematograph, and had to compete with Thurston's Exhibition of Animated Photography which was also showing national and local films with Russo-Japanese War pictures. Enoch Farrar's Royal Academy and Powell's fine art gallery completed the list of shows. There were overboats and high fliers by Parr and Harris, four small sets of horses, ten shooting galleries, a number of bottle batteries and twelve variety frames and coconut sheets.

127. Barker & Thurston's 'Twentieth Century' Gondolas, c1900

Heading south after Peterborough William Biddall arrived at Windsor in time for the fair on 22nd October, opening his Bioscope and Mexican Show in a field near St Leonards Road in company with Samuel Jones, William Hastings, Richard Matthew Warwick and M.A. Thomas. Soon all five showmen were being summoned under a similar bye-law to that in Biggleswade, viz: for 'unlawfully, in connection with a roundabout placed on certain vacant ground near St Leonard's Road, causing to be made by means of an organ a loud and continuous noise to the annoyance of residents and passengers.' One complainant, who had obviously done his homework, alleged that at six o'clock on the Saturday evening noise came from five mechanical organs, three drums, two pairs of cymbals, one

128. Dobbies (platformless horses) c1900

cornet, four rattles, two brass bells, numerous whistles and periodical revolver shots. As a result Police Sergeant Barham went to the fair field and read bye-law Number 9 to each defendant.

When charged, William Biddall pointed out that his organ was a hand organ and asked if the byelaw said anything about the distance from the road. He was told 'No'.

At the magistrates' court evidence was given that the showmen had not acted illegally because the ground in question was not 'vacant'. It was a six acre field used regularly for fourteen years past and it belonged to Colonel Bulkeley to whom they had paid £25 rent. After hearing that the showfolk had always been reasonable and conducted their business properly, the case was dismissed. (Era, 12th November 1904)

Despite this happy outcome the year ended sadly. At the beginning of December young Emily Elliott died at Old Highway, Hoddesdon, leaving her brother sole survivor of the wagon crushed in the storm. Her untimely death meant that William Biddall and John Barker had to make new arrangements for the fund set up for the orphans.

Biddalls stayed in London again that winter, in mid December managing a fair near Woolwich before moving to Deptford. They must have been glad they had turned their backs on Portsmouth's Drill Hall when they heard about the wrangling between its owner and George Beech who was being sued for non-payment of rent. Beech's case was that the Drill Hall failed to live up to expectation. For instance, among its attractions might have been three cages of wild beasts had not the management – owing to a typing error – advertised instead for 'two wagons of *bats* and one bouncer.' (*Music Hall & Theatre Review*, 3rd March 1905)

Bats or beasts made no difference to the Biddall Brothers, for they were no longer in a position to answer any such advertisement. By March 1905 they had – at last – disposed of their menagerie and were using their extended stay at Deptford to have a new and elaborate living picture show constructed for the next season.

13

Ghost Of A Former Self

I was given to understand by William Biddall himself ... that this same front had been the property of the late George Biddall, who was uncle to William.

World's Fair, 21st May 1932

Sharing Deptford showground with Roberts' Mysteries, Hastings' midgets and Miss Lambert, the Leicester giantess, Biddall Brothers opened their new bioscope on 25th March 1905. It was fronted by a magnificent gilt, wood and plaster façade with brightly painted panels, the broad wooden steps leading up to its pay box being flanked by two ornate pillars. Inside, it was equipped with a screen and projector capable of providing the public with the very latest in entertainment. On the outside, for those who looked, were large gilded letters betraying a more distant past:

PHANTOSPECTRA BIDDALLS GHOSTODRAMAS

William and Polly Biddall had bought the old front off the celebrated ghost show travelled by their Uncle George in the north.

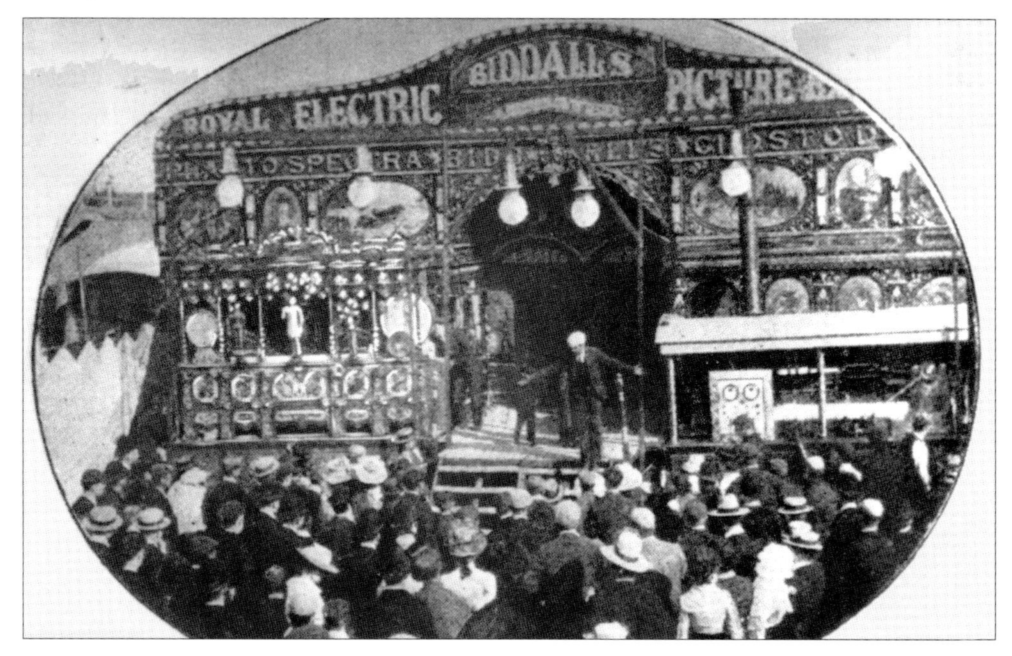

129. Biddall's new show front with John Biddall 'dooring'

130. Biddall's two shows on Hampstead Heath, 1905

At Easter Biddalls opened on Hampstead Heath, their two shows – William's Electric Empire and the Brothers' American Bioscope – doing brisk business down in the vale. Fairs had been known on the Heath since at least the seventeenth century. In about 1700 a fair held in Lower Flask Walk at the same time as races on the Heath was frowned on for bringing low company to patrons of what was then a fashionable spa. As a result the fairs were temporarily suppressed.[1] After making its comeback, however, Hampstead gradually absorbed the ancient fairs of Islington, Tottenham, Camden Town and Highgate so that by the end of the nineteenth century people were in the habit of flocking to the Heath every Easter, Whitsun and August Bank Holiday for amusement.

At Whitsun 1905 trams were packed with Londoners on their way to Hampstead for the day. One passenger noticed signs of activity connected with the fair quite a mile from the Heath. Many shops had open stalls and scores of itinerant toy and novelty-vendors were shouting their wares and doing good business. At the end of the journey vast crowds, especially family groups, thronged the streets and surged up the hill to the Heath. The first grand avenue of variety stalls and entertainments to meet their eyes included Forrests' roundabouts and Searle's aerial flight and coconut shies. Then, embowered in a beautiful valley, stood Biddall's Electrograph and Theatre of Varieties. 'This capital show was a great centre of interest, and held with its fine outside attractions a vast crowd, and the inside performance was well patronised.' (*Era,* 17th June 1905) At the largest fairground, situated at the furthest point of the Heath, were Purchase's Menagerie and Chittock's Cinematograph Exhibition, while at the Vale of Health stood H. Cox's gallopers, giant wheel, overboats and pannum stalls.

In August Biddall Brothers were back in Hampstead with their Electrograph and Variety Theatre showing to good houses from its special 'coign of vantage' in the middle of the Heath. William and Polly, on the other hand, concluded a successful tour of Kent by spending Bank Holiday at Bromley.

Afterwards their Cinematograph Theatre took private business at Farnborough before making its way to Mitcham.

Tradition names Julius Caesar's wife as the one who obtained for Mitcham Fair its first Charter Rights, the site being on Old Fair Green in the heart of the town at the junction of roads between Sutton and Tooting, Carshalton and Mitcham. By 1905 what used to be open space was already surrounded by houses. The *Era,* 19th August 1905, described the scene:

> When we visited the ancient fairground, the evening crowds were beginning to muster. Open brakes and motor cars, with their quota of eager sightseers were discharging their passengers from Tooting, Croydon, Beddington, Carshalton and Streatham. All was life and fun and good-natured merriment. What a lesson it is to notice how the people grasp at the chance of a little brightness in the routine of daily life. William Beddall's superb show, the electrograph, with animated pictures and Empire varieties, and Prof Alf Ball, with Bioscope pictures and varieties, were the principal shows; and well indeed they catered for the amusement of the people.

131. Coconut shy, early twentieth century

Whilst most of the shows went either to Weybridge or Crayford after Mitcham, William and Polly took in a short season at Westerham with smaller concerns that included Honor Matthews' Winchester range and park swings, Harvey's juvenile horses, and J. Smith's coconut shies. As usual they met up with the Brothers at Barnet where, if all the fairground stuff had been placed in one line, there were enough shows, roundabouts and stalls in 1905 to stretch two miles. One observer counted a hundred and fifty caravans, six immense shows in the first class, six in the second, four side shows, nine large roundabouts, four smaller ones, six or seven swings and twelve shooters. Before concluding that Barnet Fair in the number of attractions was Hampstead, Wanstead Flats, Wormwood Scrubs, and Blackheath rolled into one, he reported that William Biddall's Electric Empire, living pictures and variety combination was the centre-piece of its principal group of shows. (*Era,* 9th September 1905)

While William and Polly headed north after Barnet, opening at Peterborough Bridge Fair in early October together with Thurston's electrograph and Manders' Star Menagerie, the Brothers travelled into Middlesex for Uxbridge Fair. Returning to East London in time for the annual winter fair at

132. John Nail's Biograph on Wanstead Flats, Easter 1903

Stratford, they were among mourners at the funeral of John Nail, well-known bioscope owner, who died there just before Christmas. Glorious weather induced thousands to spend their holiday in the open air that year and business was exceptionally good at Mrs Jane Pettigrove's fairground in the High Street. William and Polly's Electric Picture Show also reaped advantage from the weather at the Deptford showground where it opened alongside Ridley's lady conjurors, Littlefield's assault-at-arms, and the elephant man.

The Biddalls were particularly interested in a petition debate that took place at the *Star & Garter*, Islington, in March 1906 in response to a recent London County Council regulation prohibiting the inclusion of caravans on open spaces such as Hampstead, Blackheath and Wormwood Scrubs at holiday times. Chaired by Alf Ball, those present included Tom Norman, Henry Peters, J.W. Chipperfield, Charles Biddall, Thomas Manning, J. Hastings, H. Forrest, C. Hill, Harry Taylor, George Beach, T. Irish, Tom Nigliten [possibly Knighton is meant], F.Gray, W. Bishop, J.Wilson, D. Stevens, and J. Edwards. In the course of the discussion Tom Norman urged that a distinction be made between gypsies and squatters and showmen. In response to a request, the Reverend Thomas Horne described the difference. A number of showmen who were not already members of the Showmen's Guild were then enrolled.[2]

Biddall Brothers' Bioscope and the equally big concerns of William Biddall – the Empire of Varieties and Royal Cinematograph – were among principal shows at Hampstead Heath on Easter Monday 1906 when more than 150,000 people visited. Afterwards Biddall Brothers opened at Reading May Fair but rejoined William Biddall for Whitsun at Hampstead where crowds were even larger than at Easter.

William and Polly then headed west for the Forest of Dean, opening in mid-June at Cinderford fair held in brilliant weather on a new site near the Railway Hotel. Biddall Brothers meanwhile were touring Sussex, in July occupying the premier position at Horsham where their brother-in-law John

Stroud was lessee of Jew's Meadow, a splendid site with room to build up and display all the shows and rides. Sadly, Horsham's town council thought otherwise and was trying to stop the fair.

In August William and Polly attended the Cainscross and Ebley Flower Show held in Jefferies' Field, Stroud, before heading back for Mitcham where they would meet up again with the Biddall Brothers who had meanwhile opened at Bromley Fête for the Bank Holiday.

Unfortunately for showmen the fair at Mitcham, like that in Horsham, was under threat. In 1905 the franchise to hold the fair had been sold for £950 to four trustees acting for the newly-appointed Board of Conservators of Mitcham Common. The latter were determined to abolish the fair because the traffic chaos it caused had been increased by the extension of the London tramway system to Mitcham in 1906. They therefore served notice prohibiting shows and roundabouts from pitching on Fair Green. Ignoring this order, showmen pulled on and built up as usual. Alf Ball, when interviewed by the *Daily Chronicle*, spoke up for England's fairs, saying that in recent times their tone had much improved.

'Years ago they were merely freak shows or some kind of catch-penny entertainment. Now better ideas prevail, more mechanism is used in the production of shows, and a great deal more money is expended by showmen in seeking to meet the public taste. Today many more thousands of pounds are laid out on a good travelling show ... It has become an organised, legitimate, and respectable industry.' (*Era,* 18th August 1906)

It was certainly respected by those good people of Mitcham who assembled in their hundreds in front of Alf Ball's Bioscope at 3 p.m. on 12th August to hear Mr Grange, member of the Parish Council, join with the Reverend Horne and Alf Ball to protest against the proposed abolition. They also heard Mr Watson Wright, solicitor for the Showmen's Guild, argue that the franchise had originally been granted on the understanding that a fair was to be held once a year and that it had been held on the same spot since 1599. Many in the audience, which included Mr F.H. Pedgrift of the *Era,* and Messrs Biddall, Stroud, Bailey, Hastings, Mayne, Taylor, and Matthews, were convinced of the strength of the showmen's case.

133. Rev. Thomas Horne addressing crowds from Alf Ball's Bioscope, 12 August 1906

John Stroud in particular must have felt encouraged. Still involved in his struggle against would-be abolishers of Horsham fair he was due in the High Court the following week. In the event he won a signal victory, the judge refusing to grant an injunction against the fair. Reporting on the case, the *Era* (25th August 1906) commented: 'We confidently anticipate that Mr Stroud will hear no more about it. At Horsham it was one man against a thousand, and although one man can become a thorn in the flesh to a whole town, sound sense and justice is found to win in the end against prejudice and selfish fluster.'

Together with Alf Ball, Lal Elliott, and Swales Forrest, William and Polly Biddall moved on to Strood after Mitcham. An example of what could be done when there was plenty of room, Strood Old Charter Fair was arranged as a vast quadrangle with big shows occupying the whole of one side of the square; shooting galleries and sideshows another; throwing games, dart and ring-boards another; and the remaining side given over to coconut shies and Emma sheets. The central avenues also displayed pannum, toy stalls and Japanese fish games.

134. Coconut shies, Wanstead Flats

From Strood some showmen went to Oxford but the majority, including the Biddalls, travelled to Barnet Old Fair which in 1906 was hailed as the best ever. Still important as a horse and cattle market, its pleasure fair was expanding every year. After Barnet the Biddalls parted company again, the Brothers travelling into Hertfordshire where they opened at Hemel Hempstead fair alongside Purchase's Menagerie, while William and Polly headed north towards Peterborough Bridge Fair. One of the films they were showing that season was *The Sailor's Wedding* in which a ship is seen burning at sea while on shore a young wife watches the heroic efforts of a rescue party to reach it. Her face is agonised. She begs her father to kneel with her and pray ...

During one showing, as the lecturer paused, the clear treble voice of a three-year old girl in the audience was heard saying the *Lord's Prayer*. Sitting on her mother's knee and clearly visible, she held everyone spellbound.

Enjoying something of an Indian summer, Biddall Brothers attended Salisbury's annual pleasure fair for three days from 22nd October together with Anderton & Rowland, Dooner, and William Taylor. The following week they were at Marlow together with Professor Elliott's boxing booth and John Thomas's gallopers. Their Christmas was again spent at Mrs Pettigrove's Stratford showground.

William and Polly on the other hand tried something more ambitious. They took a place at the International Fair and Christmas Carnival at Olympia in the company of showmen such as Pat Collins, Relph & Pedley, Sam Mayne, John Stroud, Alfred Bond, and Joe Matthews. Open from eleven in the morning till eleven at night, admission 6d, it attracted enormous crowds. Early in the new year they were joined at what was called *Fun City* by the Brothers Biddall who 'with their experienced showmanship and a good inside performance seem to be having a large share of public favour,' reported the *Era* (4th January 1907). A week later it was noted that 'Biddall's Mexican and Electrical Exhibition get full houses inside their pavilion and give a very interesting series of pictures and other novelties. The outside parade is wonderfully good and the younger members of the family are as talented artistes as their parents are well known and respected members of the showman world.'

Olympia proved not only popular with the public – nearly half a million people passed through its turnstiles – but also attracted showfolk from all over the country to see what was latest and best in their profession or simply to meet up with old friends. On Sunday, 6th January, the Biddalls were among those who gathered in a section of the circus at Olympia to hear the Reverend Horne conduct a special service for the Showmen's Guild. Preaching on the theme 'Christ and the pleasures of the people', he declared that to provide amusements was an important work in national life.

With so many struggles to face in coming months showmen needed encouragement. They also needed to organise. At the annual general meeting of UKSVDA[3], William Biddall was elected on to the Executive Committee. In lighter vein, the Biddall Brothers were on the Committee appointed to organise Olympia's first showmen's banquet and ball on 21st January 1907.

The Music Hall & Theatre Review (1st February 1907) reported on the event:

> Showmen have certainly nothing to grumble about in respect of their own entertainment this season. Once upon a time a day at Belle Vue or Old Pomona, Manchester, was the only relaxation the Northern showmen had. An odd day at Nottingham Goose Fair, or the old Mawguesite Fair at Charlton, Woolwich (now extinct) was the playtime of the Southern showmen.
>
> Things have moved a bit from those days. The huge gatherings of the showmen at Bolton, Olympia (London), and the Agricultural Hall, London, all go to prove this.
>
> Where were the critics who used to persistently present pen and word pictures of the showmen in a guise of ridicule at the great gathering held at the Mammoth Fun City?
>
> Fully 400 gathered at the first annual showmen's banquet and ball.
>
> The firm of Messrs Lyons was responsible for the catering – below is the menu.
>
> *Soup*
> Mock Turtle Soup
> *Poultry*
> Cold Surrey Fowl
> Ham
> Salad
>
> *Joints*
> Roast Beef
> Tongue
> Vegetables in Season
> Apple Tarts
> Cheese
>
> The chair was taken by Mr F.H. Payne in the absence of Lord George Sanger who was indisposed. Amongst others present were Sir Wm. Bull (MP for Hammersmith); Mr C.B. Cochran, Mr B.W. Rose, Mr E.H. Bostock, Glasgow; Mr F. Bostock, Paris; Mr P. Collins, Walsall; Mr William Murphy, Newcastle-on-Tyne; Mr J. Relph, London; Mr W. Sedgwick, Olympia; Mr W. Le Neve, London; Barron Bros, Yarmouth; Biddall Bros, London; Mr F. Bibby, Manchester; Mellor Bros, Oldham; Mr A. Ball, Mitcham; Mr Geo. Campbell, Newcastle-on-Tyne; Mr W. Taylor, London; Mr E. Lawrence, Plymouth; Tom Norman, Kettering; A. Dashwood, J. Allport, and S. Jeffries, Walsall. The ball was a great success and will rank as one of the best gatherings of showmen that has taken place in London.

135. Travellers at Battersea, late nineteenth century

Separating again after Olympia, William and Polly took their Electric Bioscope to Acton Green for a season, while the Brothers Biddall opened on Mrs Manley's fairground at Battersea. From here on 11th March John Freeman-Biddall and Caroline, twenty-eight year old daughter of Charles Pelham, show proprietor, set out for Wandsworth Register Office to be married.

As usual, the two Biddall bioscopes met up that Easter at Hampstead Heath where it was noted that their Electric Empire had a new series of pictures and did good business. The weather enticed many onto the Heath including Sir Joseph Ward, Prime Minister of New Zealand, who with his wife spent a glorious afternoon at the fair. "I would not have missed it for anything," he declared. "To feel myself at one with the merry-makers, to take part in the joyous din of chatter and song, and to be carried away with the hurly-burly of the roundabouts, and to be drawn a willing patron into the numerous shows was, to me, one of the most delightful experiences of my home visit." (*Era,* 13th April 1907)

William and Polly began the month of May at Reading, moving on to Bracknell and Staines, then Dorking, where they opened alongside Chris Odam's gallopers. Together with Biddall Brothers they pulled back on to Hampstead Heath for the Whit holiday.

> Motor and other 'buses, in addition to a splendid train service, brought thousands of holiday-makers to Hampstead Heath on Whit Monday. And there was plenty of fun provided. The most favoured of all were the cinematograph shows, of which there were four – Messrs. Biddall Bros, Wilson, W. Biddall and H. Chittock. A film that found great favour with the public was one exhibited by the Biddall Bros. From that celebrated firm, *Pathe frères,* it was entitled *A Bad Mother* and at its conclusion received rounds of applause. Nail Bros' Photoscope and ghost show came in for a large amount of support. There was A.W. Brown's sensational riding machine, a novelty which seemed to specially please the ladies. Mrs Cox provided roundabouts and The Little Wonder juvenile swings. (*Music Hall &Theatre Review*, 31st May 1907)

From Hampstead the Biddalls moved to Belton Road, Willesden – a showground used earlier that year by their cousins, the Scotts, whose circus had opened there in February. Wherever they went now, the singing and dancing of William and Polly's daughters evoked admiration. As well as vaudeville acts, Biddalls provided a programme of films, some exquisitely coloured which kept the audience in roars of laughter for nearly an hour. Among the most popular was *A Venetian Tragedy*.

From Belton Road William Biddall advertised for an electrician, two good knockabouts and a doorsman – applicants to apply that Friday or Saturday at Willesden, or catch up with him at Great Berkhamsted on Monday and Tuesday, or Tring the next two days. On 7th and 8th June the Biddall Brothers with their two bioscope exhibitions opened at Aylesbury Fair together with Thurston's new mountain motor-cars.

Early July found Biddall's cinematograph and variety company visiting Emsworth for three days. At the end of the month they opened at Epsom before travelling back for August Bank Holiday on Hampstead Heath where together with Chittock's they occupied the Battery Fairground, an excellent pitch within easy reach of *Jack Straw's Castle*.

William Biddall, the Biddall Brothers and many other London showmen found Dartford Fair a useful fixture between holiday fairs on Hampstead Heath, Wormwood Scrubs or Wanstead Flats and Mitcham.

Mitcham … After last year's showdown, this name sent every showman's blood racing. Twelve months had firmed their resolve. If the Conservators mounted another attack, showfolk would stand and fight for their traditional rights.

A prolonged advertising campaign succeeded in attracting the largest gathering on Fair Green on record. 'Such a large influx of caravans caused all the roads leading to Mitcham to be completely blocked for several hours on Saturday morning … Every kind of showground vehicle filled the streets, from coster barrows to the trains of enormous vans shackled together in tow of resplendent brass-bound traction engines.'

And what did the townspeople think? When asked, they were in favour of their annual carnival being retained, shopkeepers expressing the opinion that the fair put money into their pockets. 'The showmen may take some money out of the town,' they remarked, 'but on the other hand, they have to live and must therefore spend a considerable amount during their sojourn. And … a very large sum is also brought into the town by visitors.'

'Who then are the enemies of this Fair?' asked the *Music Hall & Theatre Review* reporter, 16th August 1907, before proceeding to answer his own question:

'Apparently the Common Conservators, who have been *egged on* by what one tradesman described as the *Motor Pigs* … It is these motor pigs who rush through our village at 40 miles an hour and never spend a penny in it who are doing all they can to do us out of our fair. These London gentlemen have for the last few years exercised such persuasion and flattery upon the local bigwigs as to make them feel that they are really the most important of all the great corporate bodies of the country.'

It was also pointed out that since the Fair Green was now a market place with hardly any grass the showmen could do it no harm.

On the Saturday evening a meeting convened by the Showmen's Guild took place on the Green and was addressed by the Reverend Horne and members of the Parish Council. Resolutions were passed protesting against the actions of the Conservators and expressing the willingness of showmen and townspeople to come to any reasonable arrangement for the conduct of the fair.

Nevertheless, the following day writs were served on thirty-seven showmen, chief among whom were T. Harniess, Swales Forrest, T. Knighton, F. Bailey, Professor Elliott, C. Bailey, H. Bailey, Pettigrove and Mrs C. Bird. The Biddalls and others who had been previously injuncted escaped prosecution by taking private ground close by. With fine weather and such a huge attendance, they had no difficulty in filling their large pavilion throughout the three days.

136. Biddall's Show next to King's Arms, Mitcham, 1906.
Films being shown were: 'Ship of Fire' & 'Sailor's Wedding'

Moving on to Farnborough, Kent, immediately afterwards, they advertised for:

> Good Tumbling Knockabouts, and useful people of all kinds for inside and outside Cinematograph Show. Money no object to people with drawing powers. No all-day and all-night building up and pulling down. Also a good Electrician can write in. State terms and particulars of business in first letter. Long engagement for suitable people. Join at once. Biddall, Electric Pictures, Farnboro, Kent, Saturday till Tuesday. Crayford to follow.

They were no longer asking artistes to state lowest terms and not expect fancy prices. 'Money was no object to people with drawing powers', for Biddalls had a reputation to maintain. Not just their own. After an exchange of letters about Barnet Fair in the *Daily News,* 30th August, they found themselves carrying the torch for travelling shows in general.

> Sir,
>
> The showmen are anxious to maintain their "rights". Most of us would consider the case of these gentlemen to be more justifiable if they provided a cleaner class of entertainment. The "plays" are most degrading and demoralising and would not be permitted in a permanent building. The rabble that can appreciate such "performances" is the dread of all respectable residents, many of whom go from home during the fair, while others who happen to possess an orchard naturally expect the fruit to disappear before the close of the carnival …
>
> Yours, etc. Refiner's Fire.

Reply – to the Editor of the *Daily News:*

> Sir,
>
> Your correspondent "Refiner's Fire" has all the approved methods of the anonymous critic. He has the "vasty vague" manner. Will he kindly oblige the showmen by being a bit more explicit? I was at Barnet Fair last year, and I saw most of the shows. I join issue with him, and for honesty's sake demand a plain statement. Which show was it where the "play" was degrading and demoralising? Was it the magnificent cinematograph theatre of Thurston and Sons? Was it Biddall's similar show? Was it Hastings & Whayman's theatre of varieties? Was it Chittock's Show? etc. etc.
>
> Yours faithfully, T. Horne (Chaplain to the Showmen's Guild)

Biddall's good name was also being used in publicity for Olympia's Fun City. On 31st August 1907 its proprietors (International Fairs Ltd.) announced that they were scouring the world of shows for novelties to join the proved successes of the first year's ventures: Sedgwick's Menagerie, Pat Collins's machines and Biddall's Cinematograph Theatre. They added that Pat Collins would also be bringing his magnificent coloseum of animated and vocal photography, a helter-skelter tower and several new roundabouts.

After Barnet Fair William and Polly did their usual tour, opening at Huntingdon on 28th September before moving on to Peterborough. They were still advertising for: 'Useful People, for Parading with Picture Show, those that can do a turn inside, and used to show business, preferred (singing, dancing, or tumbling), ladies & gents. Good money to right people. Terms & particulars, wire, Saturday, W. Biddall, Electric Exhibition, Huntingdon. After, Peterborough. Thoroughly experienced Traction Engine Driver (Fowler) can join at once.'

William was also wanting to sell: 'Three Good Moneytaking Novelties. A Midget Pony, 32" high, sound and perfect in every way; a Giant Rat; and a Woman in Box, as hard as stone. The above are all genuine moneytakers, and to be sold reasonably.' (*Era,* 28th September 1907)

Biddall's Royal Bioscope was described as the principal novelty at Hatfield fair the following month and provided one of two large electric bioscopes that excited audiences at Bedford fair. The other was Thurston's.

Windsor followed. Then Marlow, where the fair, driven from its streets, was now held on a splendid site off the main road. As winter season drew near – and Olympia beckoned – Biddalls were still in search of talent: 'Wanted two good Singing, Dancing, or Tumbling Comedians; used to Show Business inside & out preferred. Wire terms, particulars, Biddall, Exhibition, Fair Field, Windsor; Saturday after, Fair Field, Marlow, Bucks.' (*Era,* 26th October 1907)

'Biddall's Electric Exhibition caused a big sensation at Staines,' reported the *Era* before the Brothers repaired to Willesden to prepare for Olympia. 'Wanted to sell, New, Agent's Trap, also an 87-key Paper Organ, and quantity of music for same. Reasonable for cash. Address: Biddall, Electric Pictures, Belton Road, Willesden Green.' (*Era,* 7th December 1907)

Describing how Fun City was shaping up, the *Music Hall & Theatre Review,* 20th December 1907, mentioned that 'here will stand the Electric Empire owned by Mr William Biddall.' A week later his photograph appeared in their journal over the following article:

> Few showmen of the day are better known than William Biddall, who took to his calling quite naturally. His father and mother, the late William and Mary Biddall, were well known throughout the country with their performing ponies and variety entertainment. With them during his early years young William Biddall was associated, until a passion for knife-throwing caused him to break away and set out on his own account. He became known as one of the most successful exponents of the art. Then rejoining his father and his brothers, he assisted in the establishment of a menagerie, which set out for its first season in 1895 with a fine collection of wild beasts. Changing with fashion again, Mr William Biddall organised a cinematograph exhibition, which he does not claim to be the largest or the most pretentious on tour. What he does claim, however, is that the show he gives would be very hard to beat. Mr Biddall began his second season at the Mammoth Fun City at Olympia on Christmas Eve.

William's claim was borne out by a visitor to Olympia early in the New Year:

> The Biddall Family, both on the outside parade and in the show itself, demonstrate the hereditary ability that distinguished them amongst the cleverest combination of Show talent travelling our fairs. The cinematograph films were of the best and most up-to-date character, and the Biddalls fully deserve the patronage of the show-loving public.[4]

14

Also, A Petrified Mummy

For Sale, two Indian Serpents, 9-10 ft long, thoroughly acclimatised and good feeders.
World's Fair, 3rd February 1912

The second Olympian Banquet and Ball on 20th January 1908 became the occasion for several branches of the Biddall family to meet. As members of its organising committee and *at home* showfolk, it fell to the Biddall Brothers to entertain those from further afield, such as Albert Biddall who had made it from Dundee with latest news of their Uncle George. Among the four hundred guests in the Pillar Hall were Mr and Mrs Pat Collins, Pat Collins junior (who would marry Eliza Fossett two days later in a quiet ceremony because of serious illness in the Collins' family), Mr and Mrs Caddick, Mr and Mrs William Biddall, Mr and Mrs J. Biddall, Mr and Mrs J. Stroud, Mr and Mrs Mayne, and Mr and Mrs Bond. The Ball continued till five in the morning.

Having had no success at selling his 87 key paper organ and agent's trap at Willesden, William had taken them along to Olympia where he advertised them again. At the same time the Brothers were trying to find a buyer for a ribbed living wagon, 10ft by 6ft, two sets of white metal harness, and a good large barrel organ. Organs were becoming something of a sore point for William, who in late January was summoned at Wandsworth for being responsible for the nuisance of loud mechanical noise associated with his cinematograph exhibition. When the magistrate asked what kind of instrument was involved, he was handed a photo of the offending organ. A photo, he growled, did not convey what amount of noise the thing made. (Loud guffaws in court!)

Local authorities had in fact received so many complaints about music attached to outdoor shows that new bye-laws were being proposed. A letter to the Home Secretary in March explained that such changes were unnecessary because within the last six years the loud trumpet organ had been superseded by ingenious orchestraphones playing good music and capable of being so moderated as to meet all reasonable objections.

After Olympia the Biddall Brothers pulled into the Maplin Street showground, Mile End, to repaint their show and prepare for next season. Being settled for a few weeks gave Charles, erstwhile lion-trainer and youngest member of the family, the chance to wed. On 17th February 1908 he and Netta, twenty-seven year old daughter of John Ridley, married at the Register Office in Mile End Old Town. Their witnesses were George Brackett and Charlotte Matthews, the bride's sister.

Despite this enlargement of the family, the Brothers still advertised for two female paraders and two tumbling knockabouts before moving on to Hampstead Heath to take up their usual position near the Viaduct Pond at Easter. For neighbours they had two shows run by Jack Hastings – the midget family and Miss Lambert, the Leicester giantess. It was noticed that Biddall's looked particularly smart in its new coat of paint and 'doubtless the favourable impression created on previous visits accounted for the generous patronage.' (*Music Hall & Theatre Review*, 24th April 1908) Defying poor weather, crowds of up to 150,000 flocked to the fair.

After a brief stop at Mrs Pettigrove's Welsh Harp ground, William and Polly then set off on tour. By the time they reached Wallingford in June they seemed desperate for help. 'Wanted, 1 or 2 Knockabouts, used to Show Business, or a Juggler or a Bender and a young man to assist with electric light' … 'Wanted, thoroughly experienced Traction-Driver, must be sober and reliable man, good wages to good man … All to open at once. All state lowest terms. If necessary, rail fares arranged. Wire: Saturday, W. Biddall, Exhibition, Wallingford, Berks; Monday/Tuesday, Swallowfield, Hants; after, Fareham, Hants.' (*Era,* 20th June 1908)

But they had other problems on their minds that summer. The Movable Dwellings Bill was about to come before Parliament and showfolk resented being singled out as a class in need of special legislation with regard to health and sanitation. Were they not already subject to the ordinary laws of the land? At Dartford Fair in August, William and Polly's show became the venue for an emergency meeting of the Showmen's Guild to protest against the Bill and discuss how to defend fairs in the Metropolitan area under threat by local authorities. With the Guild's Vice-President, Alf Ball, in the chair, the Reverend Horne addressed a crowd of prominent showpeople which included the Biddall Brothers, Polly Biddall, Mr T. Manders, W. Payne and Henry Forrest.

After Dartford the Biddalls travelled on to Mitcham where the Brothers' Electrograph stood on the top of the Green while William and Polly's Royal Electric Bioscope had to pitch on the private King's Head ground because of the writ previously served on them. Noting that his show was much admired and drew big audiences, the *Era*, 15th August 1908, concluded that, 'It was easy to see that the people of Mitcham sympathised with the old tenants of the fair and that popular feeling ran high in favour of the showmen forbidden to use the Fair Green.'

Barnet Fair's opening day was ruined by rain, but on Saturday, Monday and Tuesday, fine weather attracted crowds in from London by special trains and from local towns by electric trams. Joining up with his sister Sarah Harris and the Thurstons, William Biddall opened at Stevenage later in September and Huntingdon and Peterborough the following month. Like his grandparents, he had magic in mind as he advertised for a 'Clever Card Manipulator, with good Hanky traps, must understand show business. Money no object to the right people; can open at once. Wire Saturday: W. Biddall, Electric Pictures, Huntingdon; after, Fair Ground, Peterborough.' (*Era,* 3rd October 1908)

After Bedford he joined Alf Ball at the Great Marlow Fair which in 1908 was divided in two: one part being held on the Crown field, the other in Mr Porter's meadow at the far end of town. George and Venie Biddall were meanwhile pursuing a separate route with their Electric Bioscope which was described as 'a pleasing attraction to the fairground' at Sutton. (*Music Hall & Theatre Review*, 26th February 1909)

In March William, as member of the London Committee of the Showmen's Guild, received an urgent call to meet with its Organising Chaplain at the *Era* offices in Tavistock Street to discuss Mitcham, Bedford, and other fairs under threat. It is not hard to imagine the kind of debate which ensued at Weatherhead's fairground in Deptford where Biddall's Bioscope opened for business before pulling into Green Cup Valley on Hampstead Heath for Easter. On another part of the Heath were George Biddall's striker, the 'Hackensmidt' striker and J. Freeman's doll frame and juvenile motor cars. Despite showers on Easter Monday over a hundred thousand people came to the fair.

George and Venie's Cinematograph Exhibition visited Beaconsfield in May while William and Polly headed for Dorking. After touring Surrey, they arrived at Epsom in July on the lookout as usual for fresh talent. 'Wanted, two Good Tumbling and Patter Comedians, also good Illusionist, with churn, for Picture Show. Long Engagement to suitable people; Comedians to assist with show. Write stating full particulars and lowest terms. Open Monday. W. Biddall, Exhibition, Epsom, Surrey.' (*Era*, 24th July 1909)

George and Venie meanwhile were on tour in Sussex where their Electrical Exhibition opened at Pulborough, Bognor and Brighton before joining up with William at Lindfield fair in August. Lindfield, once famous for sheep, was now known only as a pleasure fair. Held on the picturesque green, it was convenient for the village but sufficiently remote not to cause disturbance to more sedate inhabitants. In delightful weather, it proved an ideal camping-ground.

> Their caravans pitched in wooded seclusion, they [the showfolk] picnicked to perfection. They had a little grievance. Hastening to Lindfield, as usual, from Brighton Races, they were sternly excluded from the fair ground until six o'clock on Saturday morning. Then there was a rush! Actually the fair was appointed for 8th August – a Sunday. It was formally held on Monday, but it was in full swing on Saturday, liberally patronised by the 800 dragoons who happened to be in the village. Nothing impressed the visitor so greatly as the immense aggregation of *hoop-la* stands ... One end of the showground was dominated by the two spacious splendid shows of the Brothers Biddall, Purchase's menagerie and allied entertainments.
>
> (*Music Hall & Theatre Review*, 12th August 1909)

At Mitcham a few days later William's Royal Bioscope was welcomed back to its old site on Fair Green. A photograph was taken of him and his brother-in-law, John Stroud, sitting smiling on the steps of Biddall's show. Not that its owner had lost his fighting spirit, his name was again prominent amongst contributors to the Mitcham Fair Defence Fund that year.

137. Biddall's Show at Mitcham, 1909
Seated on top step are George Taylor, John Stroud and William Biddall

Biddall's Bioscope and Varieties visited Strood Fair, one of the most ancient and popular in the country, before travelling to Barnet Old Fair where there was record attendance in 1909. But the mood was spoilt by sad news.

'Mr J. Stroud of Redhill, known as "the showman's friend" died on Friday last of dropsy, at 39. Showmen assembled at Barnet have begged us to record the expression of their deep sympathy,' wrote a reporter for the *Music Hall & Theatre Review*, dated 9th September. John Stroud had been lessee of many fairs in Surrey, Sussex, Hants and Kent and energetic defender of any that came under threat. His widow, Becky, left with seven young chavvies, turned to her eldest brother for help.

138. John and Becky Stroud at Dorking Fair, 1905.
Their children (left to right):
Edward, May, Lilian, Henry, Charles (baby), Jack and Nell.

It was announced that notwithstanding the lamented death of Mr John Stroud, the fairs under his control would be carried on as usual by his widow, with the co-operation of Mr William Biddall.

After the funeral Biddall Brothers paid their usual back-end visits to Biggleswade, Sandy and Bedford before returning to Cambridge Heath Road, Bethnal Green, where they opened in company with Thurston's motor galloping horses, helter-skelter and racing birds, and Sam Mayne's juvenile horses, cars and swings. Winter spent on one of London's well-organised fairgrounds provided a good social life crowned by the Annual Showmen's Supper and Ball which William and Polly attended at Islington after Christmas.

Biddall's Royal Electrical and Mexican Exhibition opened the 1910 season at Hoddesdon, doing good business here for three weeks despite bad weather. Their success owed much to the clever Costello Brothers who were performing with them. But it was not only the Exhibition that was absorbing the family's attention. George was about to patent a new sideshow, a game entitled 'Teddy Bears from the Clouds' in which bears suspended on strings dropped down whenever a bullseye was scored. In May one of these was seen working on Hampstead Heath. Biddall Brothers had always travelled sidestuff with their main show. Now that static cinemas were being built and the future for Bioscopes seemed limited, they began to diversify and invest more in shooters, shies and throwing games.

For many showmen 1910 was to prove *annus terribilis*. The Biddalls were at Horsham fair in July when they heard that Alf Ball's spectacular Electric Lyceum had been destroyed by fire at Tilbury Docks. William immediately set up a subscription list to help his old friend. Biddalls were also among those quick to respond when Tom Norman appealed for funds to help the elderly Mr and Mrs James Chittock after their Empire Cinematograph was seized to cover debts.

Showmen at Mitcham fair in August were shocked by a row over apportionment of ground that led Henry Harris of Battersea to shoot at Fred and Harry Gray, a crime that brought him a ten-year jail sentence. Then, after Barnet fair, came news of the brutal murder of roundabout proprietor Chris Odam at Horley. Becky, who lived close by, was asked to identify the body of the man she called Uncle Chris and then to comfort his poor widow. No one was ever convicted of the crime.

139 Chris Odam's coconut shy, c1900

Perhaps counting his blessings as he remembered one tragedy averted, William Biddall gave the proceeds from his opening show in Marlow's Star Meadow that November to the Cottage Hospital. On an earlier visit to the town Marco, a black animal-trainer working in their Menagerie, had been savaged by a lion and his life saved by the staff of Marlow hospital.

Easter 1911 found the Biddalls and other London showmen with a problem. To protect soft grassland, steam road locomotives had been banned from Hampstead Heath, Blackheath and Wormwood Scrubs. Since these engines were needed for transport and to work the roundabouts and shows, alternative venues had to be sought. The result was that Wanstead Flats in 1911 had the greatest number of machines and shows ever seen there, its night sky ablaze with ten thousand electric lights and huge arc lamps. While its three largest cinematographs were provided by W. Taylor, Ball &

Sons, and Henry Thurston, among those which attracted special notice for its up-to-date enterprise was Biddall's Mexican Circus with its equestrian acts, tightrope dancing, joey pony, and the thrilling display of knife-throwing by the famous Mexican Bill (alias William Biddall.)

140. Manders & Bailey's gallopers at Wanstead Flats, Easter 1911 (Biddall's Mexican Circus in background)

As if to underline the importance of his road locomotive, William was soon advertising: 'Wanted, Experienced Traction Engine Driver for Fowler Engine, and to assist with electric plant; living wagon supplied; board in or out. Also two useful Knockabouts, Parade and Inside turns. Particulars and lowest terms. W. Biddall, Fair Meadow, Old Southgate, Saturday & Monday.' (*Era,* 6th May 1911)

A fortnight later, addressing organisers of Coronation festivities, he advertised: 'Wanted Known, The Biddall Family, open for Engagement at Fêtes, Galas or Flower Shows. First Class open-air performance; male and female performers; series of first class animated pictures at intervals. After dusk grounds illuminated for dancing, etc. with own traction engine and electric plant. For terms and particulars, apply The Proprietor, William Biddall. Next week, Leighton Buzzard. Permanent c/o *The Era.'*

In August of this coronation year (and as a sign that the Guild now had the situation under control), it was announced that the gold key ceremony at Mitcham was to be restored after four years' abeyance. The fair was duly opened with great solemnity. At twelve o'clock noon the Reverend Horne and members of the London Divisional Committee proceeded to mark the 'bounds'. With Mr R. Clasper, key-bearer, leading the procession, they entered Fair Green near the Clock Tower where the Guild Chaplain declared: 'According to the ancient use and custom, with this key as the symbol of possession for the three days of the fair, I do open the gates of the fairground. May the blessing of the Almighty be showered upon all innocent enjoyment and recreation within the confines of the fair. Amen.' (*Era,* 12th August 1911)

141. Biddall's Mexican Circus, c1912

Biddall's Mexican Circus and Picture Annexe, the Royal Bioscope, were pitched alongside Sol Elliott's School of Boxing on the Croydon Road. Afterwards they journeyed on to Strood Fair where William's show was joined by Leo Scott and partner, famous for their Magical Illusions. Barnet Fair followed in September and then the usual back-end run through Hertfordshire, Bedfordshire and Northants until they ran into trouble at Peterborough.

The fair opened smoothly enough, rivalling Mitcham with its solemn ceremony. Shortly before noon a procession of civic authorities accompanied by a posse of police left the Guildhall and made for the Town Bridge where the Crier formally exhorted everyone to behave 'soberly and civilly'. Next, the mayor and his party proceeded to the fairground and halted at the far end where the Crier repeated his proclamation amidst the shows, roundabouts and coconut shies. The procession re-formed and returned to the Guildhall where, after being regaled with a 'sausage luncheon' they drank the usual loyal toasts with the addition of 'Success to Bridge Fair'.

So far, so good. It was in the evening that William and Polly's trouble began. Shortly before nine o'clock their talented daughter Louisa went through her routine on a tightrope four feet off the ground. First she danced with the aid of a balancing pole which was long enough to get her out of trouble should she lose balance. Then, to add drama to her performance, she dropped a handkerchief across the rope and without the pole stooped to pick it up. She fell. And was caught by her father. She tried again. And fell again. This time into the arms of the clown. The spectators, now on tenterhooks, watched as the plucky little girl climbed back on the rope to try once more. And – glory be! – at last succeeded.

In the audience sat two men who were not applauding. They were Inspector Bauser from the Society for the Prevention of Cruelty to Children and Detective Sergeant Kyle who, having ascertained that Louisa was under fourteen, promptly brought charges against William under the Dangerous Performances Act.[1]

When the case was heard at Peterborough Police Court on 25th October the defence was mounted by Mr T. Watson-Wright, solicitor to the Showmen's Guild, who put father, mother, child, and clown into the witness box. All agreed on two things, viz: that it was part of the act for the performer to pretend to fall and that being caught by her father and the clown increased the drama. Polly Biddall expanded on this by describing how she and her mother, the famous Female Blondin, had done this act in the same way. It was Louisa herself, however, who proved the most persuasive witness, her clear, happy answers completely demolishing the prosecution's case.

It only remained for the Reverend Horne to testify to the excellent character of Mr and Mrs Biddall, their family, and their show. Louisa had attended both his Sunday school and the day school at Olympia and he judged her to be an extremely bright and intelligent child who so loved her parents' show that they could not have kept her out of it if they tried. The Biddalls, he said, were amongst the most talented and worthy travelling showpeople, and he could not imagine them for one moment allowing any of their children to participate in something dangerous.

After a brief consultation the Bench dismissed the case. (*Era,* 28th October 1911)

In a less co-operative mood Louisa might have told a different tale about what it was like to work on the show. Whilst open at Barnet Fair one year she and her sister Violet had been given a cup and told to help the clown collect entrance money from the queue. Adults paid twopence, children a penny, and at half-time people could enter for a ha'penny. When one gentleman gave the girls a shilling by mistake for a penny, Violet promptly gave it back. Noticing this, the clown in big boots clouted her. Violet screamed. Fond father arrived on the scene and thumped the clown. However, once the clown explained why he had hit the child, William Biddall sympathised with him.

'Wherever did you learn this nonsense?' he demanded, turning to his daughter.

'At school. You know, hang yer coat in the lobby and honesty is the best policy,' Violet sobbed, repeating two lessons that had been drummed into her.

142. On Parade - Venie and Rosie, daughters of William & Polly Biddall

143. Venie (impersonating Vesta Tilley) and Rosie

Despite the eager talent of his seven daughters and son, William was advertising for extra help early in the new year. He also set about clearing out old to make way for new – or, if not new exactly, something old enough to appear so. 'Wanted for Ghost Show, Two Young People (Lady and Gent) must thoroughly understand every branch of the business. Preference to gent able to touch up scenery. Also two good Knockabouts with good songs and patter. Join at once … W. Biddall, South Road, New Southgate, Middlesex.' (*World's Fair*, 13th January 1912) 'For Sale, two Indian Serpents, 9-10 ft long, thoroughly acclimatised and good feeders; also a midget Pony, about 9 hands, partly broken for showing, sound and in good condition; one large Barrel Organ, about six feet long, suitable for Show or machine; one small organ, lately overhauled, suitable for juvenile roundabout; one 3 octave Portable Harmonium; also a Petrified Mummy, first class Novelty for sideshow, good money-taker. All the above in good order and cheap for cash. Can be seen by appointment. Apply: W. Biddall, Hoddesdon, Herts.' (*World's Fair*, 3rd February 1912)

The petrified mummy was a figure three and a half feet long in a crouched position, with perfect hair and teeth, and according to gag cards in front of the show 'she' had been found in the workings of an old coal mine. A ghoulish exhibit that drew crowds of spectators if not many speculators, it – together with snakes, midget pony, organ and harmonium – was still on offer at Hoddesdon three weeks later.

Easter saw no return to Wanstead Flats. The LCC, learning from the previous year's mistake, had withdrawn opposition to the showmen's traction engines and allowed William Biddall's Mexican Circus and Thurston's electric coliseum to take up positions in Horseshoe Walk on Hampstead Heath. They returned at Whitsun in the company of nearly a thousand showmen who were there to cater for more than half a million pleasure-seekers.

For summer 1912 William organised a tour of the southern counties. In mid-June he was at Gosport advertising for two good Knockabouts and one or two good Step Men, 'one to describe Pictures preferred.' Travelling along the coast Biddall's Mexican Circus and Cinema Show opened near the station in Havant before moving on to Sussex. The tone of William's next advertisements suggests an unhappy experience with people recently hired. 'Wanted, two good Step Men for Picture Show; also two good Tumbling Knockabouts. Boosey Tumblers need not apply. All must assist with Show. Terms low but money sure. Wire Saturday, Fairground, Bognor; Monday, Tuesday and Wednesday, Arundel.' (*World's Fair*, 6th July 1912) 'Wanted, two good Knockabouts for Picture Show; also one or two Handy Men and Horse-keeper. All to assist with show. Fares can be arranged if required. Wire Saturday only. Wm Biddall, Mexican Exhibition, Pulborough, Sussex; Monday & Tuesday, Billingshurst.' (*World's Fair*, 13th July 1912)

At Mitcham in August Biddall's Mexican Circus was pitched among those on the old Fair Green together with George Biddall's throwing games. Again the fair was scene of a London Showmen's Protest, not against any abolition but against traffic proposals being put forward by the County Council's Association. Showmen met in Alf Ball's show on Wednesday, 14th August, to discuss which particular conditions would threaten their livelihood. For example, there were plans to penalise all tractors over fourteen tons in gross weight (to include fuel and water with the engine kit); to prohibit use of certain roads; to hike up the cost of licences and daily permits; and to give the police greater powers over traction engine users. Present at the meeting were Messrs H. Thurston & Sons, F. Gray & Son, William Wilson, William Biddall, Mrs Bird and others.

Before moving on to Barnet Fair in 1912 William's show opened at Eltham, where he advertised for some 'good Startling Acts, suitable for Small Ring or Stage; also two good Tumbling Knockabouts.' Less emphasis on the bioscope possibly reflected a current revival in small show booths. According to the *Era*, the monopoly of the picture show was over and the future lay with the showmen who could make an entertainment in a thirty foot booth. 'Every fairground this year has borne witness to the fact that pictures are merely an adjunct, not the supreme novelty they were.' (*Era*, 31st August 1912)

From Huntingdon and Peterborough William Biddall sent his message out again: 'Wanted (tumbling) two good Knockabouts for Picture Show.' Then, as he and Polly headed for Sunninghill in Berkshire, George and Venie pulled into the showground at Stratford East where that winter they tried to stage something new every week: 'Wanted ... Swimmer or Second-Sight performance, or Dogs or Monkeys. Anything that can be done in ring or on stage.' (*World's Fair*, 9th November 1912) And, 'Wanted Fresh Show Weekly, Marionette with own fit-up; write in for Christmas Week; or anything that is good, female wrestlers or strong woman. For terms, apply Biddall, Showground, Stratford.' (*World's Fair*, 14th December 1912)

But it was a miserable winter. Business was suffering from the competition of permanent cinemas and George was ill. Far from expanding his show he was soon considering selling the lot to concentrate on sidestuff. It was a sad advertisement that appeared in *World's Fair*, 11th January 1913. 'For sale: Double Wagon Canopy Front, opens out 28ft; also Shuttered Booth, 30ft x 45ft, good Tilts and Green Baize Linings, Standing Gallery and Pit, two good Trucks, one fitted with traction gear; one large Barrel Organ, two drums and cymbals; 10 Arc Lamps, Cinematograph. Volt Meter, 120 voltage; also, one Light Road Living Wagon; also a Quantity of Films, to be bought Cheap, all in good condition. Apply, Biddall, Fairground, Stratford. To be sold together or separate.'

His Cinematograph equipment and films apparently sold quickly, but the other items were to prove a drug in the market. Two weeks later George was embellishing his description: 'For sale, Double Wagon front, opens out 38ft, one-horse load; good Shuttered Booth, length 44ft, 30ft wide at front, tapers to 26ft at back, Tilts, Lining and Seating, two Trucks to carry same; large Barrel Organ; Drums and Cymbals; 10 Dickinson arc lamps. The above in splendid condition and ready for opening, suitable for any kind of show; must be sold owing to ill-health; cheap for cash, or easy terms to a responsible person.'

In March at the beginning of a long stay at the Welsh Harp, Hendon, George offered to exchange the double wagon front for a light living van and ground booth. Then he tried offering the complete show for sale together with the band organ. In May when the advert reappeared he added: 'No reasonable offer refused.' There were still no takers.

15

Still Performing Wonders

The first part of the entertainment was usually a short drama, followed by a comedy film, then came the Joey pony, wire act and finally the illustrated songs which always proved a great hit with the audience.

World's Fair, 10th February 1940

For William Biddall the New Year looked promising. At the AGM of the Showmen's Guild in January 1913 he and his cousin Albert Biddall had been numbered among the President's supporters alongside prominent men such as Mr Watson Wright and the Reverend Thomas Horne. And at his winter-quarters at Sunninghill he took advantage of a workshop on site to bring in Mr E. Fear of Bristol, painter and gilder, to redecorate his show-front. By mid-February, besides appealing for a good letterer and liner to complete the job, he was already preparing for London Easter week by advertising for four men to help generally, two tumbling knockabouts, someone who understood electric lighting, a good-looking doorsman with his own uniform, and any good act for his Mexican Show. This search for staff went on all summer. From Hampstead Heath at Whitsun he advertised for two or three useful men to assist in building up and pulling down and one to look after horses. At Pulborough in July he again wanted two or three useful men who understood building up and pulling down; also two good knockabouts who could assist with the show. He moved on to Horsham and Godstone, still advertising for the same.

After Lindfield and Mitcham, at the end of August William opened at Strood where his sister Becky was lessee, then made his way via Eynsford to Barnet for 3rd September. Gearing up for the back end run he advertised again for a sensational act suitable for ring or stage and for two good knockabouts. Stressing that the latter must be funny, he warned that 'only those who are used to parading and clever need apply.'

For George Biddall back-end meant another chance to get rid of his show. It was either that or spend good money on refurbishing. In October he advertised: 'For Sale, a Shuttered Booth, 30' x 44', good tilts and linings, pit and galleries, can be seen built up, suitable for any performance. Next week, Show Grounds, Acton Green.' (*World's Fair*, 11th October 1913) When, still at Acton, he advertised the showfront and barrel organ for sale again the following April, he described it as 'all in fairish condition and to be sold cheap.'

William Biddall on the other hand had no intention of selling up even though his show also needed attention. Pulling into Sunninghill for winter 1913-14, he was soon advertising for a good illusion or sensational act for the Christmas season. After that he set out to find two or three useful

144. Henry Stroud, helping on his Uncle William Biddall's show

145. Becky Stroud's chairoplanes which had a mellifluous Verbeeck organ

146. Becky's Fowler Road Locomotive Roseta (named after her sister Rose) which drove the chairoplanes

young men who could do a bit of chamfering and painting. With a tour up-country in mind for the new season he advertised for a traction engine driver for the Fowler: 'one that has knowledge of electric light. A single and sober young man preferred.' Whatever the man's technical skills, it appears that the new driver proved unsatisfactory in other respects. Advertising for a replacement towards the end of the summer William stressed that: 'This is a good shop for a good man. Those that are too fond of going away to oil up and cannot be sociable with other men need not apply.' Those interested were asked to apply to: 'Biddall, Fairground, West Bromwich, Staffs.' (*World's Fair*, 13th August 1914)

Returning south along the A5 William and Polly opened at Redbourn in Hertfordshire where they advertised for two or three useful men, a good horsekeeper, and a young man who understood electric light. 'Can join at once' was their urgent plea, as the show was spruced up for Barnet. Few could have foreseen that 'useful young men' would be in short supply in coming months.

147. Barnet Fair, 1914

British showmen everywhere responded to the outbreak of war by making generous contributions to the National Relief Fund. At Barnet Fair Amos Ford, chairman of the local branch of the fund, approached leading showmen and received immediate promises of help. 'Mr Frederick Gray, Mr George Sanders, and Messrs Julian and Simpson kindly offered half their takings on Monday, the 7th, and Mr W. Biddall willingly gave one-third of his takings [£3/14/2], whilst Mr Thurston, senr. and Mr J. Harris handsomely subscribed £5/5/- and £2/12/6 respectively,' he reported. (*World's Fair*, 19th September 1914)

William was in poor health that autumn, a fact noted by his old friend, Leo Scott, when he met up with him at Cottenham in Cambridgeshire. Some years later Leo, who had been agent for Thomas Fossett's circus at the time, reported that 'The William Biddall family were then doing a fine circus programme and the whole outfit was an imposing and beautiful scene.'[1] He had also noticed that their show front still bore in gold letters its old legend: *PHANTOSPECTRA GHOST O DRAMAS.*

William, still unwell in November, advertised for a steady and reliable young man to drive the Fowler traction engine: 'One used to Electric Light preferred. Lodgings found. Live in or out. State lowest terms for winter shop. Can join Monday week. Apply W. Biddall, Vine Cottage, Chase Side, Enfield, Middlesex.' (*World's Fair*, 21st November 1914)

War brought concentrations of troops and where there were young men in uniform there was need of entertainment. George and Charles Biddall spent the winter months of 1914-15 at North Camp in Farnborough where Redshirt Matthews, showman, had his head-quarters. In January 1915 George was still trying to get rid of the organ off his show.

'For Sale, large Barrel Organ, suit any purpose, cost £155, take £20. Bargain. Reason for selling, too big for business. For particulars apply: G. Biddall, Fairground, North Camp, Farnborough.' (*World's Fair*, 9th January 1915)

In November 1914 William Biddall had moved from Enfield to Braintree where about ten thousand soldiers were billeted. Although his show was built up near the town centre only six yards from Mr Cyril Getcliff's New Picture House, for the next five months it was packed to capacity by the military. So how did the Biddalls give the permanent cinema a run for its money? By calling on all their inherited skills as strollers and showfolk.

The entertainment consisted of a series of cowboy and comedy films (usually of the two or three reel variety) and a circus which included wire-walking, juggling, knife-throwing, and a performing pony. The seating was arranged in a circle and at the back of the booth a stage opened out for William and Polly's daughters to give their song and dance act. This was what the troops loved best and they packed the show every night to join in the choruses of *Keep the Home Fires Burning*, *A Long, Long Trail* and *You Know Very Well, Isobel.*

148. Venie, Rosie and Nellie parading on their father's show

Biddall's Show left Braintree the week before Easter 1915 for Wanstead Flats, the two front wagons drawn by William's splendid team of horses while the rest of the loads were pulled by the Fowler.[2] Before leaving Braintree he had advertised several times for:

'Two or three Useful Men, good Horsekeeper. Also Traction Engine Driver to take charge of 6nhp Fowler Engine. Comfortable job for competent man. State wage to board in or out. Money sure. Can join at once. Can arrange fare. Also wanted, good starting Act for small ring or stage. Those known to me please write: W.Biddall, Market Place, Braintree, Essex.' (*World's Fair*, 13th March 1915)

But suitable young men were sadly otherwise engaged. In April came news of the first showman soldier to fall in battle – Private Henry Wallser of Plymouth was killed at Neuve Chapelle. As weeks and months passed his name was joined by a legion of others.

From Wanstead Flats William journeyed to Billericay and Danbury, Essex, where he built up the show at The Bell in early May. Then he travelled into Berkshire, opening at Spital, Windsor, in June before moving on to Brookwood in Surrey. Just down the road in Farnborough George had recently made another attempt to sell the two front wagons of his old show. By now shabby, they had (he assured potential customers) 'good underworks and bodies.' There was also the large barrel organ still going cheap. His anxiety to find a buyer was soon overshadowed by a tragic event.

The Biddall family had always been close, George and his youngest brother living cheek by jowl in the yard at North Camp. One Monday morning in July Charles Biddall was on his bicycle approaching a sharp bend at Blackdown when a heavily laden motor lorry came round the corner. It was impossible to avoid a collision. Charles was knocked off his bike and under the lorry's wheels. Terribly injured, he was taken to North Camp's Connaught Hospital where he died at eleven o'clock that same night. Aged forty-two, he left Netta with five children, the eldest only seven. Nor was this the end of her suffering. Two of these children – Rhoda and three year old Charles – would die within weeks of each other in 1917.

Charles's death coincided with the end of an era for Biddall's travelling show, for William and Polly's Exhibition would remain at Brookwood for the duration of the war and not go back on the road afterwards. It is not clear whether William intended such a long stay at Brookwood. His advert in *World's Fair*, 6th November 1915, sounded equivocal:

'Wanted, Traction Engine Driver for Fowler Engine now permanent for a few months.' [!] It went on to specify: 'Comfortable job for steady man all the year round. Preference given to one with knowledge of electric light.'

Electric light – such an attraction on pre-War fairgrounds – caused William grief when he was caught infringing new government regulations. His offence was that he did not for the period from one hour after sunset till one hour before sunrise so shade or reduce the lights inside his shooting gallery that no more than a dull subdued light was visible from any direction outside. The maximum penalty if convicted was a fine of £100 or six months' imprisonment. William pleaded not guilty.

In court Police Constable Rendell testified that he had seen the shooting gallery illuminated at 7.50 p.m. There were two shaded electric lights at the far end reflecting on the bottles and white-washed back of the structure and another shaded light above the firing point. The top of the gallery was closed in, but at the firing point there were gaps for people to enter and through these light was shining. On the previous evening he had warned William Biddall's brother-in-law that they were not complying with the lighting order and risked being summoned. He admitted that the proprietor had made many alterations but all had failed to keep the light within the gallery. When asked if the alterations – additional tin shades, bulbs whitened, the lamp at the firing point fitted with a cardboard ruff – left enough light to read by, the Constable replied that he had not attempted to do so.

The case eventually hung on the fact that William, trying to comply with police instructions, had not opened the shooting gallery on the evening in question, but had been caught whilst experimenting with curtains at the entrance. He had needed lights on for this. He swore that no direct light was visible from outside the gallery and that he had obtained timber and canvas to make further alterations. In the event William was convicted but, taking into account everything he had done, only ordered to pay costs.

In the spring of 1918 George and Venie's son, George, was welcomed back to the yard at Peabody Road, North Camp, discharged after being wounded in France. War had not long been over when William and Polly moved to premises at 128 High Street, Watford, and began to invest in amusement arcades. But in September 1919 William was driving a caravan along Hempstead Road near Apsley Mills when he was involved in an accident horribly reminiscent of those that had killed Charles and Rose Hannah. After William's horse shied at a goat and threw him under the wheels, he was taken to West Hertfordshire Hospital 'in a grave condition.' Six weeks later he returned home still on crutches and only slowly recovering use of his legs.

By Christmas, however, he was up and at it, booking novelties for his new Arcadia Pastimes, 141 King Street, Hammersmith. He was also soon developing a run of gaffs for his travelling fair. And, as usual in showmen's families, fairground links were being strengthened by marriage. In this respect no union was more welcome than that between William's daughter Venie and Walter, son of James Harris (and nephew of Abraham Harris who had married Sarah Biddall in 1883). The young couple married at Hastings in July 1922.

149. Venie Biddall marries Walter Harris at Hastings, 1922. William & Polly front row, right. Bride's sisters (Violet, Nellie, Doris) front row, left. Row above: Charles Hyatt & wife, Louie, (another sister). Next to her, Rosie. Sixth sister, Polly Barron, holding child. Polly's husband, Stanley Barron, holding little girl. Back row: William Biddall, junior, stands to left of gentleman in light-coloured cap.

150. Venie Harris with daughter, Vera, and son, Walter William (Dick)

151. Dick Harris with toy spectacles and comic 'to make him sit still'

152. Dick Harris as a young man. Dick would marry Grace Gray, daughter of Jane, née Elliott, who in 1903 had survived the storm at Nether Stowey.

153. Grace Gray minding her father's wheel-'em in

Afterwards William travelled to Southsea, returning only to give evidence against Edward Ross, a former employee who had made off with £12/1/- with which he was supposed to buy swag from Brown & Sons, Hounsditch. Ross was sentenced to three months' hard labour. In May 1924 William announced that there were a few spaces to let at the fair he was holding on The Moor at Maidenhead from 6th June. It would remain for two Saturdays and the town band had been engaged for Whit Monday. In July the following year he was advertising spaces to let for up-to-date games, juvenile roundabout and swings at a whole run of fêtes and galas. 'Applications to Fête Ground, Wood Street Green, Guildford.'

154. William and Polly Biddall

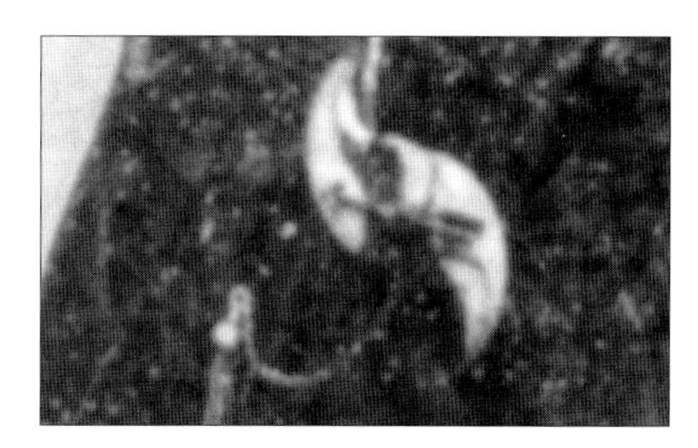

155. Polly's brooch (detail)

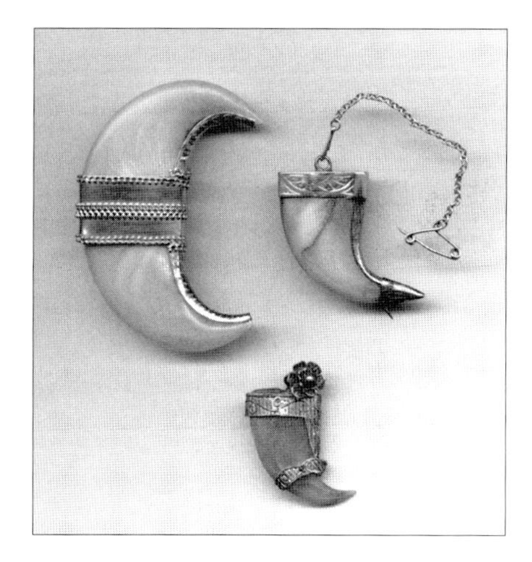

156. Claw brooches as worn by Biddalls[3]

Not only did he continue to give a benefit for the Cottage Hospital every year he returned to Marlow, he became known as someone always willing to help a needy cause. The King Edward VII Hospital, Windsor, was one among many which benefited from his generosity. But when William celebrated his sixty-second birthday on the fairground at Iver, Buckinghamshire, he was already seriously ill. It was a curious twist of fate which brought him here – to the village where his great grandparents, Moses and Mary, lay buried in the churchyard – for his last birthday. He died at the circus field, Slough, four months later and was interred at Hounslow, his famous Bowie knives being buried in a chest at the same time.

World's Fair, 30th October 1926, paid tribute to his life:

> The late Mr William Biddall ... was one of the real old type, a showman, champion knife thrower, ex-menagerie owner, and circus performer from childhood. His father and mother were both circus artistes, and he himself entered the same profession in early boyhood, and became an accomplished performer. His skill as a knife-thrower won him more than one championship medal, and what was no less remarkable was his skill as a player of the cornet. He used to travel a circus, and was a well-known and popular member of the circus fraternity ... Of late years he became proprietor of the amusement fair which had its centre in Slough and travels the towns and villages round about ... He leaves a widow and a son and seven daughters. Mrs Biddall has been, and still is, a clever tightrope performer, and the rest of the family are all connected with the business. The son intends to carry on the show in his father's place.

Polly lived on for another twenty years, dying at Ashford Hospital in 1946, aged 75. George Biddall died in November 1931, his widow Venie in February 1944 within days of her brother-in-law, John Biddall. Although this, the death of the last of the Biddall Brothers, was reported in *World's Fair* as bringing to an end 'one of the oldest families of showmen who have done so much in the past to brighten the lives of others', the valediction proved happily premature. It was but a generation that was passing and if you visit a traditional circus or fairground anywhere in the world today you are likely to come across showfolk with the blood of Freeman-Biddalls running in their veins. The name might be different – the descendants of Henry and Hannah have married with (among others) Meers, Manders, and Millers; Sangers, Sedgwicks and Scotts; Ohmys, Newsomes, and Fossetts; Testos, Ridleys, and Codonas; Silbons and Sandows – but their common legacy is clear. They have inherited that spirit of strollers and showfolk which will continue to brighten lives as long as fairs and circus survive.

157. Getting ready for the next show

Postscript

On Sunday, 4th February 2001, the third World's Fair Circus Awards was held at the Hanover International Hotel in Hinckley following the International Circus Reunion. Recognised as the British Oscars of the circus world, the intention of the awards is to reward, recognise and encourage members of the profession and spur them on to even greater things. This year, in addition to the usual humanitarian, animal husbandry, lifetime achievement and showmanship categories it was decided to make a special award to mark the end of the 20th century and start of the new Millennium. Acknowledging their debt to a performer considered to be the greatest, the committee had no doubt in naming Jimmy Freeman (Pimpo) as BRITISH CIRCUS PERFORMER OF THE CENTURY.

He was once described in *World's Fair* as the incarnation of circus in all its aspects and when he died in 1961 it was said there was none greater than this talented performer, an all-rounder without a superior or equal. There was nothing in circus that this man could not do and extraordinarily well and no performer of the past century more deserving of the title of fine performer. His whole life was linked to just one famous circus family, that of Sanger, and he became a clown, rider, trapeze artiste, animal trainer, acrobat, second to none, as well as displaying those necessary talents of a real circus man. As a blacksmith, saddler, sailmaker, groom, propmaker and cobbler, he was able to turn his hand to virtually any task. He was Jimmie Freeman, destined to be the second man to bear the title of the clown Pimpo and the most celebrated clown in British circus history. He married into the Sanger circus family but today there is not a Sanger to be found in the circus business. However, his two grandsons, Michael and Peter, keep family tradition going with their exceptional comedy dog acts as Mike Sanger and Old Regnas respectively.

(*World's Fair,* 16th February 2001)

Appendix

TRACTION ENGINES OWNED BY BIDDALLS

BURRELL

Burrell No.2173 (1899) *Flora*, formerly *The Empress*. Devonshire class. 6 nhp, single-crank compound engine with 5.5in x 9in x 10in cylinder. Purchased by JAMES BIDDALL (Ceres) from Smith & Whittle, Woking, Surrey and rebuilt with dynamo.

Burrell No.2355 (1901) *Mons Star*, formerly *Lord Roberts*. 8 nhp, double-crank compound engine with 6.5in x 11in x 12in cylinder. Registration No.XH 8048 (LCC). Built for W.C.& S. Hancock and owned by Fred Gray before being purchased c 1943 by JOHN BIDDALL (Hampstead). This engine was used on demolition work and in 1947 sold to Hardwicks of West Ewell, Surrey, for scrap.

Burrell No.3341 (1911) *St Bernard*. 4 nhp, double-crank compound 5 ton tractor with 4.5in x 7.5in x 8.5in cylinder. Built for Marshall Hill, Bristol, and purchased in 1914 by George Baker & Sons, Southampton, before being bought by JOHN BIDDALL (Hampstead). Then sold to W. Thomas, Feltham, in 1938.

FOWLER

Fowler No.6927 (c1893) *Roseta*. This road locomotive was owned by REBECCA STROUD-TAYLOR in 1930s and named after her sister, Rose Hannah. It was used to drive her chairoplanes.

Fowler No.9887 (1903) *The Mexican*. A4 class, double-crank compound engine. Built for BIDDALL BROS (Deptford), sold in 1921 and later registered BL 8500 (Berkshire C.C.)

Fowler No.9387 (1904) *Queen Alexandra*. A5 class, double-crank compound engine. Purchased by BIDDALL BROS (Deptford) in 1905 from J. Studt, Cardiff, later sold to White's of Leith and registered SR 2234 (Angus C.C.)

Fowler No.10694 (1906) *Evening Star*. R class double-crank compound engine. Built for GEORGE BIDDALL (Scotland) in 1906 and later sold to John Evans & Son Ltd, Edinburgh.

Fowler No.14873 (1917 W.D.) *Empress*. Owned by REBECCA STROUD-TAYLOR and sold to A.Greenway, 1936.

Fowler No.14916 (1917) *Demolicious*. TE2 class, registered NO 1246. Built as a road locomotive for Ministry of Munitions and after the war sold to G.E.Millbank, Hatfield Heath. Then sold on to Fred Gray, Kensal Green, who converted it to a showman's road locomotive. Purchased by JOHN BIDDALL (Hampstead) in 1945, the engine acquired her name from being used to demolish bomb-damaged buildings for the LCC. Later sold to Hardwick, West Ewell, for scrap.

Fowler No.15324 (1919) *Renown*. Registered KE 3895 (Kent C.C.). Converted to a showman's engine in 1923 by Charles Openshaw, Reading. Purchased by JOHN BIDDALL (Hampstead) and later sold to Hewitt & Irvin of Hounslow who used it in 1941/2 to demolish bomb-damaged buildings in London.

McLAREN

McLaren *Stella Matina*. Owned by GEORGE BIDDALL (Scotland). No further information, but probably the McLaren engine pictured below.

RUSTON, PROCTOR

Ruston, Proctor No.29777 (1905). 5D class, 3 ton tractor. Purchased by JAMES FREEMAN (Ceres) in 1913 from an Essex market gardener and sold the following year to J.Freeman, Glasgow.

WALLIS & STEEVENS

Wallis & Steevens No.7130 (1910) *Minoru*. 8nhp, double-crank compound engine. Registered HT 3796 (Bristol C.C.) Built for Marshall & Ernest Hill, Bristol, and named after King Edward VII's 1909 Derby winner. Updated in 1912 with a dynamo to work their four-abreast gallopers. Purchased in 1934 by Mrs A.Brown, Guildford, and sold on to JOHN BIDDALL (Hampstead) in 1941. Used by Biddalls to demolish bomb-damaged buildings and scrapped in 1948 by Hardwicks, West Ewell.

Notes

Chapter 1: The Wizard That Was

1. *Era*, 20th November 1864
2. Record of sexton's fees kept by Iver parish clerk – Buckinghamshire Record Office Ref:PR115/8/2
3. Information about the Freeman family was found in Gloucestershire Record Office. *Monumental Inscriptions of Gloucestershire*, first published in 1791, records a tomb in Bisley churchyard erected over the remains of 'John Freeman, of this Parish, clothier, died August 5, 1710; Joan, his Wife died June 7, 1692, and Rowland their Son died May 6, 1713.' John and Joan had three sons – William, Rowland and Anthony. When William died in 1738 he left a Will making it clear that he had already advanced a considerable loan to his son John (viz. £43), from which the latter was expected to pay legacies to his own five children – Moses (born 1716), Mary, Ann, Elizabeth and John. Whether these legacies were forthcoming is not recorded, but what is clear is that John Freeman (born 1691) made good use of his father's loan and died a comparatively wealthy man in 1763. Among several properties left in the neighbourhood of Bisley and Avens Green, he bequeathed a cottage at the Lynch to his grandson, Moses Freeman, who was ten years old when his grandfather died.
4. *World's Fair*, 19th May 1934
5. Hannah's nephew was Tom Baker, circus owner and father of the famous Baker Boys, equestrian artistes.
6. Whimsical Walker, *From Sawdust to Windsor Castle* (London: Stanley Paul & Co, 1922)
7. George Sanger, *Seventy Years A Showman* (London: Dent & Sons, 1926)
8. The origin of Henry Freeman's middle name St Clair (as recorded on his death certificate) remains a puzzle. There was a famous wizard, Professor Charles Sinclair (1827-90), who appeared at Newcastle in January 1858; Dudley Castle Fetes in June 1862; and Cremorne Gardens in July 1865. His name was variously spelt Sinclair or St Clair and it is possible that this was the wizard whom Henry Freeman impersonated.

Chapter 2: Rise to Fame

1. *Oxford Chronicle*, 17th September 1853
2. *World's Fair*, 10th November 1956
3. *Blocksidge's Dudley Almanack*, 21st August 1860
4. *World's Fair*, 30th May 1970

Chapter 4: A Clown is Born

1. C.H.Lea, *PIMPO – Famous Clown's Life Story* (*World's Fair*, 26th January 1935)
2. Details gathered by author in conversation with the late Victoria Freeman.
3. *World's Fair*, 30th April 1910
4. W.G.Bosworth, *Wagon Wheels: The Romance of the Circus* (London: 1935)
5. M.Willson Disher, *Greatest Show on Earth* (London: Bell, 1937)
6. *World's Fair*, 4th February 1961
7. *World's Fair*, 4th February 1961

Chapter 5: Biddall's Ghost

1. *Annandale Oberver*, 14th October 1938
2. *World's Fair*, 7th May 1932
3. *Era*, 8th July 1877
4. *World's Fair*, 7th May 1932
5. *World's Fair*, 24th April 1909

Chapter 6: Almost the First

1. *People's Journal*, 14th August 1937
2. *Eskdale & Liddesdale Standard*, May 1958
3. Information about the Scottish Round taken from *Era*, 25th March 1899
4. Beacon Museum, Whitehaven, WHHMG.1994.369.5
5. *News & Star*, 30th September 1994

Chapter 7: There's No Fun Like Work

1. *Whitehaven News*, 23rd November 2000
2. *World's Fair*, 14th January 1950
3. Beacon Museum, Whitehaven, WHHMG 1982.63
4. *World's Fair*, 6th December 1952
5. *Our Wee Toon*, A Collection of Images & Memories from Annan's past. 1994
6. Advertisement, 1914, from *Biddall's Kinema, Part of a Remarkable Family Story* (Annan Historic Resources Centre)
7. *World's Fair*, 25th June 1949
8. Newspaper cutting, 28th December 1928 (Annan Historic Resources Centre)
9. Advertisement for *Loose Ends* and *Viennese Nights*, and other details from *Biddall's Kinema, Part of a Remarkable Family Story* (Annan Historic Resources Centre)
10. Draft letter, undated. (Annan Historic Resources Centre)
11. *World's Fair*, 27th November 1954

Chapter 8: Cockney Nank

1. *West Sussex Gazette*, 20th July 1882
2. *Era*, 26th January 1884
3. *Daily Telegraph*, 29th December 1883; *Islington Gazette*, 31st December 1883
4. *Daily News*, 21st January 1884
5. *Islington Gazette*, 31st December 1884
6. *Islington Gazette*, 14th February 1895
7. *World's Fair*, 15th December 1934
8. *World's Fair*, 7th July 1951

Chapter 10: Wanted, a Lion-Tamer

1. *World's Fair*, 15th December 1934
2. *Strand Magazine*, 1896

Chapter 11: Bioscope Days

1. *World's Fair,* 11th August 1951
2. Francis Ferrari (1862-1914) married Emma Warwick, sister of Eliza, wife of Tom Baker. In 1892 he purchased the show then known all over Europe as Biddle's French Menagerie. When this show was photographed on the Flat Iron Market, Salford, in the early 1890s it featured the name 'Biddells' over the entrance but 'Biddales' on its posters. It probably took its name from the celebrated French lion-trainer and menagerist, Francois Bidel (1839-1909), and had no obvious connection with the Freeman-Biddall family.

Chapter 12: Join at Barnet Fair

1. Henry Freeman died, aged 82, in 1935. His death was registered at Pontypridd where Mary Wallser had died suddenly of heart failure in 1887. Henry's son, William Henry Freeman, was aged 82 when he died at Abergavenny in 1956.
2. *World's Fair*, 5th February 1949

Chapter 13: Ghost of a Former Self

1. *The Heathside Book of Hampstead & Highgate*, (1962)
2. *Music Hall & Theatre Review*, 30th March 1906
3. United Kingdom Showmen and Van Dwellers' Association formed in 1889. Its name was changed to the Showmen's Guild in 1910.
4. *Era*, 8th February 1908

Chapter 14: Also, a Petrified Mummy

1. Children's Dangerous Performance Act came into operation on 1st January 1880. It prohibited children under the age of fourteen from taking part in any public exhibition where life or limb might be endangered. See *Era,* 4th July 1880.

Chapter 15: Still Performing Wonders

1. *World's Fair*, 21st May 1932
2. *World's Fair*, 14th May 1932
3. In picture no. *155* Polly appears to be wearing a double claw brooch. Tiger-claw brooches were treasured by circus families and tradition held that they should only be worn by women with circus blood in their veins. A matching pair of claws was particularly prized.

Index

Italic numbers refer to illustrations

Details of other books by Frances Brown

FAIRFIELD FOLK – A HISTORY OF THE BRITISH FAIRGROUND & ITS PEOPLE
Hardback, 176 pages with more than one hundred photographs. Price: £15.95
This second edition of FAIRFIELD FOLK traces the history of the Matthews family from the early nineteenth century to the present. The book describes their way of life, the changes and developments of the fairground and contains a wealth of original photographs. It has been hailed as a fairground classic.

THE HARESFOOT LEGACY
Paperback price: £5
This historical novel is based on the lives of the author's ancestors. First published by Headline, this book has since appeared in a World Book Club edition and was reprinted by Brockhampton in 1997.

DANCING ON THE RAINBOW
Hardback price: £15. Paperback price: £5
This novel (the second in the trilogy) was inspired by the life of the Female Blondin, one of the great tightrope walkers of the Victorian age. First published in 1991 by Headline and reprinted by Brockhampton in 1997.

THE OTHER SISTER
Hardback price: £15. Paperback price: £5
The concluding volume of Frances Brown's family saga was inspired by her father's circus background. First published in 1992 by Headline, it was reprinted in 1997 by Brockhampton.

All prices include postage and packing and the books are available from:

Ronda Books
Sandings Farm
Lydeard St Lawrence
Taunton
TA4 3RD

Tel/Fax: 01984 667276